APPLICATION OF IT AND MANAGEMENT IN ECONOMIC GROWTH

APPLICATION OF IT AND MANAGEMENT IN ECONOMIC GROWTH

S.K. Sinha

RANDOM

RANDOM PUBLICATIONS

NEW DELHI - 110 002 (INDIA)

Application of IT and Management in Economic Growth

ISBN 978-93-51116-74-5

Published in 2015 in India by

RANDOM PUBLICATIONS

4376-A/4B, Gali Murari Lal, Ansari Road
New Delhi-110 002
Phone: +9111-43580356, 23289044
E-mail: randomexports@gmail.com; sales@randompublications.com;
info@randompublications.com

Type Setting by: Friends Media, Delhi-110089
Digitally Printed at: Replika Press Pvt. Ltd.

Preface

Information technology (IT) is the application of computers and telecommunications equipment to store, retrieve, transmit and manipulate data, often in the context of a business or other enterprise. The term is commonly used as a synonym for computers and computer networks, but it also encompasses other information distribution technologies such as television and telephones. Several industries are associated with information technology, including computer hardware, software, electronics, semiconductors, internet, telecom equipment, e-commerce and computer services.

Information technology (IT) has become a vital and integral part of every business plan. From multi-national corporations who maintain mainframe systems and databases to small businesses that own a single computer, IT plays a role. The reasons for the omnipresent use of computer technology in business can best be determined by looking at how it is being used across the business world. The exponential improvements in the power of digital technologies have been remarkably consistent for over 40 years, but the economic effects of these advances are much larger in recent years. Digitization has led to an acceleration in productivity growth in the global economy overall, and particularly for the companies that use information technology most intensively. Information technology is both an industry and a modernizing force. In most countries, IT spending grows at two to five times the rate of overall economic growth. To the extent that the spending is on locally produced products and services, the industry provides employment, tax revenues and a generally expanded industrial base. According to economic theory, technology stimulates economic growth both directly and indirectly. For many companies, email is the principal means of communication between employees, suppliers and customers. Email was one of the early drivers of the Internet, providing a simple and inexpensive means to communicate. Over the years, a number of other communications tools have also evolved, allowing staff to communicate using live chat systems, online meeting tools and video-conferencing systems. Voice over internet protocol (VOIP) telephones and smart-phones offer even more high-tech ways for employees to communicate. Storing data is only a benefit if that data can be used effectively. Progressive companies use that data as part of their strategic planning process as well as the tactical execution of that strategy. Management Information Systems (MIS) enable companies to track sales data, expenses and productivity levels. The information can be used to track profitability over time, maximize return on investment and identify areas of improvement. Managers can track sales on a daily basis, allowing them to immediately react to lower-than-expected numbers by boosting employee productivity or reducing the cost of an item. Smart use of IT can raise productivity levels, which has direct impact on the bottom line. Also, The Internet presents new opportunities to drive new businesses, create new models of governance, and help jump start the economies of even the least developed nations of the world.

This book is an effort to examine the impact IT has on politics, education, sociology, and technology. Focuses on the benefits of IT for developing countries, whose problems must be solved, and obstacles overcome in order to further IT advancement.

I thank all members of my team who have helped in the preparation of the book. My special thanks go to "Random Publications" who have published the book.

— S.K. Sinha

Contents

Chapter 1

Introduction

Computer Science

Computer science programmes prepare people to work with computing problems and solutions. Students learn computer systems design. They study software and hardware design. They also learn to profile the needs of specific end-user situations.

It's become a cliche, that once you buy a computer, it's already outdated within about two weeks. Technology keeps advancing faster and faster. Computers that used to take up a whole room now fit into the palm of your hand! We now think of typewriters as artifacts from the dark ages! Today we live in the Information Age. Computer scientists take technology and bits of plastic to give us more ways to digitize our world. With a degree in computer science, you can work as entry-level programmers and network administrators. You can work for all kinds of organizations, from small businesses to software start-ups to government agencies. After all, nearly every professional organization uses computers to keep things running. That means people are needed to keep the computers running themselves. In computer science programmes, you might be surprised to learn that you take several math courses, including advanced algebra, statistics and calculus. This is because math is the basis for most computing languages. Of course, you take several computer science courses. This includes learning different programming languages, such as Java and C++. You take courses about computer networks, database management and operating systems (think Mac OS X or Windows 2000). You also learn how computers are built and how to develop new computer technology.

In addition, many programmes allow you to specialize in a specific area of computer science. These can include artificial intelligence, computer graphics and numerical analysis, to name a few.

Most four-year colleges and universities offer bachelor's degrees in computer science. Most community colleges offer two-year programmes that can be transferred to a four-year school.

Many schools offer graduate degree programmes in computer science. These programmes take from two to five years after you finish your bachelorÆs degree. Most people who get graduate degrees in computer science become high-level computer scientists or professors."

College Preparation: For this programme, schools recommend that you know how to use a computer and the Internet.

You can prepare for this programme by taking courses in high school that prepare you for college. This typically includes four years of English, three years of math, three years of social studies and two years of science. Some colleges also require two years of a second language.

- Network Technology
- Computer Science and Programming
- Advanced Algebra courses
- Calculus
- Probability and Statistics

Undergraduate Special

Many programmes require you to apply for admission even after you've been admitted to the school. Typically you must complete introductory computer science courses. You may also have to take courses in logic, calculus and physics.

Graduate Admissions

Admission to graduate programmes is competitive. You need a bachelor's degree in computer science or a similar field, good grades and good test scores

Additional requirements at some schools include:

- Graduate Record Exam (GRE) General
- Graduate Record Exam (GRE) Computer Science
- Letters of recommendation
- Personal statement

Typical Course Work

This undergraduate programme typically includes courses in the following subjects:

- Analysis of Algorithms
- Calculus
- Computer Architecture
- Computer Graphics
- Computer Networks
- Computer Organization
- Database Systems
- Introduction to Computer Science
- Operating Systems
- Programming Languages
- Software Engineering
- Statistics

Graduate programmes that lead to a master's or doctoral degree typically include:

- Required courses
- Thesis (master's degree)
- Preliminary exams (doctoral degree only)
- Dissertation and dissertation defense (doctoral degree)

Things to Know

Computer science programmes are often called "Computer Information and Science" or "Computer Science and Engineering. Although it's true that a bachelor's degree in computer science will teach you a variety of skills that many employers value, it is becoming more common for employers to require a master's degree for many jobs.

One reason might be that technology is becoming more complex. Therefore, you need more time to focus on a particular area.

Computational Mathematics

Computational mathematics programmes teach people to use math to design and build computers. Students also learn how to use computer technology to create models and simulated experiments. They also learn how to use algorithms and binary code.

If you're interested in several different scientific disciplines, computational mathematics might be a good choice of study for you. Computational mathematics is related to several other disciplines, including mathematics, computer science, physics, astronomy, astrophysics and geoscience. Computational mathematics teaches you to study and attempt to solve problems in science and engineering. For example, you can study turbulence in order to make air travel safer. You also learn computer-aided graphic design. You can use your math, computing and engineering skills to work in a variety of fields. You can work for a computer hardware company, developing high-performance computer chips. Or, you can work for a genetic engineering lab, studying how DNA functions and develops.

In computational mathematics programmes, you take courses in several areas of math. This usually includes statistics, several kinds of mathematical analysis and computer modelling and simulation. Nearly all of your courses will include heavy use of computers, since many programmes use sophisticated software to teach mathematical concepts. In turn, students become skilled in using computers. Several schools offer bachelor's degrees in computational mathematics. In some cases, you can minor in computational mathematics while getting your undergraduate degree in math or a related field. However, usually you get a bachelor's degree in math and then decide to specialize in computational mathematics during your master's studies. About 30 schools offer master's and doctoral degrees in computational mathematics. These programmes take from two to five years after you finish your bachelorÆs degree. Most people with graduate degrees in computational mathematics become professors and researchers."

College Preparation: For this programme, schools recommend that you know how to use a computer and the Internet.

You can prepare for this programme by taking courses in high school that prepare you for college. This typically includes four years of English, three years of math, three years of social studies and two years of science. Some colleges also require two years of a second language.

- Computer Science and Programming
- Physics
- Pre-Calculus
- Calculus
- Probability and Statistics

Graduate Admissions

Admission to graduate programmes is competitive. You need a bachelor's degree, good grades and good test scores

Additional requirements at some schools include:

- Graduate Record Exam (GRE) General
- Letters of recommendation
- Personal statement
- Undergraduate major or significant course work in math, including calculus, linear algebra and statistics

Typical Course Work

This undergraduate programme typically includes courses in the following subjects:

- Applied Analysis
- Complex Analysis
- Computational Linear Algebra
- Computer Programming
- Differential Equations
- Modelling
- Nonlinear Equations
- Numerical Analysis
- Optimization
- Probability and Statistics
- Real Analysis
- Wavelet and Multi-Resolution Analysis

Graduate programmes that lead to a master's or doctoral degree typically include:

- Required courses
- Thesis (master's degree)
- Preliminary exams (doctoral degree only)
- Dissertation and dissertation defense (doctoral degree)

Things to Know

Computational mathematics is often considered a subset of applied mathematics. Often, they are combined into a single degree programme.

Computer Engineering Technology

Computer engineering technology programmes prepare people to help engineers design and build computer systems. Students learn to install and maintain equipment. They also learn to write and test software programmes.

What does it mean to engineer a computer? You may imagine somebody tinkering with the chips and the connections inside a computer system to get it to run with maximum efficiency. And that's partly right.

But in many computer engineering technology programmes you spend much more time on software. That's because engineering is about applying the scientific method to solve practical problems, so it can be done to software as well as to hardware.

In this programme, you start by studying math and physics. Physics helps you understand the workings of electronic circuits. Just as important, it teaches you how to solve problems by experimenting, gathering data and testing theories. You take more specialized courses that teach you how circuits can represent logical operations. You learn what actually goes on inside those amazing chips. And you study how data is communicated over networks. You learn a few programming languages. You also study how popular kinds of software store and process data.

If your programme focuses on engineering technology, you study the logical processes that go on before any code is written; that is, you study how to solve a problem by creating an algorithm. You learn skills you will use in research and development. With two or three years of full-time study beyond high school, you can earn an associate degree in a programme of this kind. This will qualify you to work as a technician within an engineering team. A four-year programme will earn you a bachelor's degree and you can work as an engineering technologist. In some states, you may be able to work as an engineer. This programme is available at about 80 colleges. Much more common are programmes that prepare you to work as a computer technician. You install and repair computer systems, networks and peripherals. You troubleshoot, consult manuals and online help, run tests and load software. You show workers how to use the computer equipment and software. About 300 colleges offer a two-year programme of this kind, leading to an associate degree."

College Preparation: You can prepare for this programme by taking courses in high school that prepare you for college. This typically includes four years of English, three years of math, three years of social studies and two years of science. Some colleges also require two years of a second language.

- Computer Science and Programming
- English Composition
- Biology
- Chemistry
- Physics
- Trigonometry

Typical Course Work

An associate degree programme in this field typically includes courses in the following subjects:

- College Algebra
- College Trigonometry
- English Composition
- Engineering Physics
- Electronic Circuits
- Digital Logic
- Introduction to Computer Science
- Programming in C++ and/or Visual Basic

A programme that emphasizes software also includes courses such as the following:

- Algorithm Design and Analysis
- Data Communications
- Machine and Assembly Language
- Networking and Internet Technologies

A programme that emphasizes hardware also includes courses such as the following:

- Computer-Assisted Circuit Design
- Microprocessor Technology
- Solid State Devices

A bachelor's degree programme in this field usually emphasizes engineering technology.

It often assumes that you have taken the math courses listed above while in high school. It typically includes the other core courses listed above. It also includes those listed for the software emphasis, plus the following:

- Applied Differential Calculus
- Chemistry
- Data and File Structures
- Operating System Design
- Microcomputer-Based System Design
- Software Engineering
- Senior Design Project

Things to Know

You need good communications skills to succeed in this field. A writing course and probably a public speaking course, should be part of your programme even if they are not required.

Consider taking some business courses. Engineering technologists often work closely with management. In addition, the skills you learn in these courses may later help you make a career shift into management. This can be a logical and fulfilling career path, especially if you are uninterested in becoming a licensed engineer (or if your state does not allow it).

A lot of people are unclear about the difference among an engineer, an engineering technologist and an engineering technician. All work as part of an engineering team. Together, they solve practical problems by applying principles of science and math. The engineer tends to work more in theoretical terms and is more concerned with design. The engineering technologist tends to work more in practical terms and is more concerned with putting the design into practice. The technician gathers data and works with equipment to make the implementation work.

With a bachelor's degree in an engineering technology, you may be able to work either as an engineer or as a technologist. Your options depend on where you live. About one-third of the states do not allow engineering technology graduates to be licensed as engineers. Other states allow the license but restrict what you can do. Without a license, you still can have a rewarding job as part of the engineering team.

If you want a license and you are allowed by your state to seek one, you usually must have a bachelor's degree from an engineering technology programme recognized by the Accreditation Board for Engineering and Technology. (In this field, there are fewer than 20.)

Then, you need several years of work experience and must pass an exam. Often you can take the exam in two stages. Your best bet is to take the first exam when you graduate or soon afterward.

Computer Installation and Repair

Computer installation and repair technology programmes prepare people to install, maintain and repair computers. Students learn how to programme and network computer systems. They learn about computer components such as power systems, chips and buffers.

It can be exciting to purchase a new computer. More memory, more RAM, better graphics, more bells and whistles! Yet it can also be intimidating to bring that big box home and try to set it up. You need to make sure that the monitor, CPU, keyboard and mouse all "talk" to each other the right way. And then there's the issue of setting up your Internet and e-mail access and getting connected to your printer. Sometimes, you think, it'd just be so much easier to pay someone else to do this for you!

What if you had to set up computers for a whole company? So many employees, so many computers! Not to mention the fact that each terminal must connect to the others so that files and information can be shared. And what if one computer breaks down? What happens if you need an important document that happened to be stored on that computer's hard drive?

Enter computer installation and repair technicians. These are the people who can help. They've studied how computers are put together and how to fix common computer problems. They aren't afraid of handling memory problems, error messages, or setting up your new personal digital assistant (PDA) so that it can upload files from your desktop. They understand how things connect and what phrases such as "network interface cards" and "computer architecture" mean.

In computer installation and repair programmes, you learn how to put together and take apart different kinds of computers. You also learn how to install, operate, maintain and repair them. You take courses about electronics, operating systems and programming. You also study computer networks, memory and peripheral equipment (*e.g.*, PDAs, printers). You learn how to fix common computer problems and how to interact with clients.

Computer installation and repair technology programmes are offered at about 25 community colleges, technical institutes, vocational centres and occasionally through high schools. They typically take from two months to a year to complete. In addition, some schools offer associate degrees in this field. These usually take one to two years to complete. However, most programmes are at the certificate level. As with many jobs, people with degrees in the field are usually able to advance to higher level positions.

With a background in computer installation and repair, you can work nearly anywhere that computers are used. You can work for large or small businesses as part of the team that handles the computer network. Many people start their own business or become independent contractors. This means that you work for hire."

College Preparation: For this programme, you should be comfortable using computers and the Internet. You should also be familiar with different operating systems. You can prepare for this programme of study by completing your high school degree or getting a GED.

- General Computer Applications
- Computing Systems
- Computer Science and Programming
- Electricity
- Pre-Calculus

Typical Course Work

This programme typically includes courses in the following subjects:

- Advanced Configuration
- Computer Architecture
- Computer Hardware
- Computer Information Systems
- Computer Memory
- Computer Programming
- Computer Software
- Customer Relations
- Digital Electronics
- Network Management
- Operating Systems
- Peripheral Equipment
- Principles of Computer Repair
- World Wide Web and the Internet

Things to Know

Many computer support technicians decide to become certified. There are several different types of certification, but usually you must complete course work in computer installation and repair and have at least six months' work experience.

Computer Systems Networking

Programmes in computer systems networking and administration prepare people to manage linked systems of computers and devices. Students learn to design, implement and run these systems. They learn to evaluate security needs and develop safeguards. They also learn to manage computer usage.

When people think of the Internet, they often think of their favourite web site. Or, they think of it as a place to research and find information. But do you ever think about the fact that the Internet is one giant computer network? After all, the information and your favourite web sites have to come from somewhere. In fact, they're stored on servers all around the world. When you look up how to get to the Picasso museum in Barcelona, Spain, for example, your computer is connecting to another computer in another continent!

Network and systems administrators are people who manage computer networks and systems. They make sure that the links between computers, software, servers and printers and other equipment are working properly. They make sure that data is stored and backed up. They also make sure that information is kept secure. This includes keeping hackers out of sensitive files that include personal data. Overall, network and systems administrators want to keep the flow of information between computers smooth and safe and effortless for end users to the people who use the individual computers that are part of the larger network.

In computer systems networking and administration programmes, you study the basics to computer programming, operating systems and hardware and software. You also take courses about database management, security issues and ways to fix problems. Most importantly, you learn about different kinds of servers and networks. You learn about making networks run smoothly and efficiently. In addition, you study techniques for updating systems and storing data. You learn how to use computer equipment "off the shelf" as well as designing original software or equipment for different network and system needs.

Community colleges, technical colleges and vocational schools offer programmes ranging from one to two years. They are designed to prepare students for jobs as entry-level network or systems administrators. Many colleges and universities offer bachelor's degree programmes. Graduates of these programmes are prepared with a broad base of knowledge of the networks and servers that they can apply to business activities. With a degree in computer systems networking and administration, you can be called many titles: systems administrator, network analyst, project manager, or probably the most common term: "the computer person."

Because new kinds of computers, servers and network systems are constantly developed or updated, many network and systems professionals choose to become specialized in addition to getting a degree in the field. Without specialized certification, it would be nearly impossible to keep up with all the changes in computer technology. Specialized certificate programmes in computer systems networking are usually offered through community colleges, technical institutes, or vocational schools. Some programmes are offered through online courses or proprietary schools. These programmes vary in length from a few weeks to a year or more. Common certifications are for Microsoft, Cisco, Nortel, Enterasys and Linux/UNIX networks and software. Keep in mind that you don't just become a Cisco certified administrator, for example. There are different types of certifications for each vendor. These certification programmes focus on different applications, from wireless networking to firewalls.

In general, your courses will concentrate on the specific computer networks and systems you wish to specialize in. You also study how to troubleshoot and debug network and system setups. This means that you learn how to test them for errors before they go live. You can concentrate on local area and wide area networks, or LANs and WANs. You can concentrate on Internet applications, such as e-commerce. Or, you can specialize in data security and storage.

In general, most two-year degrees can be transferred to four-year colleges and universities. In addition, graduate study is possible through programmes in computer science or management information systems. Check out these programmes of study for further information on a master's or doctorate degree."

College Preparation: For this programme, schools recommend that you know how to use a computer and the Internet.

You can prepare for this programme by taking courses in high school that prepare you for college. This typically includes four years of English, three years of math, three years of social studies and two years of science. Some colleges also require two years of a second language.

- Computing Systems
- Network Technology
- Computer Science and Programming
- Advanced Algebra courses
- Calculus

Undergraduate Special

For admission to specialized certification courses and programmes, you usually are required to have taken several courses in computer programming and general computer science. Depending on the certification you are seeking, you may need a degree in the field or networking experience.

Typical Course Work

This undergraduate programme typically includes courses in the following subjects:

- Computer and Network Security
- Computer Architecture
- Computer User Support
- Data and Computer Communications
- Database Administration
- Internet and World Wide Web
- Introduction to Computer and Network Administration
- Local Area Networks (LAN)
- Network and Systems Repair
- Operating Systems
- Peripheral Installation
- Programming Languages
- System Analysis and Design
- Unix Programming
- Wide Area Networks (WAN)

Things to Know

It is common for employers to require you to have a bachelor's degree in computer network systems administration to gain entry-level work in the field. Certificate programmes in computer network systems administration are often offered. These are usually for people who already have a bachelor's degree in a related field and have professional computer experience.

Computer Networking

The need for seamlessly moving information across the globe for many to use and share through computers and Internet has given birth to computer networking. Networking is changing the world of consumer electronics, biomedicine, industrial automation, super computing and defence. With the advent of Ethernet-enabled sensors and controllers, companies are increasingly looking at hooking their factory floor to their executive offices and beyond. Enterprise management is another widespread application made possible by networking.

The Work: Computer network management is a purely technical function. In a world where connectivity is the key, expertise in networking can take you places. There are several career avenues within networking, some of which are the following: Instead of working in a bank, credit card company or telecom company where you get to interact face-to-face with the custom

Network Administration: Working from the concept upwards, network administration involves configuring and managing LANs (Local Area Networks), WANs (Wide Area Networks) and VPNs (Virtual Private Networks). You will be responsible for analysing, installing and configuring the company's network even from a remote location. Monitoring network performance, troubleshooting problems and maintaining network security has to be done on a daily basis. With the proliferation of B2C (business to customer) websites, e-commerce, e-governance, VPN (Virtual Private Networks) and other Internet and telecom-based applications like remote servicing and IVR (Interactive Voice Response) the demand for network administrators is expected to peak in the next couple of years.

Familiarity with the intricacies of the specific systems being used by a company: Windows NT, Novell, Unix, Linux and so forth, thorough knowledge of networked applications, security and virus-protection schemes, system diagnostic utilities and experience with routers, hubs and bridges is also necessary.

Network Technicians: Focus more on the set up, troubleshooting and repair of specific hardware and software products.

Service Technicians: Visit customer sites to perform "field" upgrades and support functions.

Network Programmers and Analysts: Write software programmes or scripts that help evaluate third party products and integrate new software technologies into an existing or new network environment.

Network Managers: Supervise the work of administrators, engineers, technicians and programmers. They also work at long-range planning and strategy. At the entry level you will be focusing on tasks such as troubleshooting, monitoring, LAN performance, adding or deleting users, adding new servers, etc.

Network Security: As more and more organisations move their offline transactions online and vast quantities of vital and sensitive data travels through networks, the need for developing "fool proof" e-security systems to safeguard the networks and databases from rampant cracking has emerged as the number one IT concern globally. And consequently, it is one of the hottest and most sought-after specialities. With over 300 new viruses released everyday and rampant hacking (82,000 recorded cases, according to a Carnegie Mellon University study, governments and corporations have beefed-up their IS spend and tightened access to their systems and core applications. They are looking for people who can administer their enterprise network security safely and securely as a strategic priority. To excel in this field, you must be as familiar with system programming and administration as with security configuration and firewalls. This also includes knowledge of advanced TCP/IP, security fundamentals, security implementation, router security and attack routes.

Employment Opportunities: The Indian market for computers and peripherals has been growing at a rapid pace. In fact, the networking market is one of the fastest growing segments in the industry. Over three million units were sold in FY 2003-04 and the figure is expected to grow by 40 per cent crossing the 4.2 million mark in 2004-05. Driving this boom are technological innovations and a drop in prices, thanks to the IT agreement under the WTO, which will soon come into effect (translating into a PC penetration of 20 per 1000). Going by the average requirement of one hardware engineer for every 50 machines, the demand for networking professionals is bound to increase.

Moreover, Internet usage is increasing by the day and correspondingly the need for larger bandwidth for simultaneous transfer of data, voice and visuals (still and streaming video). The spurt in demand, has in turn, spurred the need for next generation data services like broadband access, virtual private networking, Voice over Internet Protocol (VOIP) and hi-tech Video Conferencing. With the tremendous growth in telecommunications and networking, people with good knowledge of computer network management on various platforms are in high demand. No doubt then, that there's a considerable demand gap in the availability of networking professionals globally. Whereas over 1,00,000 networking technicians and engineers are required, there are barely 50,000 of them presently.

What it takes?: Knowledge of computer hardware is the foundation for a career in computer networking. A good course will familiarise you with the basics of operating systems, microprocessors, peripheral devices, computer architecture, assembly and disassembly, installing various software, configuring PCs, preventive maintenance and troubleshooting. This can be followed by a relevant course/s or certification in networking to gain expertise in LAN and WAN, which is in high demand.

LAN shares the information and resources within the premises through the intranet with the help of products like Windows NT or Windows 2003 from Microsoft, Unix from SCO, Solaris from Sun Microsystems, Netware from Novell, etc. It can be further connected to the Internet through internet working devices such as Routers and Switches. WAN is a combination of Internet and Intranet — a network of networks, as it were.

Vendor certifications like Microsoft's MCSE or Cisco's CCNA or CCNP or CCIE, or Novel's CNE or Sun Microsystems' Sun Solaris Administrator at the higher end, are increasingly sought by recruiters.

What you'll Make?: Entry level salaries can be as high as Rs.20,000–25,000 for those with relevant vendor certifications like CCNA, etc. Diploma holders could expect to earn Rs.7,000–10,000. At the higher end a CTO (Chief Technology Officer) would get Rs 40,000. Those with good knowledge of ISPs, TCP/IP and the three-odd protocols, lease lines, particularly Microsoft Exchange Server 2003, command anything between Rs.75,000 upto 1.5 lakh+ (plus hefty perks).

Where to Study?: The basic qualification for getting into networking is preferably a Degree/Diploma in Computer Sc/Electrical/ Electronics/Telecommunication followed by a course in computer hardware.

People with non-engineering background who possess good knowledge of computer fundamentals can also enter this field.

In addition, recruiters prefer certain global certifications.

Some of the popular International Certifications available for LAN/ WAN Administration are MCSE, UNIX Admin, LINUX Admin, CNE, etc., whereas for WAN Administration you need CCNA, CCNP, CCDA, CCDP, CCIE.

Internet Security is an emerging technology in networking, which can be implemented by using Firewalls. A large part of the firewall implementation worldwide is done by Checkpoint/Computer Associates.

However, the most preferred certification is VUE Prometric as it covers most certifications — irrespective of the vendor platform.

Coaching facilities for clearing the various online tests for certification are offered at a number of Authorised Training Centres (ATCs) of the company. You can clear the (somewhat tough) test within 6 months of gaining some practical hands-on experience at any hardware establishment specialising in system integration.

Computer, Automated Teller and Office Machine Repairers

Significant Points: Workers qualify for these jobs by receiving training in electronics from associate degree programmes, the military, vocational schools, equipment manufacturers, or employers.

Job growth reflects the increasing dependence of businesses and individuals on computers and other sophisticated office machines.

Job prospects will be best for applicants with knowledge of electronics as well as repair experience.

Nature of the Work: *Computer repairers,* also known as *computer service technicians or data processing equipment repairers,* service mainframe, server and personal computers; printers; and disc drives. These workers perform primarily hands-on repair, maintenance and installation of computers and related equipment. Workers who provide technical assistance, in person or by telephone, to computer system users are known as computer support specialists or computer support technicians. Automated teller machines (ATMs) allow customers to carry out bank transactions without the assistance of a teller. ATMs now also provide a growing variety of other services, including stamp, phone card and ticket sales. *Automated teller machine servicers* repair and service these machines.

Office machine and cash register servicers work on photocopiers, cash registers, mail-processing equipment and fax machines. Newer models of office machinery include computerized components that allow them to function more effectively than earlier models. To install large equipment, such as mainframe computers and ATMs, repairers connect the equipment to power sources and communication lines that allow the transmission of information over computer networks. For example, when an ATM dispenses cash, it transmits the withdrawal information to the customer's bank. Workers also may install operating software and peripheral equipment, checking that all components are configured to function together correctly. The installation of personal computers and other small office machines is less complex and may be handled by the purchaser.

When equipment breaks down, many repairers travel to customers' workplaces or other locations to make the necessary repairs. These workers, known as *field technicians*, often have assigned areas in which they perform preventive maintenance on a regular basis. *Bench technicians* work in repair shops located in stores, factories, or service centres. In small companies, repairers may work both in repair shops and at customer locations.

Computer repairers usually replace subsystems instead of repairing them. Replacement is common because subsystems are inexpensive and businesses are reluctant to shut down their computers for time-consuming repairs. Subsystems commonly replaced by computer repairers include video cards, which transmit signals from the computer to the monitor; hard drives, which store data; and network cards, which allow communication over the network. Defective modules may be given to bench technicians, who use software programmes to diagnose the problem and who may repair the modules, if possible.

When ATMs malfunction, computer networks recognize the problem and alert repairers. Common problems include worn magnetic heads on card readers, which prevent the equipment from recognizing customers' bankcards and "pick failures," which prevent the equipment from dispensing the correct amount of cash. Field technicians travel to the locations of ATMs and usually repair equipment by removing and replacing defective components. Broken components are taken to a repair shop, where bench technicians make the necessary repairs. Field technicians perform routine maintenance on a regular basis, replacing worn parts and running diagnostic tests to ensure that the equipment functions properly.

Office machine repairers usually work on machinery at the customer's workplace; alternatively, if the machines are small enough, customers may bring them to a repair shop for maintenance. Common malfunctions include paper misfeeds caused by worn or dirty parts and poor-quality copy resulting from problems with lamps, lenses, or mirrors. These malfunctions usually can be resolved simply by cleaning the relevant components.

Breakdowns also may result from the failure of commonly used parts. For example, heavy use of a photocopier may wear down the printhead, which applies ink to the final copy. In such cases, the repairer usually replaces the part instead of repairing it. Workers use a variety of tools for diagnostic tests and repair. To diagnose malfunctions, they use multimeters to measure voltage, current, resistance and other electrical properties; signal generators to provide test signals; and oscilloscopes to monitor equipment signals. To diagnose computerized equipment, repairers use software programmes. To repair or adjust equipment, workers use handtools, such as pliers, screwdrivers, soldering irons and wrenches.

Working Conditions: Repairers usually work in clean, well-lighted surroundings. Because computers and office machines are sensitive to extreme temperatures and to humidity, repair shops usually are air-conditioned and well ventilated. Field repairers must travel frequently to various locations to install, maintain, or repair customers' equipment. ATM repairers may have to perform their jobs in small, confined spaces that house the equipment.

Because computers and ATMs are critical for many organizations to function efficiently, data processing equipment repairers and ATM field technicians often work around the clock. Their schedules may include evening, weekend and holiday shifts, sometimes assigned on the basis of seniority. Office machine and cash register servicers usually work regular business hours because the equipment they repair is not as critical. Although their job is not strenuous, repairers must lift equipment and work in a variety of postures. Repairers of computer monitors need to discharge voltage from the equipment to avoid electrocution. Workers may have to wear protective goggles.

Training, Other Qualifications and Advancement: Knowledge of electronics is necessary for employment as a computer, automated teller, or office machine repairer. Employers prefer workers who are certified as repairers or who have training in electronics from associate degree programmes, the military, vocational schools, or equipment manufacturers. Employers generally provide some training to new repairers on specific equipment; however, workers are expected to arrive on the job with a basic understanding of equipment repair. Employers may send experienced workers to training sessions to keep up with changes in technology and service procedures.

Most office machine and ATM repairer positions require an associate degree in electronics. A basic understanding of mechanical equipment also is important, because many of the parts that fail in office machines and ATMs, such as paper loaders, are mechanical. Entry-level employees at large companies normally receive on-the-job training lasting several months. Such training may include a week of classroom instruction, followed by a period of 2 weeks to several months assisting an experienced repairer.

Field technicians work closely with customers and must have good communications skills and a neat appearance. Employers normally require that field technicians have a driver's license. Various organizations offer certification. To receive certification, repairers must pass qualifying examinations corresponding to their level of training and experience. Newly hired computer repairers may work on personal computers or peripheral equipment. With experience, they can advance to positions maintaining more sophisticated systems, such as networking equipment and servers. Field repairers of ATMs may advance to bench technician positions responsible for more complex repairs. Experienced workers may become specialists who help other repairers diagnose difficult problems or who work with engineers in designing equipment and developing maintenance procedures. Experienced workers also may move into management positions responsible for supervising other repairers.

Because of their familiarity with equipment, experienced repairers may move into customer service or sales positions. Some experienced workers open their own repair shops or become wholesalers or retailers of electronic equipment.

Employment: Computer, automated teller and office machine repairers held about 168,000 jobs in 2004. Wholesale trade establishments employed about 35 percent of the workers in this occupation; most of these establishments were wholesalers of professional and commercial equipment and supplies. Many workers also were employed in electronics, appliance and office supply stores. Others worked in electronic and precision equipment repair shops and computer systems design firms. A small number found employment with computer and peripheral equipment manufacturers, government agencies and Internet service providers. About 15 percent of computer, automated teller and office machine repairers were self-employed, which is more than twice the proportion for all installation, maintenance and repair occupations.

Job Outlook: Employment of computer, automated teller and office machine repairers is expected to grow more slowly than the average for all occupations through 2014. Limited job growth will be driven by the increasing dependence of business and individuals on computers and other sophisticated office machines. The need to maintain this equipment will create new jobs for repairers. In addition, openings will result from the need to replace repairers who retire or transfer to new occupations. Job prospects will be best for applicants with knowledge of electronics as well as repair experience.

Although computer equipment continues to become less expensive and more reliable, malfunctions still occur and can cause severe problems for users, most of whom lack the knowledge to make repairs. Computers are critical to most businesses today and will become even more so to companies that do business on the Internet and to individuals that bank, pay bills, or make purchases online.

People also are becoming increasingly reliant on ATMs. Besides offering bank and retail transactions, ATMs provide an increasing number of other services, such as employee information processing and distribution of government payments. Improvements in ATM design have increased reliability and simplified repair tasks, reducing the number and extent of repairs. However, opportunities for ATM repairers should still be available arising primarily from the need to replace workers who leave the specialty, rather than from employment growth. Conventional office machines, such as calculators, are inexpensive and often are replaced instead of repaired. However, digital copiers and other, newer office machines are more costly and complex. This equipment often is computerized, designed to work on a network and capable of performing multiple functions. The growing need for repairers to service such sophisticated equipment should result in job opportunities for office machine repairers.

Earnings: Median hourly earnings of computer, automated teller and office machine repairers were $16.90 in May 2004. The middle 50 percent earned between $13.11 and $21.36. The lowest 10 percent earned less than $10.31 and the highest 10 percent earned more than $26.28. Median hourly earnings in the industries employing the largest numbers of computer, automated teller and office machine repairers in May 2004 are shown below:

Professional and commercial equipment and supplies merchant wholesalers	$18.51
Computer systems design and related services	18.08
Office supplies, stationery and gift stores	15.69
Electronic and precision equipment repair and maintenance	14.95
Electronics and appliance stores	14.04

Assembly Technician

Computer assembly technicians build computers from their parts, such as circuit boards, disk drives, cables and switches. When they have put the parts together, they test the computer and correct any faults.

Work Activities: Computer assembly technicians build complete computers from their parts. For an ordinary PC (personal computer), these would include:

- external case
- power supply unit
- disk drives
- processor
- circuit boards
- cooling fan
- cables and switches.

Computer assembly technicians gather the necessary items from stockrooms and warehouses as required. They fit the parts and wire them up, then test that the finished computer is working correctly. If it is not, they perform a series of further tests to discover where the fault lies and correct the fault. Technicians working for a computer manufacturer typically assemble a series of machines with identical specifications. If they work for a smaller specialist supplier or retailer, they may construct each machine according to a different set of specifications as required by the customer. In such cases, assembly technicians may also become involved in dealing with customers and perhaps servicing and upgrading existing machines.

They use tools such as screwdrivers and soldering irons and electronic testing equipment such as multimeters and oscilloscopes. Some of the components used in computers are quite delicate and sensitive, so they may have to wear special outer clothing to reduce the risk of contamination by dust or dirt. Also, static electricity can damage some circuit boards, so they may have to avoid wearing certain items (for example, man-made fabrics such as nylon) which can allow static to build up. They may also have to wear anti-static wristbands and other static-reducing items.

Personal Qualities and Skills: As a computer assembly technician, you will need an interest in computers and electronics. You will also need good manual dexterity, as many of the parts are small and delicate. You must also be able to work reasonably quickly.

You will need a methodical approach and the ability to follow written instructions precisely. You will also have to be conscientious and careful, as mistakes made during assembly can be costly and time-consuming to put right later. When a newly-built machine fails to work properly, you may need patience and perseverance to identify the source of the problem and fix it.

A reasonable level of physical fitness/stamina is desirable, as computer assembly technicians spend much of their day performing repetitive manual tasks such as soldering and inserting circuit boards. You may also have to carry heavy computers or computer components to and from stockrooms and workshops.

Pay and Opportunities: The pay rates given below are approximate. Computer assembly technicians earn £200—£230 a week, rising to £290—£350 a week. Higher earners can make around £400 a week.

Assembly technicians typically work 39 hours, Monday to Friday. Shift work and early morning starts may be required. Part-time work and overtime may be available. Employers include large computer manufacturers and firms that supply electronic parts and assemblies to them. The following information is sourced from government statistics. The government's definition of types of job is slightly different to that used in this programme. For this type of job, the most relevant government-defined occupation is 'Assemblers (electrical products)'. In 2001 there were 3,600 people working as 'Assemblers (electrical products)' in Scotland. 16 in every 10,000 employees working in Scotland were employed as 'Assemblers (electrical products)'.

Estimates of projected future job openings requiring new entrants to the jobs market are available, but not at the level of detail of 'Assemblers (electrical products)'. Employment levels for the broader occupational type of 'Assemblers and Routine Operatives' are projected to decline over the five years between 2003 and 2008 and there will be limited job opportunities for new employees.

3 out of every 20 employees work part time in this type of job.

Entry Routes and Training: New entrants may be able to train through a Skillseekers/Modern Apprenticeship. This combines on-the-job training with off-the-job training at a college or training centre and leads to SVQ levels 2/3.

Qualifications: There is no minimum entry requirement for this occupation. Applicants may have to perform an aptitude test to check whether they have the skills and dexterity needed for this career.

According to government statistics, employees in this type of job have the following qualifications. Higher Education: Fewer than one in ten employees have their highest level of qualifications attained at degree level or equivalent or higher. Post-16 or Further Education: 2 out of 10 employees have their highest qualification at a level below a degree or higher degree or equivalent, but gained after the age of 16. School leaving age (16) qualifications or qualifications at SVQ3: 7 out of 10 employees gained their highest qualification at the age of 16 or have gained another qualification lower than a VQ level 3 since they were 16.

Computer Games Designer

Computer games designers devise the concept for computer games and help determine the way they look and play. They begin with an outline of the game and use a variety of tools to produce a final script for the game.

Work Activities: Computer games have become a familiar aspect of life in modern Britain. Computer games designers are the people who dream up these games and help determine the way they look and play. Games are developed for a number of different 'platforms' (types of computer). The most important are PCs (personal computers) and consoles (dedicated games machines). A growing number of games are now also played online via the Internet. Computer games designers devise the basic concepts for these games. The original inspiration may be a book, film or short story, or it may come entirely from the designer's own imagination.

Typically, they begin with an outline that sets out the story of the game in linear form. However, because computer games are interactive (the player's actions play a crucial part in determining how the story unfolds), they develop from this a complex script showing all the options a player might take and the consequences, leading to one or more different conclusions. To do this, they use tools such as flowcharts, storyboards and index cards. Many of these tools are available in the form of computer programmes. Eventually, perhaps working with one or more writers, they produce a final script for the entire game.

In association with the art director, computer game designers are also responsible for the overall look of a game. To this end, they may produce sketches and storyboards and design the 'interface', which is what a player sees while actually playing the game. The interface is a crucial part of any game design, because it determines how it feels to play the game and the kind of choices that a player has available at any time.

Games designers also increasingly use 'level editors' which provide a user-friendly interface between 'old-fashioned' coding and a standard graphic design programme. Level editors are used for building up a game's 2D or 3D world. Level editors often come packaged with the game at retail, allowing players to design their own levels for games. This can be a good way for aspiring designers to improve their skills and build up a portfolio of work.

Computer game designers work in a tightly-knit team, which also includes graphic artists, writers, musicians and programmers. The team is led by a project manager. In practice, many team members will have a range of skills and the industry is full of writer-designers, artist-programmers, designer-producers and so on. Different designers have different skills and strengths, some leaning more towards the writing, others more towards visual aspects of the design.

Personal Qualities and Skills: As a computer games designer, you will need an interest in computers and a good knowledge of (and enthusiasm for) computer games. You will require a strong visual imagination and the ability to work with highly complex, multi-stranded scripts and programmes. A logical, methodical approach is therefore essential. You will also need to be patient and painstaking, as developing a new game from scratch is a lengthy and demanding process.

You will need to be a good team worker. Artistic/design skills are essential and for some types of computer game, script-writing skills are also important. Some programming knowledge/ability is desirable. However, computer games designers do not necessarily have to be expert computer programmers.

Pay and Opportunities: The pay rates given below are approximate. Salaries for computer games designers are in the range of £19,500—£25,500 a year, rising to £38,000. Higher earners can make around £49,500 a year. Salaries may include performance-related pay, profit sharing or company bonuses. Games designers usually work a basic 37-hour week, Monday to Friday. However, late finishes and weekend work may be required, especially as deadlines approach. Self-employed designers may work longer and more irregular hours.

The UK has a small but thriving computer games industry and skilled personnel are much in demand. There are also good opportunities to work in France, the USA and Japan, where many more computer games companies are based. Employers range from large firms involved in creating, publishing and marketing new games, to smaller software publishing houses that specialise in a particular range of games. Vacancies are published in the national press and also in specialist magazines such as 'Edge' and 'Computer Trade Weekly', both of which have online internet recruitment sections.

Some designers are employed on a short-term or fixed-term contract basis. The following information is sourced from government statistics. The government's definition of types of job is slightly different to that used in this programme. For this type of job, the most relevant Government-defined occupation is 'Software professionals'.

In 2001 there were 17,200 people working as 'Software professionals' in Scotland. 80 in every 10,000 employees working in Scotland were employed as 'Software professionals'. Estimates of projected future job openings requiring new entrants to the jobs market are available, but not at the level of detail of 'Software professionals'. It is estimated that over the five years between 2003 and 2008 there will be a need for 7,000 new employees to fill vacancies in the broader occupational type of 'Information & Communication Technology'.

1 out of every 20 employees works part time in this type of job.

Entry Routes and Training: While there are no formal entry qualifications, some hold a degree or Higher National qualification in computer-related subjects, such as computer science, computer visualisation and animation, digital arts or computer graphics. Others are graduates of art and design courses. Mature entrants need relevant skills and experience to enter the industry.

Qualifications: There are no formal minimum requirements for entry to this work. Applicants with an interest in computer game design, coupled with a good imagination and plenty of fresh ideas, can be as successful as those who hold formal qualifications such as a Higher National Diploma or a degree in graphic design.

For entry to a degree course the minimum requirement is 3 Highers (A-C) plus Standard Grades (1-3) in 2 other subjects.

However, entry requirements vary between courses and alternative qualifications may be accepted—check prospectuses for details.

According to government statistics, employees in this type of job have the following qualifications. Higher Education: 7 out of 10 employees have their highest level of qualifications attained at degree level or equivalent or higher.

Post-16 or Further Education: 2 out of 10 employees have their highest qualification at a level below a degree or higher degree or equivalent, but gained after the age of 16. School leaving age (16) qualifications or qualifications at SVQ3: 2 out of 10 employees gained their highest qualification at the age of 16 or have gained another qualification lower than a VQ level 3 since they were 16.

Computer Games Programmer

Computer games programmers turn the ideas of games designers into games that people can actually play. They do this by writing computer code or using a range of programming tools that generate code for them.

Work Activities: Computer games programmers develop games for a number of different 'platforms' (types of computer). The most important are PCs (personal computers) and consoles (dedicated games machines). A growing number of games are also now played online via the Internet.

Computer games programmers work as members of a tightly-knit production team, which normally also includes designers, writers, musicians and graphic artists. The team is led by a project manager. The programmer provides the technical expertise to turn the ideas of the designer, writer and other production team members into reality on the computer screen.

To do this, programmers either write the code in an appropriate computer language such as C/C++, Java or Pascal, or they use a range of special programming tools that generate the actual code for them.

Modern computer games are extremely complex, so there is usually a team of programmers working on each one. The actual programming is divided into a number of tasks, with each one assigned to a different programmer. This requires efficient teamwork and co-ordination and special CASE (computer-assisted software engineering) tools are often used to ensure consistency is achieved and that programmers are not duplicating each other's work. Once the coding is complete, the programmer tests the application to make sure that it works correctly and there are no faults. This 'de-bugging' can prove a time-consuming process, though most programming applications include special software tools to assist in the process.

Personal Qualities and Skills: As a computer games programmer, you will need an interest in computers and a good knowledge of (and enthusiasm for) computer games. Advanced programming skills, preferably in a number of different computer languages, are essential. As with most computer-related jobs, you will require a logical, methodical approach to your work. You will also need to be patient and painstaking, as developing a new game from scratch is a long and demanding process.

You will need to be a good team worker, able to get along with others and meet deadlines. You must also be willing to spend many hours sitting at a computer developing code. Good problem-solving abilities are essential when attempting to remove 'bugs' and to find ways to solve complex programming challenges.

Pay and Opportunities: Salaries for computer games programmers vary depending on the range of their responsibilities and the size and type of company they work for. The pay rates given below are approximate. Salaries are in the range of £19,500—£25,500 a year, rising to £38,000. Higher earners can make around £49,500 a year. Salaries may include performance-related pay, profit sharing or company bonuses.

Computer games programmers usually work 35—37 hours, Monday to Friday. However, late finishes and some weekend work are often required, especially as deadlines approach.

The UK has a small but thriving computer games industry and skilled personnel are much in demand. There are also good opportunities to work in France, the USA and Japan, where many more computer games companies are based.

Employers range from large firms involved in creating, publishing and marketing new games, to smaller software publishing houses that specialise in a particular range of games. Self-employment is possible for experienced programmers. Short-term contract work can be available through specialist IT recruitment agencies.

The following information is sourced from government statistics. The government's definition of types of job is slightly different to that used in this programme. For this type of job, the most relevant Government-defined occupation is 'Software professionals'.

In 2001 there were 17,200 people working as 'Software professionals' in Scotland. 80 in every 10,000 employees working in Scotland were employed as 'Software professionals'.

Estimates of projected future job openings requiring new entrants to the jobs market are available, but not at the level of detail of 'Software professionals'. It is estimated that over the five years between 2003 and 2008 there will be a need for 7,000 new employees to fill vacancies in the broader occupational type of 'Information & Communication Technology'.

1 out of every 20 employees works part time in this type of job.

Entry Routes and Training: There are no formal minimum entry requirements for this occupation, though in practice most programmers possess at least one or two Highers or a relevant vocational qualification. A growing number possess a degree or Higher National Diploma in a computing subject. More important than formal qualifications in this field is the possession of relevant skills and/or experience.

Qualifications: For entry to a degree course the minimum requirement is 3 Highers (A-C) plus Standard Grades (1-3) in 2 other subjects. Other relevant qualifications at National Certificate, Higher National Certificate or Higher National Diploma level may also be considered. However, it may be possible to enter this work with no formal qualifications if you have relevant skills and/or experience.

According to government statistics, employees in this type of job have the following qualifications. Higher Education: 7 out of 10 employees have their highest level of qualifications attained at degree level or equivalent or higher. Post-16 or Further Education: 2 out of 10 employees have their highest qualification at a level below a degree or higher degree or equivalent, but gained after the age of 16. School leaving age (16) qualifications or qualifications at SVQ3: 2 out of 10 employees gained their highest qualification at the age of 16 or have gained another qualification lower than a VQ level 3 since they were 16.

Computer Hardware Engineer

Computer hardware engineers work on the design, development and manufacture of computer hardware. They may specialise in areas such as communications, control systems, robotics, microprocessors or semi-conductor devices.

Work Activities: Some hardware engineers research and design very advanced and sophisticated technology. For example, hardware engineers are working on using different wavelengths of light on one optical fibre to increase the amount of data that can be transmitted at once. Engineers make most computers by buying microprocessing chips, assembling components and equipment and linking them up together to form a system. The process may begin with the computer systems analyst providing an outline specification for a computer system to meet a particular need. A team of logic designers works on the initial logic design and produces detailed specifications. They translate the ideas into detailed drawings and circuit diagrams.

A team of hardware engineers takes the design and builds and tests a prototype or working model. They buy the computer chips, assemble the hardware components and build the necessary interfacing equipment. They test the prototype to make sure it meets the specification requirements; they carry out any necessary modifications to the design.

Personal Qualities and Skills: To be a computer hardware engineer, you need strong technical knowledge of computers and electronic systems. You must have a flair for turning system requirements into detailed designs. You need to be able to work to deadlines and budgets; you may also need to consider the cost and availability of components. Computer hardware engineers must be able to work as part of multi-disciplinary teams;.you must have strong oral and written communication skills.

Pay and Opportunities: Salaries for engineers vary. The pay rates given below are approximate. Computer hardware engineers earn £21,000—£25,000 a year, rising to £29,500—£36,500 . Higher earners can make around £47,000 a year. Hardware engineers usually work up to 37 hours, Monday to Friday.

Employers are computer manufacturers, electronics companies, retailers and distributors of computers, information technology consultants and software or systems houses. The following information is sourced from government statistics. The government's definition of types of job is slightly different to that used in this programme. For this type of job, the most relevant government-defined occupation is 'Software professionals'.

In 2001 there were 17,200 people working as 'Software professionals' in Scotland. 80 in every 10,000 employees working in Scotland were employed as 'Software professionals'. Estimates of projected future job openings requiring new entrants to the jobs market are available, but not at the level of detail of 'Software professionals'. It is estimated that over the five years between 2003 and 2008 there will be a need for 7,000 new employees to fill vacancies in the broader occupational type of 'Information & Communication Technology'.

1 out of every 20 employees works part time in this type of job.

Entry Routes and Training: Computer hardware engineers normally complete an appropriate degree. Relevant course titles include Electronic and Computer Engineering and Computer Systems Engineering. It is essential to consult prospectuses to make sure the course you choose is appropriate to the branch of engineering you want to follow.

Computer hardware engineers can gain Chartered Engineer and Incorporated Engineer status, which are both highly regarded by employers throughout industry.

To register with the Engineering Council (UK) as a Chartered Engineer (CEng) or Incorporated Engineer (IEng), you must apply through an appropriate engineering professional institution. To register as a Chartered Engineer, the usual route is to complete first an accredited degree, as listed on the Engineering Council (UK) website, *e.g.*. an M.Eng.

To register as an Incorporated Engineer, the usual route is to complete first an accredited degree, as listed on the Engineering Council (UK) website, *e.g.* a B.Eng. After gaining your degree, you will undergo Initial Professional Development (IPD). This involves accredited training and responsible experience in the workplace. This is followed by a Professional Review with interview to assess your competence and commitment to Continued Professional Development (CPD).

Qualifications: The usual qualification for entry into this career is a degree. However, it is possible to enter through completion of a Higher National Diploma or Higher National Certificate.

The usual entry requirements for a degree in Computer Engineering are 3/5 Highers (A-C). Higher Maths is often essential and Physics or Computing may also be recommended.

The usual entry requirements for an HNC/HND are 1/3 Highers and Standard Grades. However, entry qualifications vary between courses and alternative qualifications may be accepted—check prospectuses for details.

According to government statistics, employees in this type of job have the following qualifications. Higher Education: 7 out of 10 employees have their highest level of qualifications attained at degree level or equivalent or higher.

Post-16 or Further Education: 2 out of 10 employees have their highest qualification at a level below a degree or higher degree or equivalent, but gained after the age of 16. School leaving age (16) qualifications or qualifications at SVQ3: 2 out of 10 employees gained their highest qualification at the age of 16 or have gained another qualification lower than a VQ level 3 since they were 16.

Helpline Operator: Computer helpline operators deal with telephone calls from people who are having computer problems. They find out what the problem is and then try to find a solution for the caller. They work for manufacturers of hardware and software, Internet service providers and large organisations whose staff use computers in their work.

Work Activities: Computer helpline operators help people overcome problems they may have while using a computer. Such problems may be related to the computer itself, but more often concern one or more specific applications. The latter might include:

- accounting programmes
- databases
- spreadsheets
- word processing programmes
- desktop publishing programmes
- computer-aided design (CAD) programmes
- computer games
- Internet-related software

Their work requires them to have an in-depth knowledge of the machines and/or applications enquirers are using. This is normally gained through a combination of on-the-job and off-the-job training, plus in many cases direct personal experience of working with the applications concerned. Helpline operators work on 'help desks', taking telephone enquiries from users while wearing hands-free headsets. They first establish the nature and cause of users' problems and then talk them through the steps necessary to solve them. They have a computer in front of them from which they are able to obtain information and perhaps reproduce users' problems.

In some cases, problems may be due to mistakes made by the user, but in others they may be caused by a fault in the user's computer or the software. In such cases operators may have to advise users to return the item concerned to the supplier for a repair or refund. Computer helpline operators work for a variety of institutions, including computer manufacturers/retailers, Internet access providers and software suppliers. They are also employed by some large organisations to provide help for staff who have to use computers in the course of their work.

Personal Qualities and Skills: As a computer helpline operator, you will need an interest in computers and a good knowledge of the applications concerned (though training will normally be provided). You will require a logical, methodical approach, as identifying the cause of a problem sometimes requires a certain amount of detective work.

Good communication skills and patience are important and you will need a calm, clear telephone manner.

Pay and Opportunities: Salaries for computer helpline operators vary depending on the size and type of company they work for and the level of technical competence required for the job. The pay rates given below are approximate. Helpline operators earn in the range of £16,000—£18,000 a year, rising to £23,500—£29,500. Higher earners can make around £36,000 a year. Salaries may include performance-related pay, profit sharing or company bonuses. Computer helpline operators work a basic 35-hour week, Monday to Friday. Early starts, late finishes, weekend work and shift work may be required.

Employers, throughout the UK include computer manufacturers, software suppliers and Internet service providers. Firms in industry and commerce, including banks, building societies and insurance companies and those in the public sector; local and central government departments, the NHS and public utilities.

The following information is sourced from government statistics. The government's definition of types of job is slightly different to that used in this programme. For this type of job, the most relevant Government-defined occupation is 'IT user support technicians'.

In 2001 there were 4,000 people working as 'IT user support technicians' in Scotland. 18 in every 10,000 employees working in Scotland were employed as 'IT user support technicians'.

Estimates of projected future job openings requiring new entrants to the jobs market are available, but not at the level of detail of 'IT user support technicians'. It is estimated that over the five years between 2003 and 2008 there will be a need for 6,000 new employees to fill vacancies in the broader occupational type of 'IT Service Delivery Occupations'. 2 out of every 20 employees work part time in this type of job.

Entry Routes and Training: Most computer helpline operators have at least 4 or 5 Standard Grades (1-3) including Maths and English.

Many entrants train through a Skillseekers/Modern Apprenticeship. This combines on-the-job training with off-the-job training at a college or training centre and leads to SVQ levels 2/3.

It may be possible to work towards SVQs in Information Technology subjects at levels 2/3.

Qualifications: There are no minimum qualifications for entry to this work. However, employers are likely to ask for some Standard Grades (1-3) including English and Maths. Many entrants have at least 4 or 5 Standard Grades at 1-3.

It is not uncommon for people with higher qualifications, such as Highers and National Certificate/Higher National Certificate/Higher National Diploma qualifications to enter this work.

According to government statistics, employees in this type of job have the following qualifications. Higher Education: 5 out of 10 employees have their highest level of qualifications attained at degree level or equivalent or higher. Post-16 or Further Education: 2 out of 10 employees have their highest qualification at a level below a degree or higher degree or equivalent, but gained after the age of 16. School leaving age (16) qualifications or qualifications at SVQ3: 3 out of 10 employees gained their highest qualification at the age of 16 or have gained another qualification lower than a VQ level 3 since they were 16.

Computer Operator

Computer operators control the processing of work through large, mainframe computers. They load discs or tapes and run programmes. Operators take action when faults occur.

Work Activities: Computer operators control the processing of work through a mainframe computer. This is a large computer that is responsible for the central processing of an organisation's data. Usually, organisations that have to process a large volume of data use mainframe computers, for example, banks, local authorities, the Inland Revenue and the police. Operators start up the mainframe computer (unless it runs constantly). Then they load data and programmes from magnetic tapes or discs and start up the process operation.

They control and check operations from a console, using a keyboard to type instructions to the computer and its peripheral (related) equipment. Older computer systems need the operator to type in commands at several stages. Modern systems are more automated. The operator may need only to load a special operations programme or type in an initial set of instructions for the computer to run a whole sequence of operations. Operators have to check that the system, including the peripheral equipment, is working smoothly. For example, they must check that the printer is producing good quality printouts. If a fault occurs, operators have to find the problem. If the fault is with the hardware (the computer itself), they may have to carry out simple repairs. The operator has to make sure all data is saved on storage discs (or 'backed up') in case the system goes down.

This work also includes routine maintenance tasks such as checking the temperature and humidity in the room (mainframe computers need a carefully controlled environment). Operators run housekeeping programmes and clean equipment. They monitor how well the system works, keeping records to make sure the computer processes data as efficiently as possible.

Many organisations have replaced the mainframe computer with a system that allows individual computers to process data. This has significantly reduced the number of opportunities for computer operators.

Personal Qualities and Skills: As a computer operator, you will need strong technical knowledge. You must be able to work logically and methodically. You will also need the patience to make routine checks on the system. You must be able to cope well with pressure, for example, if the mainframe computer goes down. This means you need initiative, an analytical mind and good problem solving skills.

You should also have good communication skills to explain problems clearly and concisely to people who are not computer experts.

Pay and Opportunities: Salaries for computer operators vary depending on the range of their responsibilities and the size and type of company they work for. The pay rates given below are approximate. Salaries are in the range of £11,000—£12,500 a year, rising to £15,000—£21,500 a year. Higher earners can make around £29,000 a year.

Computer operators usually work 35—37 hours, Monday to Friday. Shift work, including weekend work on a rota basis, is common.

Employers, throughout the UK, are organisations that use a mainframe computer system, for example, local authorities, the Inland Revenue and the police and those in industry and commerce, such as oil companies, banks, building societies and insurance companies. Since one mainframe computer department can service an entire company's needs, staffing levels tend to be small.

The following information is sourced from government statistics. The government's definition of types of job is slightly different to that used in this programme. For this type of job, the most relevant Government-defined occupation is 'IT operations technicians'.

In 2001 there were 7,500 people working as 'IT operations technicians' in Scotland. 35 in every 10,000 employees working in Scotland were employed as 'IT operations technicians'.

Estimates of projected future job openings requiring new entrants to the jobs market are available, but not at the level of detail of 'IT operations technicians'. It is estimated that over the five years between 2003 and 2008 there will be a need for 6,000 new employees to fill vacancies in the broader occupational type of 'IT Service Delivery Occupations'.

2 out of every 20 employees work part time in this type of job.

Entry Routes and Training: New entrants may be able to train through a Skillseekers/Modern Apprenticeship. This combines on-the-job training with off-the-job training at a college or training centre and leads to SVQ levels 2/3.

A National Certificate/Qualification course in Computing/ Information Technology is an alternative starting point. Some employers may ask for Highers.

Qualifications: Entry requirements vary. It may be possible to enter this job with no formal qualifications and receive on-the-job training. Some employers ask for some Standard Grades or qualifications such as a National Certificate/Qualification course in Computing/Information Technology. According to government statistics, employees in this type of job have the following qualifications. Higher Education: 5 out of 10 employees have their highest level of qualifications attained at degree level or equivalent or higher.

Post-16 or Further Education: 2 out of 10 employees have their highest qualification at a level below a degree or higher degree or equivalent, but gained after the age of 16. School leaving age (16) qualifications or qualifications at SVQ3: 3 out of 10 employees gained their highest qualification at the age of 16 or have gained another qualification lower than a VQ level 3 since they were 16.

Computer Service Technician

Computer service technicians maintain, update and service computer equipment and software in the organisations where they work or in third party organisations.

Work Activities: When new computers arrive from suppliers, computer service technicians check that they are as ordered, then connect and test them to make sure that they are working properly. They install any specialist software which the user may need (such as computer-aided design or e-mail programmes). They may also install the equipment at the user's workstation and perhaps provide basic instruction on how to use it.

Technicians also repair and upgrade older machines. This might involve such tasks as:

- installing extra RAM (memory)
- fitting a new hard disk
- repairing a faulty monitor
- connecting a new soundcard
- fitting a CD-ROM or DVD drive
- installing extra equipment, such as a scanner.

They may also work on other computer-related equipment, such as printers, scanners and digital cameras.

Where computer networks are used in the organisation, technicians may be responsible for administrative tasks such as issuing passwords and performing a daily backup, as well as dealing with any problems that crop up. If their main task involves supporting computer networks, they are likely to be given the job title network technician or network administrator. Many computer service technicians are 'on call' for part or all of their working time to support users who have problems. This might involve explaining how a particular programme function works, or identifying and eradicating a computer virus. In some cases, computer service technicians may be able to talk users through their problem on the phone, but in others they may need to visit them personally. Where they cannot solve a particular problem, technicians may need to talk to suppliers and manufacturers' support staff to try to find a solution.

Personal Qualities and Skills: As a computer service technician, you will need an interest in computers and a logical, methodical approach to your work. Patience and perseverance are important. You will also need a good understanding of the hardware and software used in the organisation (though training is likely to be provided). Good communication skills are important when speaking to users or clients. Some may not be able to explain their problem clearly, so you will need to be patient, asking questions to help clarify the nature of the problem, then suggesting steps they can take to overcome it. A reasonable level of physical fitness/stamina is desirable, as computer service technicians may have to carry computers and other heavy equipment to and from storerooms and to users' offices. For some jobs, you may need a driving licence.

Pay and Opportunities: Salaries for computer services technicians vary, depending on the size and type of company they work for. The pay rates given below are approximate. Computer service technicians earn in the range of £14,500—£17,500 a year, rising to £22,500—£27,500. Higher earners can make around £35,500 a year. Computer services technicians usually work a 37-hour week, Monday to Friday. Late finishes, on-call and weekend work may be required from time to time.

Employers throughout the UK are firms in industry and commerce, including banks, building societies and insurance companies and in the public sector with local and central government departments, the NHS and public utilities.

The following information is sourced from government statistics. The government's definition of types of job is slightly different to that used in this programme. For this type of job, the most relevant government-defined occupation is 'IT operations technicians'.

In 2001 there were 7,500 people working as 'IT operations technicians' in Scotland. 35 in every 10,000 employees working in Scotland were employed as 'IT operations technicians'.

Estimates of projected future job openings requiring new entrants to the jobs market are available, but not at the level of detail of 'IT operations technicians'. It is estimated that over the five years between 2003 and 2008 there will be a need for 6,000 new employees to fill vacancies in the broader occupational type of 'IT Service Delivery Occupations'. 2 out of every 20 employees work part time in this type of job.

Entry Routes and Training: There are no set routes into this career although most computer service technicians have Standard Grades or equivalent. Many have additional qualifications such as a National Certificate in computing.

SVQs are available at levels 1 to 3 in subjects including Operating IT Systems, Implementing Information Technology Solutions and Installing and Supporting IT Systems.

Qualifications: There are no minimum academic requirements for entry into this career. However, most entrants have Standard Grades, including Maths and English.

According to government statistics, employees in this type of job have the following qualifications. Higher Education: 5 out of 10 employees have their highest level of qualifications attained at degree level or equivalent or higher. Post-16 or Further Education: 2 out of 10 employees have their highest qualification at a level below a degree or higher degree or equivalent, but gained after the age of 16. School leaving age (16) qualifications or qualifications at SVQ3: 3 out of 10 employees gained their highest qualification at the age of 16 or have gained another qualification lower than a VQ level 3 since they were 16.

Computer Support Services Engineer

Computer support services engineers help customers with their computer needs. They install, demonstrate, maintain and update computer equipment. This work often involves travelling to the customer's home or business premises. Some support services engineers staff telephone helplines.

Work Activities: Computer support services engineers help customers to get the best performance from their computer equipment and overcome any technical problems they have in using it. They demonstrate, install and maintain hardware/software systems, products and services and their 'upgrades' (improved versions).

Support services engineers give advice on all aspects of the installation and use of computers. They may provide support through a telephone help line, answering the whole range of customers' enquiries from simple questions to complex, highly technical problems. Some support engineers install software on customers' premises, making sure that it works. Under aftersales service contracts, they provide regular maintenance and servicing of the computer equipment to minimise breakdowns and malfunctions.

This work involves routine testing, identification of faults and, where this is relatively straightforward, the replacement of faulty components. If the computer breaks down during operation, a computer support services engineer visits the customers' premises to diagnose and repair any minor faults on-site. They may have to refer more complex faults back to the manufacturer. Through working with customers, support engineers identify potential software development and sales opportunities for the future. Computer support services engineers may also produce technical material including manuals to help customers understand their software. They may be required to travel to clients' premises locally or nationally.

Personal Qualities and Skills: You need a sound technical background in practical electronics. You need to be knowledgeable about the products or services provided to customers. You must keep up-to-date with new developments. You'll need to understand both hardware and software; both can cause operating faults.

You'll need strong communication skills, tact and consideration to work with both technical and non-technical clients. You need to keep clear and up-to-date records and report faults back to your customer service manager or service engineer manager for any further action.

Pay and Opportunities: Salaries for engineers vary. The pay rates given below are approximate. Salaries for computer support services engineers are in the range of £14,500—£17,500 a year, rising to £22,500—£27,500. Higher earners can make around £35,500 a year. Salaries may include performance-related pay, profit sharing or company bonuses.

Computer support services engineers typically work 35 hours Monday to Friday, but early starts, late finishes, on-call and weekend work may be required.

Employers, throughout the UK, vary from large multinational corporations to small computer-system suppliers.

The following information is sourced from government statistics. The government's definition of types of job is slightly different to that used in this programme. For this type of job, the most relevant government-defined occupation is 'Computer engineers, installation and maintenance'.

In 2001 there were 2,200 people working as 'Computer engineers, installation and maintenance' in Scotland. 10 in every 10,000 employees working in Scotland were employed as 'Computer engineers, installation and maintenance'.

Estimates of projected future job openings requiring new entrants to the jobs market are available, but not at the level of detail of 'Computer engineers, installation and maintenance'. Employment levels for the broader occupational type of 'Electrical Trades' are projected to decline over the five years between 2003 and 2008 and there will be limited job opportunities for new employees.

1 out of every 20 employees works part time in this type of job.

Entry Routes and Training: A relevant degree or Higher National Diploma is often an advantage, although there is no formal academic requirement for entry to this work. In general, technical degrees such as Electronic Engineering and Computer Science are preferred for management positions. Most training is given on the job.

Modern Apprenticeships, leading to SVQ level 3, may be available in your area.

Qualifications: There is no formal academic requirement for entry into this career. However, most entrants have at least Standard Grades (1-3) including Maths and English. Many have additional qualifications including a Higher National Certificate/Higher National Diploma or a degree in, for example, Electronic Engineering.

According to government statistics, employees in this type of job have the following qualifications. Higher Education: 1 out of 10 employees have their highest level of qualifications attained at degree level or equivalent or higher.

Post-16 or Further Education: 6 out of 10 employees have their highest qualification at a level below a degree or higher degree or equivalent, but gained after the age of 16. School leaving age (16) qualifications or qualifications at SVQ3: 3 out of 10 employees gained their highest qualification at the age of 16 or have gained another qualification lower than a VQ level 3 since they were 16.

Computer Technical Sales Manager

Computer technical sales managers sell computer hardware and software to commercial customers. They give advice about appropriate equipment. The work may involve negotiating contracts. They also provide an after-sales service.

Work Activities: Computer technical sales managers are responsible for the sale of computer hardware and software to other organisations. They persuade customers that they will benefit from buying new computer systems or adding to the systems that they already have. To do this, technical sales managers have to understand the customer's organisation. They work out what the customer needs to help their business run smoothly and then choose a computer system to help them achieve this. Technical sales managers need to give a lot of information to the customer. For example, they tell them what effect new systems will have on their organisation. They also prepare reports and presentations to persuade managers to buy their products.

When they have made a sale, technical sales managers keep in contact with the customer after the installation of the system, providing technical advice and support in case problems develop. This contact also enables them to find out if the organisation has any further need for new computer equipment.

You may need to travel locally or nationally.

Personal Qualities and Skills: As a computer technical sales manager, you will need excellent communication skills. You must be able to describe or explain technical ideas in everyday language. The ability to persuade and negotiate is very important, as are patience and persistence because some negotiations last several months.

Pay and Opportunities: Salaries for computer technical sales managers vary widely depending on the size and type of company they work for. The pay rates given below are approximate. Sales managers earn in the range of £24,000—£30,000 a year, rising to £40,000—£57,000. Higher earners can make around £80,000 a year. Salaries may include performance-related pay, profit sharing or company bonuses. Technical sales managers usually work office hours, Monday to Friday. However, you may need to do early starts and late finishes from time to time and occasional nights away from home.

Employers, throughout the UK, are manufacturers of computers and/or related equipment, dealers, software houses or consultancies. They may specialise in a particular market, such as health care.

The following information is sourced from government statistics. The government's definition of types of job is slightly different to that used in this programme. For this type of job, the most relevant Government-defined occupation is 'Marketing and sales managers'.

In 2001 there were 20,900 people working as 'Marketing and sales managers' in Scotland. 97 in every 10,000 employees working in Scotland were employed as 'Marketing and sales managers'. Estimates of projected future job openings requiring new entrants to the jobs market are available, but not at the level of detail of 'Marketing and sales managers'. It is estimated that over the five years between 2003 and 2008 there will be a need for 21,000 new employees to fill vacancies in the broader occupational type of 'Functional Managers'.

1 out of every 20 employees works part time in this type of job.

Entry Routes and Training: Direct entrants to technical sales are likely to need a degree or Higher National Diploma (computer science or other technical subjects may be preferred), but Highers may be enough for less technically complex products.

People often enter sales work as a career change or development from other work in the computer industry, such as systems analysis. People with degrees and HNDs in business and marketing related qualifications also enter this career.

If you are completely new to computing work, you will follow an extensive training programme. Such programmes cover product and company knowledge, understanding the business world in general terms, learning about existing and potential customers and selling and negotiating skills. You may receive training in-house; regular training throughout your career is essential to keep you up to date with technical developments.

Qualifications: For entry to a degree course the minimum requirement is 3 Highers (A-C) plus Standard Grades (1-3) in 2 other subjects. However, entry requirements vary between courses and alternative qualifications may be accepted—check prospectuses for details. Higher National Diplomas/Higher National Certificates and degrees in non-computing subjects could be relevant for employment.

According to government statistics, people working in this type of job have the following qualifications. Higher Education: 6 out of 10 employees have their highest level of qualifications attained at degree level or equivalent or higher. Post-16 or Further Education: 2 out of 10 employees have their highest qualification at a level below a degree or higher degree or equivalent, but gained after the age of 16. School leaving age (16) qualifications or qualifications at SVQ3: 3 out of 10 employees gained their highest qualification at the age of 16 or have gained another qualification lower than a VQ level 3 since they were 16.

Computer/IT Support Manager

Computer/IT support managers are responsible for the provision of IT (Information Technology) advice and support to IT users within their organisation.

Work Activities: Computer/IT support managers are responsible for the provision of IT advice and support to IT users within their organisation. Typically, they manage a small team of staff, who may include helpline operators, computer service technicians and network technicians/administrators. They work for a wide range of organisations, ranging from private sector companies to local government and the civil service.

Particularly in smaller departments, computer/IT support managers may provide some day-to-day support themselves. This may involve them working on a 'helpdesk', taking calls from users, getting details of problems they may be experiencing and talking them through the steps necessary to resolve them. In many cases, telephone advice may be enough, but in others, they may have to go to the user's own office and work directly on their computer.

An important aspect of their work is managing the staff and the resources of their section or department. These responsibilities are likely to include such matters as:

- Recruiting new staff.
- Organising helpdesk rotas.
- Budgeting and forward planning.
- Organising and (in some cases) delivering training.
- Preparing management reports, *e.g.* on the number and nature of support requests received.
- Reviewing the effectiveness of existing systems.

They may also be involved in deciding which hardware/software to buy to meet the organisation's needs. Other responsibilities can include negotiating service level agreements with external suppliers of IT-related services and disaster recovery if the system crashes (breaks down).

When problems arise due to technical issues, computer/IT support managers work with other IT staff within the organisation to resolve them. These include the computer network manager/administrator when a network-related problem arises. They may also have to liaise with external hardware and software suppliers and specialist agencies such as internet access providers.

When the introduction of new hardware or software is planned, computer/IT support managers need to become familiar with this as soon as possible (or delegate a member of the staff team to become familiar with it), so that they can provide the right level of support to users. They may be asked to advise on the introduction of new systems and often become members of planning/consultative groups concerning the use of new technology. They need to keep up to date with developments in the IT field, as changes are happening all the time. Finally, some computer/IT support managers also take responsibility for network management. This means that, as well as the duties listed above, they are also responsible for the efficient and secure operation of any computer networks used within their organisation.

Personal Qualities and Skills: As a computer/IT support manager, you will need an interest in computers and a detailed knowledge of computer hardware and software. You will also need good business knowledge and management skills.

You will require a patient, methodical approach, as identifying the cause of a user's problem sometimes requires a degree of detective work.

For managing staff and liaising with users and suppliers, good written and spoken communication skills are important.

You will need to be calm and conscientious and able to cope with a degree of stress, especially when problems arise (such as network failures) that are outside your control.

Pay and Opportunities: The pay rates given below are approximate. Salaries for support managers are in the range of £24,500—£32,000 a year, rising to £42,500—£57,000. Higher earners can make around £76,000 a year. Salaries may include performance related pay, profit sharing or company bonuses.

Computer/IT support managers usually work a basic 37-hour week, Monday to Friday. Late finishes and weekend work may be required and in some circumstances, they may be called out to deal with emergencies.

Jobs exist throughout the UK with employers in industry and commerce, including banks, building societies and insurance companies and in the public sector with local and central government departments, the NHS and public utilities. Some experienced support managers work on a freelance basis—usually on short term contracts. The following information is sourced from government statistics. The government's definition of types of job is slightly different to that used in this programme. For this type of job, the most relevant Government-defined occupation is 'Information and communication technology managers'.

In 2001 there were 9,400 people working as 'Information and communication technology managers' in Scotland. 43 in every 10,000 employees working in Scotland were employed as 'Information and communication technology managers'. Estimates of projected future job openings requiring new entrants to the jobs market are available, but not at the level of detail of 'Information and communication technology managers'. It is estimated that over the five years between 2003 and 2008 there will be a need for 21,000 new employees to fill vacancies in the broader occupational type of 'Functional Managers'.

1 out of every 20 employees works part time in this type of job.

Entry Routes and Training: Most computer /IT support managers possess a relevant degree or Higher National Diploma.

Those planning a career in IT are advised to take a degree or HND course accredited by the British Computer Society. Different courses have different emphases and it is important to check the prospectuses of the institutions concerned to identify those courses most likely to meet your future career aspirations. For computer/IT support management, relevant topics would include computer systems architecture, systems analysis and design and human-computer interaction. This is not normally an entry-level job, however and you would usually gain experience in a role such as systems analyst or network administrator before obtaining a position as a computer/IT support manager.

Many computer/IT support managers study part-time for further qualifications, for example the professional qualifications of the British Computer Society (BCS) and the Institute for the Management of Information Systems (IMIS). These can be studied full time or part time, by distance learning or at a local college.

They may also study for qualifications relevant to the specific networks and systems used in their organisation, *e.g.* Microsoft Certified Support Engineer (MCSE) or Certified Novell Engineer (CNE). Studying for these qualifications typically involves attending short, intensive courses at specially accredited training centres.

They are also likely to have to attend short courses provided by suppliers and external training organisations to help familiarise them with new hardware and software prior to its introduction within their organisation.

Qualifications: Most computer/IT support managers are graduates. Employers are also likely to want you to have experience in a role such as systems analyst or network administrator.

For entry to a degree course the minimum requirement is 3 Highers (A-C) plus Standard Grades in 2 other subjects.

However, entry requirements vary between course and alternative qualifications may be accepted—check prospectuses for details.

According to government statistics, people working in this type of job have the following qualifications. Higher Education: 6 out of 10 employees have their highest level of qualifications attained at degree level or equivalent or higher. Post-16 or Further Education: 2 out of 10 employees have their highest qualification at a level below a degree or higher degree or equivalent, but gained after the age of 16. School leaving age (16) qualifications or qualifications at SVQ3: 3 out of 10 employees gained their highest qualification at the age of 16 or have gained another qualification lower than a VQ level 3 since they were 16.

Computer/Software Sales Assistant

Computer/software sales assistants work in stores selling computers and computer-related goods. They help customers choose the products that best meet their needs and perform all the tasks necessary to complete the sale.

Work Activities: Computer/software sales assistants work in stores selling computers and computer-related goods. They help customers choose those products which would best meet their needs and perform all the tasks necessary to complete the sale. The range of products likely to be on offer in a computer/software store include:

- computers
- printers
- scanners
- accessories
- consumables (paper, toner cartridges, etc.)
- books on computing
- computer software (such as word processing packages and games).

Many customers will not have a detailed knowledge of computers, so the assistant may need to spend a while talking to them to find out their needs. Customers may be planning to spend hundreds or even thousands of pounds so they will expect in-depth information and informed advice. In many cases, the customer will also want the assistant to demonstrate the hardware or software concerned.

When a sale has been made, assistants take the payment and record the sale on an electronic cash register. Where a customer pays by cheque or debit/credit card, the assistant will need to get payment authorisation from the card company or via a cheque clearance agency such as Transax. At the end of the transaction, the assistant will give the customer a detailed receipt and perhaps a separate guarantee.

As well as their direct selling responsibilities, computer/software shop assistants are generally expected to perform a range of other duties. These may include:

- dusting and tidying the products on display
- replacing products sold with new products from the stockroom
- setting up display machines and making sure they work properly
- unpacking deliveries from suppliers or the company warehouse
- checking that all goods on display have price tickets and security tags
- dealing with customer complaints and returned goods
- keeping an eye open for shoplifters.

Many computer/software shops also have associated mail order and Internet operations. In such cases, assistants' responsibilities may also include taking telephone orders and enquiries, answering letters and emails, processing orders and general post room duties.

Personal Qualities and Skills: As a computer/software sales assistant, you will need an interest in computers and a good knowledge of the products on sale (training will be provided in this). You will need to be clean and tidy in appearance and friendly and polite.

Good communication skills are essential, both when listening to customers to try to understand their needs and when explaining sometimes complex technical matters to them. You will need to remain calm and courteous at all times, even when you are under pressure or feel that a complaining customer is in the wrong. You must enjoy working in a close-knit team and be prepared to be adaptable, covering other people's jobs when they are off sick or on holiday and willing to move at short notice to another section or department if you are needed. Like all shop workers, you will need to be punctual and trustworthy. Finally, physical fitness/stamina is important, as computer/software shop assistants are on their feet for most of the day. They may also be required to carry heavy boxes containing computers and other equipment to and from the stockroom and to customers' cars.

Pay and Opportunities: Computer/software sales assistants earn in the range of £180—£200 a week, rising to £250—£310. Higher earners can make around £430 a week. Sales assistants usually work a basic 35—39 hours per week. However, they may be required to work in the evenings or at weekends and receive overtime pay or time off in lieu. Many retail assistants are employed on a part-time basis and there may be opportunities for casual work during busy periods, for example, at Christmas. Computer sales assistants work in a range of outlets: small specialist computer shops, chain stores selling electronic goods, office supply companies and even supermarkets and large department stores. Promotion opportunities, depending on experience, are available with most of the larger employers. The following information is sourced from government statistics. The government's definition of types of job is slightly different to that used in this programme. For this type of job, the most relevant Government-defined occupation is 'Sales and retail assistants'. In 2001 there were 95,900 people working as 'Sales and retail assistants' in Scotland. 44 in every 1,000 employees working in Scotland were employed as 'Sales and retail assistants'.

Entry Routes and Training: There are no formal entry requirements for this occupation. Computer/software sales assistants are trained by their employers in matters such as product knowledge, customer service and use of the cash register. In large stores, a group of trainees starting at the same time may complete an induction course conducted by the training manager away from the sales floor. Assistants may also attend short product knowledge courses run by major suppliers such as computer manufacturers. New entrants may be able to train through a Skillseekers/Modern Apprenticeship. This combines on-the-job training with off-the-job training at a college or training centre and leads to SVQ levels 2/3.

Qualifications: Requirements vary for entry to this work depending on the company you apply to work for. It may be possible to enter this occupation without any formal educational qualifications, but often employers prefer applicants to have some Standard Grades (1-3) including Maths and English.

Data Input Operator

Data input operators use a keyboard to type data into computers. They deal with text and numerical data, putting the information in the required format. Many operators also have other office duties.

Work Activities: Data input operators transfer written information into a computer or visual display unit (VDU), so that it can be stored in the machine's memory. Eventually, someone can retrieve the information on screen or print it out on paper. Data input operators may deal with words, for example, reports, lists and standard letters, or with numerical data on spreadsheets. The operator types or 'keys in' these details according to a set format. Often, they input data into spaces or 'fields' on the computer. A simple example is an address list, where the operator enters a person's first name into one field, the surname into another, the postcode into another and so on.

Sometimes operators input the data in code form. For example, they may key in standard information such as a commonly used street name under a one or two digit code. By inputting the information in exactly the right order, operators enable others to recall data for specific tasks, for example, printing off quarterly sales figures.

Many data input operators also spend part of their time on other office duties like word processing and clerical tasks.

Personal Qualities and Skills: As a data input operator, you should be able to work quickly and accurately, often under pressure or to a deadline. The work can sometimes be monotonous but still needs good powers of concentration and attention to detail. This work may present difficulties for anyone who suffers from eye strain or poor eyesight, because it involves constant use of a computer screen. You will also be dealing with a variety of paperwork.

You'll need to have good literacy and number skills. Ideally, you should also have a fairly logical mind and some understanding of how computers work. This will enable you to use a variety of different databases and to cope with any day-to-day problems with the system you are using. You need keyboard or typing skills (at least 25—30 words per minute).

Pay and Opportunities: The pay rates given below are approximate. Starting salaries can depend on age and experience. Salaries are in the range of £11,000—£12,500 a year, rising to £15,000—£21,500. Higher earners can make around £24,000 a year.

Data input operators usually work 35—39 hours from Monday to Friday and some work shifts. Full-time, part-time, temporary and flexible working arrangements may be available.

Employment throughout the UK is with commercial organisations, some public utilities and government departments. The following information is sourced from government statistics. The government's definition of types of job is slightly different to that used in this programme. For this type of job, the most relevant Government-defined occupation is 'Database assistants/clerks'.

In 2001 there were 4,100 people working as 'Database assistants/ clerks' in Scotland. 19 in every 10,000 employees working in Scotland were employed as 'Database assistants/clerks'. Estimates of projected future job openings requiring new entrants to the jobs market are available, but not at the level of detail of 'Database assistants/clerks'. It is estimated that over the five years between 2003 and 2008 there will be a need for 7,000 new employees to fill vacancies in the broader occupational type of 'Administrative Occupations: Records'. 6 out of every 20 employees work part time in this type of job.

Entry Routes and Training: Entry routes vary depending on the type of data inputting involved. You may be able to enter this work directly but some employers prefer those who have taken a relevant college course. Many entrants train through a Skillseekers/Modern Apprenticeship. This combines on-the-job training with off-the-job training at a college or training centre and leads to SVQ levels 2/3.

Qualifications: Employers may ask for 3/4 Standard Grades (1-3) including English. However, in some cases it may be possible to enter with no formal qualifications. Typing or keyboard skills of at least 25-30 words per minute are also required.

According to government statistics, employees in this type of job have the following qualifications. Higher Education: 2 out of 10 employees have their highest level of qualifications attained at degree level or equivalent or higher.

Post-16 or Further Education: 2 out of 10 employees have their highest qualification at a level below a degree or higher degree or equivalent, but gained after the age of 16. School leaving age (16) qualifications or qualifications at SVQ3: 6 out of 10 employees gained their highest qualification at the age of 16 or have gained another qualification lower than a VQ level 3 since they were 16.

Multimedia Specialist

Multimedia specialists make computer programmes that use text, sound, graphics and pictures to entertain, educate or inform the user.

Work Activities: Multimedia specialists create products that use more than one way to communicate information. For example, they may use sound, text, graphics, animation and video pictures. They bring these different types of communication together using a computer.

Multimedia specialists work on games, educational software, websites, film, television and video. Their products may go on CD-ROMS or the Internet. Producing a multimedia product is a team effort. Writers, artists, graphic designers, animators and sound engineers make the content of the files.

The multimedia specialist plays a vital role in translating this information into a language that the computer can understand. Everyone works very closely together under the direction of a producer. As the work progresses, they attend meetings to discuss and sort out problems. Once the team has written the programme, multimedia specialists test it to identify and fix any errors they have found in the content or programme. Multimedia specialists may design and write web pages, programme the links to company databases, or create graphic effects for film studios. Some multimedia specialists produce images for company presentations.

Personal Qualities and Skills: To be a multimedia specialist, you will need a strong interest in information technology, although it's just as important to be creative and enthusiastic. You will need an open mind to grasp the future possibilities of multimedia.

It is very important that you are a good team worker because multimedia specialists usually work in small project teams with other experts, including artists, graphic designers and sound engineers.

You'll need strong communication skills to swap ideas and to explain your work clearly and concisely to people who may not have much computer knowledge. You should enjoy solving problems and working on a project from start to finish.

Good organisational skills will help you to plan your work and to meet deadlines. You must be able to work well under pressure.

Pay and Opportunities: Starting salaries can depend on age and qualifications. The pay rates given below are approximate. Multimedia specialists earn in the range of £15,000—£17,500 a year, rising to £22,500—£27,500. Higher earners can make around £37,000 a year. Multimedia specialists usually work 35—37 hours Monday to Friday, although you may need to do some late finishes as deadlines approach.

There are opportunities with multimedia publishers, software producers, website design companies and television and film companies. Consultancy and fixed-term contract work can be available for experienced multimedia designers and programmers.

The following information is sourced from government statistics. The government's definition of types of job is slightly different to that used in this programme. For this type of job, the most relevant Government-defined occupation is 'Graphic designers'.

In 2001 there were 4,600 people working as 'Graphic designers' in Scotland. 21 in every 10,000 employees working in Scotland were employed as 'Graphic designers'. Estimates of projected future job openings requiring new entrants to the jobs market are available, but not at the level of detail of 'Graphic designers'. It is estimated that over the five years between 2003 and 2008 there will be a need for 3,000 new employees to fill vacancies in the broader occupational type of 'Design Associate Professionals'.

3 out of every 20 employees work part time in this type of job.

Entry Routes and Training: Most people need a degree or Higher National Diploma in a relevant information technology subject to enter this career. Course titles vary, some having more emphasis on hardware issues, some on systems engineering and others on analysis and design. You must check college and university prospectuses carefully. Degree course titles include Multimedia Computing and Multimedia Design; there are HNDs with titles like Multimedia or Design Technology.

If you have a degree in a non-related subject, you could still find a way into this career. Some employers offer the chance to gain IT skills under graduate training programmes.

Qualifications: For entry to a degree course, the usual minimum requirement is 3 Highers (A-C) and Standard Grades (1-3) in 2 other subjects, including English.

However, entry requirements vary between courses and alternative qualifications may be accepted—check prospectuses for details.

According to government statistics, employees in this type of job have the following qualifications. Higher Education: 6 out of 10 employees have their highest level of qualifications attained at degree level or equivalent or higher. Post-16 or Further Education: 2 out of 10 employees have their highest qualification at a level below a degree or higher degree or equivalent, but gained after the age of 16. School leaving age (16) qualifications or qualifications at SVQ3: 2 out of 10 employees gained their highest qualification at the age of 16 or have gained another qualification lower than a VQ level 3 since they were 16.

Telecommunications Engineer

Telecommunications engineers work on the different types of technology that enable us to communicate over distance. They may deal with satellite and cable systems, mobile phones, radio waves, the

Internet and electronic mail. The world of telecommunications is changing very rapidly; it involves very sophisticated equipment and the latest technology.

Work Activities: Telecommunications engineers research and develop innovative products, as well as working on ways to improve existing technology, like fibre optic cables. Some telecommunications companies design, build and install telecommunications systems for their clients. Increasingly, networks are inter-linked; for example, engineers have developed systems where a mobile telephone user can access the Internet. Digital television systems can be interactive; users can have high-speed access to the Internet and e-mail.

Engineers may work on ways to provide solutions for business and private customers. For example, engineers may help a company to handle high volumes of telephone calls, perhaps by setting up or helping to improve a call centre. Engineers work closely with their clients, discussing solutions like Computer Telephony Integration (CTI). Telecommunications engineers have installed video conferencing links in hospitals. Surgeons can perform operations under the supervision of experts at another hospital, using the video-link to hear and see their colleagues. Engineers work on services like mobile communication, high-speed data and fax transmission and radio paging. They may install the equipment needed for these types of communication. Some engineers are responsible for routine maintenance and repair work, to make sure the system does not break down. Engineers may run centres or work on help desks, to respond quickly to repair or deal with any disruptions to the network.

Some telecommunications engineers travel around locally to make sure that all the sites of the network are working properly. They may use computer software to see if any part of the network is 'weak' and therefore more likely to break down.

Personal Qualities and Skills: You must be willing to learn and develop new knowledge, to keep up to date with advances in areas such as satellite technology, electronic commerce and mobile telephone networks. Also, you must have an investigative mind and excellent problem solving skills. Telecommunications engineers need management and organisation skills, to plan networks. For example, they may need to map cable networks.

Some telecommunications engineers work closely with sales and marketing departments. They may answer customer enquiries and could be involved in selling networks to new clients. You therefore need the ability to build up comprehensive product knowledge;

persuasive sales skills are useful. Engineers need computer software skills because computers are often used to control telecommunications systems.

Pay and Opportunities: Salaries vary depending on the company and level of responsibility. The pay rates given below are approximate. Telecommunications engineers earn in the range of £21,500—£25,000 a year, rising to £31,000—£37,500. Higher earners can make around £46,500 a year. Most work 35—40 hours, Monday to Friday. However, early starts, late finishes and some weekend work may be required. Telecommunications engineers work in research and development, as well as manufacturing and installation. Employers are public service providers who run the public telephone system, cable TV companies, cellular radio system providers and manufacturers of electronic communications products.

Companies with complex telecommunication requirements may employ their own engineers (for example, multinational oil companies). Opportunities for telecommunications engineers are fast increasing as the industry expands into global markets. The following information is sourced from government statistics. The government's definition of types of job is slightly different to that used in this programme. For this type of job, the most relevant government-defined occupation is 'Electrical engineers'.

In 2001 there were 1,500 people working as Electrical engineers in Scotland. 7 in every 10,000 employees working in Scotland were employed as Electrical engineers.

Entry Routes and Training: Telecommunications engineers usually complete an appropriate engineering degree or Higher National Diploma. There are a number of specialist courses, with titles like BSc Telecommunications Engineering at Glasgow Caledonian University and B.Eng Electronics and Electrical Engineering (Communications) available at Edinburgh University. UHI Millennium Institute offer a course in HND Engineering Telecommunications.

Many telecommunications engineers have backgrounds in electronic engineering, although entrants may also be graduates in other engineering disciplines, including mechanical engineering. Some entrants may also have backgrounds in computer science, mathematics and physics. It is essential to consult prospectuses to make sure the course you choose is appropriate to the branch of engineering you want to follow. Many graduates go on to join manufacturers' Graduate Training Schemes, which offer structured training and learning.

Depending on their level of entry, telecommunications engineers can gain Chartered Engineer or Incorporated Engineer status. Both are highly regarded by employers throughout industry.

Chartered Engineers (CEng) normally have the greatest level of responsibility for engineering projects. They plan and manage engineering activities and functions and lead the development of new technologies. They make sure that a project is completed on time and within budget. Chartered engineers work at the highest management levels. Incorporated Engineers (IEng) normally have a specific level of responsibility for engineering projects. They may work as team leaders or deal with technical aspects of complex technologies. They may supervise quality assurance procedures and manage and develop test and inspection programmes. Incorporated engineers generally work at middle management levels and some of their work overlaps with that of Chartered Engineers.

To register with the Engineering Council (UK) as a Chartered Engineer (CEng) or Incorporated Engineer (IEng), you must apply through an appropriate engineering body. The usual route to CEng status is to complete first an accredited degree in engineering, as listed on the Engineering Council (UK) website, *e.g.* an MEng. The usual route to IEng status is to complete first an accredited degree in engineering, as listed on the Engineering Council (UK) website, *e.g.* a B.Eng.

After gaining your degree, you will undergo Initial Professional Development (IPD). This involves accredited training and responsible experience in the workplace, followed by a Professional Review with interview to assess your competence and your commitment to Continued Professional Development (CPD).

Qualifications: The usual qualification for entry into this career is a degree. However, it may be possible to enter with a Higher National Diploma or Higher National Certificate.

Entry to a relevant engineering degree is normally with 3/4 Highers (A-C) plus Standard Grades (1-3) in 1/2 other subjects. At Higher, Maths and a science subject (normally Physics) are often preferred and may be essential. Entry to a relevant HNC/HND is normally with 1/3 Highers and Standard Grades. Entry requirements vary between courses and alternative qualifications may be accepted—check prospectuses for details.

Website Designer

Website designers use a combination of design and IT skills to produce Web pages for the Internet. They need to achieve a balance between interesting design and ease of use.

Work Activities: Website designers use a combination of design and computer skills to produce websites for the Internet.

To create a website, designers have to think carefully about the end product (the user interface). They need to achieve a balance between attractive design and delivering clear, easy to understand information. The most successful sites allow people to travel around them easily. Many designers make their websites as interactive as possible. This means that there is a two-way flow of information between the user and the website; the computer responds to the user's requests. Website designers can use a number of different ways to communicate information; this means that they use multimedia. For example, their website may have text, speech, graphics, animation or video pictures.

Website designers may use HTML (Hypertext Markup Language) to create text; they may use other programming languages, such as Java, to add a level of interactivity to a website. Also, they may use specialist Web design tools. Some companies ask website designers to manage the sites they have created. They must make sure that site information is up-to-date and relevant. To do this, they work closely with colleagues, including public relations staff and software engineers.

Personal Qualities and Skills: To be a website designer, you must have a strong interest in information technology. It is equally important to have strong design skills and be creative and enthusiastic. You should be skilled in computer languages like HTML and Java, or be willing to learn and develop these skills.

You'll need an open mind to grasp the future potential of the Internet and to think about the best way to use multimedia technologies like graphics, video and sound. Good teamwork skills are very important; you may be working closely with public relations staff, marketing departments or other IT specialists. Designers who work on a freelance basis need the skills to run their own business.

Pay and Opportunities: The pay rates given below are approximate. Website designers earn in the range of £15,000—£17,500 a year, rising to £22,500—£27,500. Higher earners can make around £37,000 a year.

Website designers usually work 35—37 hours Monday to Friday, though some late finishes may be required as deadlines approach.

Opportunities occur with employers in every area of industry and commerce, including retail and broadcasting industries and charity organisations and in the public sector, in local and central government. Other opportunities are with advertising agencies and specialist website design agencies. Some designers work independently on a freelance basis. Opportunities are increasing as more and more organisations realise the marketing potential of the Internet. Consultancy and fixed-term contract work can be available for experienced web designers, including through specialist IT recruitment agencies.

The following information is sourced from government statistics. The government's definition of types of job is slightly different to that used in this programme. For this type of job, the most relevant Government-defined occupation is 'Graphic designers'.

In 2001 there were 4,600 people working as 'Graphic designers' in Scotland. 21 in every 10,000 employees working in Scotland were employed as 'Graphic designers'. Estimates of projected future job openings requiring new entrants to the jobs market are available, but not at the level of detail of 'Graphic designers'. It is estimated that over the five years between 2003 and 2008 there will be a need for 3,000 new employees to fill vacancies in the broader occupational type of 'Design Associate Professionals'.

3 out of every 20 employees work part time in this type of job.

Entry Routes and Training: There is no set route into this job. However, most entrants have a degree or Higher National Diploma in a computer related subject.

There is a variety of degree level courses that teach the combined skills of design and computing. They have titles like Multimedia Computing, Design with Multimedia Studies, Multimedia Graphics, Interactive Systems Design and Electronic Media Design.

HNDs that may be useful have course titles such as Multimedia Information Technology, Multimedia with Web Development and Electronic Graphics.

You may be able to enter this career with a degree in a non-IT subject; some employers give IT training to people with a background in more traditional design subjects.

Qualifications: This is a relatively new job, so there is no formally recognised pathway into it. Some people enter with a degree or Higher National Diploma in a computer or design related subject.

For entry to a degree course the minimum requirement is 3 Highers (A-C) plus Standard Grades (1-3) in 2 other subjects.

However, entry requirements vary between courses and alternative qualifications may be accepted—check prospectuses for details.

Prospective entrants to Design courses usually need to present a portfolio of examples of their work.

According to government statistics, employees in this type of job have the following qualifications. Higher Education: 6 out of 10 employees have their highest level of qualifications attained at degree level or equivalent or higher.

Post-16 or Further Education: 2 out of 10 employees have their highest qualification at a level below a degree or higher degree or equivalent, but gained after the age of 16. School leaving age (16) qualifications or qualifications at SVQ3: 2 out of 10 employees gained their highest qualification at the age of 16 or have gained another qualification lower than a VQ level 3 since they were 16.

Chapter 2

Role of E-Business in the New Economy

In context of the electronic revolution taking place in our economy we must recognize these changes take place in a larger economic context. Global competition, interest rates, laws and regulations, social concerns, industry traditions, consumer preferences etc., are all part of environment affecting business activities. Besides, electronic and non electronic businesses share available economic resources including natural resources, equipment, telecommunication employees' skills etc. E-business, globalization and internet are interdependent. The more global players exist, the more business they want to do which will attract more people to get direct internet access. There are many categories of e-business such as e-commerce, e-marketing, e-mailing, e-auction, and e-supply and so on. The integration of these categories through internet enhances existing business or to create new virtual business.

E-business commonly referred to as "e-Business" or "e-business enable companies to link their internal and external data processing systems more efficiently and flexibly, to work more closely with suppliers and partners, and to better satisfy the needs and expectations of their customers.

In practice, e-business is more than just e-commerce. While e-business refers to more strategic focus with an emphasis on the functions using electronic capabilities, e-commerce is a subset of an overall e-business strategy. E-business involves business processes spanning the entire value chain: electronic purchasing and supply chain management, processing orders electronically, handling customer service, and cooperating with business partners. E-business can be conducted using the Web, the Internet, intranets, extranets, or some combination of these.

Benefits of e-Business

Expand Market Coverage E-Business eliminates these limitations of geography and time zones. The whole world is the available market, 24 hours a day, 7 days a week, 365 days in a year. Worldwide business professionals, buyers, and decision-makers have access to the Internet, spanning all time zones. The buyer conducts business "where" and "when" they want to without traditional limitations. So, with e-Business a firm creates a global, "365x24x7" availability to its customers. The firms can offer complimentary and supplementary products, and add-on promotions as buyers make selections. This leads to a larger volume of ordering, creating a higher revenue stream at a marginally low cost per transaction. It makes previously uneconomical markets attractive. This increases the size of the available market by turning marginal segments into profitable ones. This ability to turn frogs into princes is powered by e-Business's low variable costs for addressing marginal segments. The power of the add-on products can also be sold into these previously unprofitable segments, turning them into substantially profitable ones.

Reduce Costs: The major cost-reduction benefit is the promise of changing the distribution of products and services to customers. Products requiring little or no experience in the buying cycle can be purchased by the customer on the Internet and delivered directly without intermediaries. The elimination of various layers of distribution is the major cost reduction benefit to the market.

The National Association of Purchasing Management outlines the following benefits:

- Reduction in process variations
- Reductions in costs and errors
- Vendor sourcing strategy support
- Improvements in process capability
- Procurement paradigm shift from passive to acti
- Elimination of unwanted paper trail
- Improved access to information
- Reduction in costs and cycle times.

Strengthen Customer Relationships

The purpose of a business is to find and keep customers. E-Business has the ability to deliver benefits that can address both aspects of this statement, by delivering better purchase experiences to the buyer. Buyers are migrating to Internet buying in situations when it's faster, better, and cheaper than traditional methods. Faster e-Business assures faster delivery of products and services by speeding up order fulfillment, and delivering into just-in-time upstream processes, particularly in Business-to-Business environments.

Better Paper and client-server based systems with their "version control" limitations created problems that set limits to their efficiency. The "write-once, read-many" environment of e-Business assures that internal and external audiences see and work with the same up-to-date, accurate data. Additionally, where little customer-vendor interaction is required, e-Business creates an opportunity for virtual self-service counters.

Cheaper The Internet turns every vendor into an equal in a competitive bid. The customer now has more choice in suppliers. The customer has more alternate vendors, and lower prices are anticipated in all e-Business driven markets.

E-commerce is the process of buying, transferring, or exchanging products, services, and/or information via computer networks, including the internet, seeks to add revenue streams, build and enhance relationships with clients and partners and to improve efficiency. E-Commerce that is conducted between businesses is referred to as business-to-business or B2B. B2B can be open to all interested parties (e.g. commodity exchange) or limited to specific, pre-qualified participants (private electronic market). Electronic commerce that is conducted between businesses and consumers, on the other hand, is referred to as business-to-consumer or B2C. This is the type of e-commerce conducted by companies such as Amazon.com. E-Commerce is generally considered to be the sales aspect of e-business. It also consists of the exchange of data to facilitate the financing and payment aspects of the business transactions.

E-mail is a method of exchanging digital messages. E-mail systems are based on a store-and-forward model in which e-mail computer server systems accept, forward, deliver and store messages on behalf of users, who only need to connect to the e-mail infrastructure, typically an e-mail server, with a network-enabled device for the duration of message submission or retrieval. Email advertising becoming widely used as a means of distributing advertising messages to people on internet. Email advertising is being tied to the use of promotions and gimmicks. The main advantage of email advertising is that it is cheap to implement and can include feedback facility.

E-mailing Postal services and telecommunications companies are losing market share to the electronic communication, especially, e-mail. It combines the strength of a phone call is its immediacy and the letter has the advantage that everything is in written form. The internet enables instant communication in written form, either by e-mail or on line chat.

More and more businesses are talking digitally to each other. Other than a phone call, e-mails can contain more than just a text. It is possible to attach files like formatted documents, presentation, images or sound. Information can be shared much more easily-mail does also change the way to people communicate. Instead of writing down every aspect in a single letter; thoughts may be spread over multiple e-mails.

E-procurement The registered users look for buyers or sellers of goods and services. They may specify costs or invite bids. Transactions can be initiated and completed. Ongoing purchases may qualify customers for volume discounts or special offers. E-procurement software may make it possible to automate some buying and selling. Companies can control inventories more effectively, reduce purchasing agent overhead, and improve manufacturing cycles.

There are seven main types of e-procurement

- Web-based ERP Creating and approving purchasing requisitions, placing purchase orders and receiving goods and services by using a software system based on Internet.
- E-MRO (Maintenance, Repair and Overhaul) same as web-based ERP except that the goods and services ordered are non-product related MRO supplies.
- E-sourcing Identifying new suppliers for a specific category of purchasing requirements using Internet.
- E-tendering Sending requests for information and prices to suppliers and receiving the responses of suppliers through Internet.
- E-reverse auctioning Using Internet to buy goods and services from a number of known or unknown suppliers.
- E-informing Collection and distribution of purchase information both from and to internal and external parties.
- E-market sites buying communities can access preferred suppliers' products and services, add to shopping carts, create requisition, and seek approval, receipt purchase orders and process electronic invoices with integration to suppliers' supply chains and buyers' financial systems.

The e-procurement value chain consists of Indent Management, e-Tendering, e-Auctioning, Vendor Management, Catalogue Management, and Contract Management. Elements of e-procurement include Request For Information, Request For Proposal, Request For Quotation, RFx (the previous three together), and eRFx (software for managing RFx projects).

E-shopping is the process of purchasing products or services over the Internet. An online shop, e-shop, e-store, internet shop, web shop, web store, online store, or virtual store evokes the physical analogy of buying products or services at a bricks-and-mortar retailer or in a shopping mall. The metaphor of an online catalogue is also used, by analogy with mail order catalogues. All types of stores have retail web sites, including those that do and do not also have physical storefronts and paper catalogues. Online shopping is a type of electronic commerce used for business-to-business (B2B) and business-to-consumer (B2C) transactions.

E-auction is a type of auction in which the roles of buyers and sellers are reversed. In an ordinary auction which is also known as a forward auction, buyers compete to obtain a good or service, and the price typically increases over time. In a reverse auction, sellers compete to obtain business, and prices typically decrease over time. A buyer contracts with a market maker to help make the necessary preparations to conduct the reverse auction. This includes: finding new suppliers, training new and incumbent suppliers, organizing the auction, managing the auction event, and providing auction data to buyers to facilitate decision making. Reverse auction is a strategy used by many purchasing and supply management organizations for spend management, as part of strategic sourcing and overall supply management activities.

The prices that buyers obtain in the reverse auction reflect the narrow market which it created at the moment in time when the auction is held. Thus, it is possible that better value-i.e. lower prices, as well as better quality, delivery performance, technical capabilities, etc.-could be obtained from suppliers not engaged in the bidding or by other means such as collaborative cost management and joint process improvement.

The buyer may award contracts to the supplier who bid the lowest price. Or, a buyer could award contracts to suppliers who bid higher prices depending upon the buyer's specific needs with regards to quality, lead-time, capacity, or other value-adding capabilities.

Reverse auctions are used to fill both large and small value contracts for public and private commercial organizations. Buyers, sellers, and market makers should adhere to auction rules and industry codes of conduct for the use of reverse auctions, if they exist. Problems arise when one or more parties fail to conform to auction rules. Buyers should not assume that reverse auctions will, in every case, deliver savings-either on a unit price or total cost basis. Reverse auction savings can range from negative to neutral to positive savings.

E-auctioning benefits include;

- Helps to reduce prices up to 35%
- Shorten the negotiation process
- Comprehensive dynamic pricing engine
- Multi attribute multiproduct, multi language and multicurrency
- Several auction timing models to fit our needs on an auction basis
- Full support of total cost of ownership calculations
- Free training support tools
- Customizable to suit our company image.

E-banking means any user with a personal computer and a browser can get connected to his bank-s website to perform any of the virtual banking functions. All the services that the bank has permitted on the internet are displayed in menu. Any service can be selected and further interaction is dictated by the nature of service. Once the branch offices of bank are interconnected through terrestrial or satellite links, there would be no physical identity for any branch. It would a borderless entity permitting anytime, anywhere and anyhow banking. The network which connects the various locations and gives connectivity to the central office within the organization is called intranet. E-banking facilities include

- Access accounts round the clock, even on weekends
- See balances online and find out clearance of cheque deposit
- Transfer funds between accounts
- Download information directly into personal finance software
- Receive or pay bills online.

The Reserve Bank of India constituted a working group on Internet Banking. The group divided the internet banking products in India into 3 types based on the levels of access granted. They are:

Information Only System General Purpose information like interest rates, branch location, bank products and their features, loan and deposit calculations are provided in the banks website. There exist facilities for downloading various types of application forms. There is no interaction between the customer and bank's application system. No identification of the customer is done. In this system, there is no possibility of any unauthorized person getting into production systems of the bank through internet.

Electronic Information Transfer System The system provides customer-specific information in the form of account balances, transaction details, and statement of accounts. The information is still largely of the 'read only' format. Identification and authentication of the customer is through password. The application systems cannot directly access through the internet.

Fully Electronic Transactional System This system allows bi-directional capabilities. Transactions can be submitted by the customer for online update. This system requires high degree of security and control. It comprises technology covering computerization, networking and security, inter-bank payment gateway and legal infrastructure.

- Automated Teller Machine (ATM) It is operated by plastic card with its special features. The plastic card is replacing cheque, personal attendance of the customer, banking hour's restrictions and paper based verification. ATMs used as spring board for Electronic Fund Transfer. It can provide information about customers account and also receive instructions from customers.It is capable of handling cash deposits, transfer between accounts, balance enquiries, cash withdrawals and pay bills. It may be on-line or 0ff-line.
- Credit Cards/Debit Cards The Credit Card holder is empowered to spend wherever and whenever he wants with his Credit Card within the limits fixed by his bank. Credit Card is a post paid card. Debit Card, on the other hand, is a prepaid card with some stored value. Every time a person uses this card, the Internet Banking house gets money transferred to its account from the bank of the buyer. The buyers account is debited with the exact amount of purchases. The customer can never overspend because the system rejects any transaction which exceeds the balance in his account. The bank never faces a default because the amount spent is debited immediately from the customers' account.
- Smart Card Banks are adding chips to their current magnetic stripe cards to enhance security and offer new service, called Smart Cards. Smart Cards allow thousands of times of information storable on magnetic stripe cards. In addition, these

cards are highly secure, more reliable and perform multiple functions. They hold a large amount of personal information, from medical and health history to personal banking and personal preferences.

E-stock trading Companies such as e-trade, datek online allow us to trade stocks, bonds, mutual funds etc. on the internet. These companies offer to trade at a small cost compared to discount brokers. The steps involved are-place a request to trade-the system responds with current prices on the web-confirm trade or cancel.

The benefits of such trading are;

- Reduced cost
- Convenience of trading from anywhere
- Access to variety of information in different sites.

E-employment Several kinds of services are provided here;

- sites give advice on developing our resumes and to post our resumes on the web
- recruiters use website to post available jobs
- match making facilities for jobs and jobseekers based on a specifications
- use of agents to do the search.

E-retailing offers the following benefits;

- Provision of online catalogue to browse different categories of goods
- Provision of search engine
- Provision of shopping cart
- Personalization of store layouts deals, promotions
- Distribute digital goods directly
- Online salesperson to help customers to navigate through the site
- An order status checking facility.

Decide Suitable Distribution Mechanism

E-stores and e-malls sell a large number of product lines rather than very few. In an e-mall, cyberspace is rented out to cyber e-stores that wish to sell their goods. Several product lines can be present in a single e-mall in an e-mall; each store is under its own management. Mall management is responsible only for creating the cyber sites that-can be rented and can support services and marketing of the mall. It provides webhosting services. They also provide software tools, which can be utilised by a prospective e-store-to create and maintain its e-store. The advantage is that it is grouped together with other stores in a well known e-mall site.

E-brokers Brokers provide comparison shopping, ordertaking and fulfillment and services to a customer. The models of e-brokers include;

- Provide registration service
- Directory search facilities-payment facilities
- Ascertain requirement such as price
- Provide comparison-shopping between products.

E-CRM solutions can be deployed and managed to provide increased revenues and reduced costs. E-CRM goals can be achieved with internet business strategies, web based CR M specification development, web system design and project management electronic publishing and interactive interface.

They are valuable to companies face the following circumstances

- Business is driven by mission-critical customer service requirements
- Current costs for crm run high
- Large volume of information is distributed
- A complete customer care solution is required.

E-directories Telephone directories with white pages for private telephone numbers and the yellow pages for the businesses is essential to locate a person of business. Now the telephone companies allowed people to call in and ask for information. The data base is located in a single place providing a centralized functionality, offering to anyone at anytime, thus making a decentralized solution. The internet facilitates replication of phone directories without hassles. The internet makes the retrieval easier as well as more difficult.

E-engineering has also changed dramatically in the recent years. Internet changed the speed of the design. It enabled electronic collaboration to much a higher degree than n before. The location of the engineer s has become easier. The internet changed the speed of the design. It enabled electronic collaboration to a much higher degree than was possible ever before. The location of the engineers does not play a role anymore. Everyone with an internet connection is able to take part in the development. New tools concurrent development has been developed to support the possibilities of the internet. Through the internet has also become possible to develop continuous engineer ring by letting engineers participate from all overt the world. Open source development is done that way very efficiently. Anybody is able to take part and can donate a piece of code whenever there has been some time to programme it. This will vary for every person involved.

E-franchising The re-sellers are called franchising partners. By offering a set of products and brands the franchising company guarantees a certain success for the retailer as people tend to like buying these products, as the brands are well known. The advantage of the franchising companies is that they do not need to invest in shop personnel, for example, the franchising g partners is responsible or the employees and financial success of the single outlet. Electronic franchising works very similarly. It has become much easier on the internet. Moving digital products, processes and brands is extremely easy. The affiliation programmes of the large book sellers on the internet have their own store. But they allow franchising partners to exclusively distribute their products on the partner's websites. The advantage of this system is that there is no distribution costs involved. It is possible to link to the original products without letting the customers know.

E-gambling Although there is a moral issue about gambling, it is one of the most profitable businesses on the internet. In the real world gambling is restricted by many laws, making it difficult to access the casinos. The owners of the games often need to pay high taxes to the state, which makes it so difficult to create competition. Gambling is still not legal in some states and the taxes are still high in these states, but the business has moved to places where gambling is legal and only low taxes need to paid. The companies who operate the gambling websites are able to provide the full program of games, without any restrictions. As the owners have their companies in countries where gambling is legal, they are able to operate without fearing the intervention of the state. But other than the real world casinos which are restricted to the geographical location, online casinos are able to attract gamblers from all over the world with a mouse click.

E-learning is a revolutionary way to empower, a work force with the skills and knowledge it needs to turn changes to on advantages.It is faster chapter and more productive then class room instruction.Electronic learning educating employees using web enabled materials deployed via the net offers in its most sophisticated incarnations such bells and whistles as streaming audio and video, built –in power point presentation, hot links to related information the web, animation, flipbooks and self-running screen-capture display programme. E-learning is a significantly cheaper and more protective and can be delivered with more timeliness than either classroom learning or traditional computer-enhanced teaching.

E-Marketing is a traditional marketing using electronic methods affecting traditional marketing in two ways. It increases efficiency in established marketing function and transforms many marketing strategies. Internet serves as efficient marketing tools for both secondary and primary data collection. In addition electronic technologies affect the 4ps.

- Product Internet technologies spawned a variety of innovative product for creating, delivering and reading messages as well as services such as reverse auctions, business to business (B 2 B), market exchanges and interactive games.
- Pricing The net turned pricing strategies upside down. Bartering, bidding, dynamic pricing, and individualized pricing are now quite on line.
- Place The e-marketeers used the net for direct distribution of digital productsand for electronic retailing.
- Promotion The net assists with two way communication; one to one web pages-mail conversations, and e-main conferencing via news group and mailing lists. E-marketers also use the net for promotions, and sending electronic coupons and digital products samples directly to consumers.

E-Operational Resource Management Beside the goods that are needed for production, companies need to buy operational resources, these are the non production goods are services that are required and managed on a daily basis to run the day-to –day business. Operational resources allow companies to manage operational resources more strategically, by using the internet and its connectivity to provide a communication infrastructure, where buyer and supplier can together on a direct basis without losing control over the spending. E-Supply Manufacturers, logistics companies, senders, receiver and retailers all work together to co-ordinate the order generation and order taking. The order fulfillment and the distribution of the products, services, or information are organized together by the supply chain management. By digitalizing the products, the processes and the communication the internet has a great potential linking and managing this organization.

E-Trading Before the internet, buying and selling stock war restricted to people with access to financial network. The internet has changed the way stocks are traded. E-trading also called E-brokering offers the real –time stock price to every desk throughout the world.

People are able in real time to change in the stock market. Every one with on internet bank account is able to buy and sell stock. This enables anyone to participate in the stock market and earn money by investing.

The Basic E Business Models

The emerging e-business market affords companies of all sizes and types the opportunity to leverage their existing assets, employees, technology infrastructure, and information to gain or maintain marketshare. For example, in the telecommunications industry, service, rather than technology, is now the key differentiator. With lower barriers to entry, new competitors are rapidly entering the market offering new services, such as online bill presentment and payment, and leveraging their unique digital assets.

Information technology research analysts agree that e-business is any net-enabled business activity that transforms internal and external relationships to create value and exploit market opportunities driven by new rules of the connected economy. However, today's e-business requires more. Industry analysts further point out that e-business involves the continuous optimization of an organization's value proposition and value-chain position through the adoption of digital technology.

The challenge for an organization is to turn the vision and the market opportunity into a viable business. Developing the marketing strategy and plans and designing and deploying the business solution is key. Those who successfully architect, develop, and deploy e-business solutions will need to formulate and adopt a comprehensive business plan. Because of the critical role of Internet technologies and integration requirements, it is recommended that organizations need a comprehensive planning framework—an actual e-business model. This structured planning approach enables the organization to assess, plan for, and implement the multiple aspects of an e-business.

Building an e-business (an integrated value chain) that leverages the Internet's communications capabilities is a complex undertaking. The complex integration requirements of the business solutions, all performing at extremely high levels of availability and scalability, require an e-business model architectural approach. The value chain (comprised of the traditional supply chain management functions, planning, procurement, and inventory management, coupled with the customer-facing functions, typically referred to as customer relationship management) has integration and performance demands that exceed the requirements seen in traditional businesses. In a successful e-business, all of these areas are tightly integrated to provide an organization the ability to quickly and efficiently sell, manufacture, and deliver products or services.

Furthermore, in a successful e-business, this value chain rests on a foundation that leverages the organization's existing core operational business systems, as well as meets the new business-critical operational requirements for reliability, scalability, flexibility, and 24 × 7 × 365 availability in a highly volatile, electronic marketplace. An e-business model includes three essential elements:

- Solid strategies
- Knowledge management techniques applied to a company's information and intellectual assets
- Effective e-business processes typically grouped in the customer relationship management (CRM), supply chain management (SCM), and core business operations domains.

Solid Strategies

Strategy and execution are key to developing and sustaining a successful e-business. Only those organizations that successfully integrate key business strategies and processes dramatically increase their efficiencies. To be successful, organizations must also form the right strategic relationships and develop efficient business processes with robust backend solutions that are able to meet users' demands for real-time service today and into the future.

In the past, businesses had the luxury of developing business strategies in the boardroom and IT strategies in the IT department. They then brought these strategies together to run the overall business. E-businesses cannot afford this luxury. The ability to react and change direction is critical. Speed is everything. Grounding the organization with sound, winning strategies is key.

In the new economy's competitive electronic environment, it is easier for an organization to be global, but it is also harder to maintain consistency in the levels of services offered around the world. E-businesses must be ready and able to adjust their business and IT strategies rapidly, depending on unpredictable competitors and market pressures. Today's e-business climate requires the continuous optimization of an organization's business and IT strategies. Because IT now has such a significant impact on every business process (from order taking to inventory to billing), both business and IT strategies are now developed in parallel.

The best example of this is Dell Computer. From the start, the company's business strategy was tightly aligned with its IT strategy, allowing Dell to successfully integrate every aspect of its business (from order taking to inventory to billing) with both its customers and suppliers. Dell vaulted to the forefront of its industry when it came to market with a winning strategy, the unique just-in-time-delivery model. Unlike traditional computer suppliers, Dell's business strategy was founded on the premise of zero inventory.

Similarly, online brokerage companies have been leaders in the area of integrating IT and business strategies. The rapid adoption of Internet technologies combined with market globalization, industry deregulation, and media convergence has afforded these companies the opportunity to gain share and create value in the e-business marketplace.

Turning an organization's intellectual assets into knowledge is a key business differentiator. In addition to a continually optimized business strategy, successful e-businesses must establish solid knowledge management practices. Knowledge management is the definitive way to leverage an organization's information and intellectual assets for business advantage. It is the formalized, integrated approach that every organization must take to "know" its business.

Knowledge Management Techniques

Every business has both tacit and explicit knowledge. One is undocumented, and the other is documented about what is "known" in the company. This knowledge may include information about products and services or information about how the company works with a particular supplier. No matter what type of knowledge an e-business has, the company must put into place processes for organizing that knowledge.

Knowledge management includes managing intellectual capital, such as best practices, critical business processes, and operating metrics. Establishing ongoing processes for acquiring, organizing, and distributing this knowledge about customers, products, and processes is critical to success. The business domains, CRM, SCM, and core business operations, are dependent on this information and these intellectual assets.

Effective E-Business Processes

In every successful e-business, the business process domains (CRM, SCM, and core business operations) are an integral part of the continuous optimization process. The advantage and, thus, the return on investment for an e-business integrating its business process domains is that it extends the organization's business directly to customers and suppliers.

When business process domains are integrated, they can increase productivity and improve customer and supplier satisfaction. For example, when a repeat customer views a successful e-business's Web site, an integrated CRM system presents that individual with offers or items of interest based on previous orders. After the customer places an order, this same e-business allows that individual to view the status of his order in real time as it moves through the supply chain.

Business process domains are aggregations of core business processes. Although there is growing popularity of business process domains as their own entities (CRM, SCM, and core business operations), they are commanding a mind-share in the marketplace (and each has attracted various vendors and products to support it). These domains must operate together as a key component to the overall e-business strategy. In a successful e-business, convergence is the driving connection of all of the business process domains. When there appears to a customer or a supplier to be no barrier between departments, the business process domains are tightly integrated with the business and IT strategies.

Customer Relationship Management

Customer relationships are becoming a more important factor in differentiating one business from another. In order to stay competitive, e-businesses in every industry have begun to analyse these relationships with customers using CRM solutions.

In the past, customers would place an order via the telephone and wait until the company's purchasing department processed and shipped the order. Today's customers place an order electronically and then demand to be able to check the status of their order within minutes.

CRM enables an organization to adopt a comprehensive view of the customer and maximize this relationship. These CRM systems enable a business to identify, attract, retain, and support customs centres, direct mail, and retail facilities. In an efficient e-business, there are CRM processes in place to handle:

Analytical CRM: The analysis of data created on the operational side of the CRM equation for the purpose of business performance management; utilizing data warehousing technologies and leveraging data marts

Customer interactions: Sales, marketing, and customer service (call center, field service) via multiple, interconnected delivery channels and integration between front office and back office.

Operational CRM: The automation of horizontally integrated business processes involving "front office" customer touch points.

Personalization: The use of new and traditional groupware/Web technologies to facilitate customer and business partner communications.

Supply Chain Management

Integration of the SCM functions is emerging as one of the greatest challenges facing today's e-businesses. SCM is the integration of business processes from end user through to original supplier. The goal of SCM is to create an end-to-end system that automates all the business processes between suppliers, distribution partners, and trading partners. The new mantra for this process, according to industry analysts, is "replacing inventory with information." In an effective e-business, the following SCM independent processes must be highly integrated.

Demand management: These are shared functions, including demand planning, supply planning, manufacturing planning, and sales and operations planning.

Inbound/outbound logistics: These include transportation management, distribution management, and warehouse management.

Supply management: These include products and services for customer order fulfillment.

Core Operations

E-businesses also need to develop and operate complex transaction processing systems that support their core business operations. These core operations include the operational systems that support their particular business, such as claims processing, trade execution, enterprise resource planning (ERP), and enterprise resource management (ERM).

Whether a company is just beginning to transform its business into an e-business or is an e-business strengthening its market position, organizations must put in place architectures that support large and complex integrated solutions. E-businesses must address the performance requirements for reliability, scalability, and high availability. These systems also require a high level of flexibility, integration, and often the added complexity of operating in a global business environment. These e-businesses need to integrate their customer relationship management, supply chain, and core business operational systems such as enterprise resource planning, accounting, and general business support systems to operate efficiently.

Marketing in the New Economy-Online Marketing

Before going into the topic let us understand the basic difference between Internet and World Wide Web.

The internet is a worldwide network of computers networks. And the World Wide Web is one of the Internet's most popular services, providing access to over two billion Web pages.

Do you think there is any difference between E-Business and E-commerce?

What is E-Business?

E-business primarily concerns the applications of digital technologies to business within the firm. E-business refers primarily to the digital enablement of transactions and processes within a firm, involving information systems under the control of the firm. It does not include commercial transactions involving an exchange of value across organizational boundaries. For example, a company online inventory control mechanisms are a component of e-business, but such internal processes do not directly generate revenue for the firm from outside business or consumers. E-business applications turn into e-commerce precisely when an exchange of value occurs.

And e-commerce and e-business systems can and do blur together at the business firm boundary, at the point where internal business systems link up with suppliers, for instance.

We are living in an exciting time. The Power, capabilities, and worldwide reach of the Internet are quickly changing the way the world does business. E-business means any business conducted using electronic media such as the Internet, other computer networks, wireless transmissions, etc. It also stands for electronic business and refers to any kind of sales, services, purchasing or commerce on the Internet.

What is E-commerce?

E-commerce means the use of internet and the web to transact business. E-commerce primarily involves digitally enabled commercial transactions between and among organisations and individuals.

What is E-marketing?

Marketing deals with identifying and meeting human and social needs. One of the shortest definitions of marketing is "meeting needs profitably". The newest channels for direct marketing are electronic. E-business describes a wide variety of electronic platforms, such as the sending of purchase orders to suppliers via electronic data interchange (EDI) or extranets; the use of fax and e-mail to conduct transactions; the use of ATMs, and smart cards to facilitate payment and obtain digital cash; and the use of the Internet and online services. All of these involve doing business in a "market space" as compared to physical "market place".

The Internet today functions as an information source, an entertainment source, a communication channel, a transaction channel, and even a distribution channel. One can use it as a shopping mall, a TV set, a news paper, a library, or a phone. Users can send e-mail, exchange views, shop for products, and access news, recipes, art and business information.

The internet provides marketers and consumers with opportunities for much greater interaction and individualization. Companies in the past would send standard media –magazines, newsletters, ads-without any individualization or interaction. Today these companies can send individualized content and consumers themselves can further individualize the content; and today companies can interact and dialogue with much larger groups than ever in the past.

Very simply put, eMarketing or electronic marketing refers to the application of marketing principles and techniques via electronic media and more specifically the Internet. The terms E-Marketing, Internet marketing and online marketing, are frequently interchanged, and can often be considered synonymous.

E-Marketing is the process of marketing a brand using the Internet. It includes both direct response marketing and indirect marketing elements and uses a range of technologies to help connect businesses to their customers. By such a definition, eMarketing encompasses all the activities a business conducts via the worldwide web with the aim of attracting new business, retaining current business and developing its brand identity.

The seven unique features of E-commerce Technology

1. *Ubiquity:* E-commerce liberates the market from being restricted to a physical space and makes it possible to shop from our desktop, at home, at work, or even from our car. From customer point of view, ubiquity reduces transaction costs, (the cost of participating in a market) time spend and money travelling to a market.

2. *Global reach:* E-commerce permits transactions to cross cultural and national boundaries far more conveniently and cost effectively than is true in traditional commerce.
3. *Universal standards:* The technical standards for conducting e-commerce are universal standards. The standards are shared by all nations around the world. The universal technical standards of e-commerce greatly lower market entry costs and search costs for customers by creating a single, one-world market space where prices and product descriptions can be displayed for all to see.
4. *Reachness:* During the traditional market it was not possible to reach up to the different places of the market but e-commerce enables the businessman to reach out even to the last customer living at the end of the world at any time with the development of the web.
5. *Interactivity:* E-commerce makes it possible for two-way communication between businessman and customers which was not possible in traditional market. Customers are able to get the latest of information about the product that they want to use at any time, sitting at any corner of the world.
6. *Information density:* E-commerce technologies reduce information collection, storage, processing and communication costs. At the same time increase greatly the currency, accuracy an d timeliness of information –making information more useful and important than ever. In e-commerce markets, prices and costs become more transparent. Therefore the consumer and the merchant both are benefited by e-commerce.
7. *Personalization/Customization:* E-commerce technologies permit personalization. Merchants can target their marketing messages to specific individuals by adjusting the message to a person's name, interests and past purchases.

Types of E-commerce

There are different types of e-commerce. Following are the lists of five major types of e-commerce.

Business-to-Consumer e-commerce (B2C)

In this type, online business attempt to reach individual consumers to sell out the goods. The most frequent online consumer purchases have been books, music, software, air tickets, PC peripherals, clothing, videos, hotel reservations, toys, flowers and consumer electronics.

Business-to-Business e-commerce (B2B)

In this type businesses focus on selling to other business. There are number of B2B business models developed, including e-distributors, B2b service providers, matchmakers, and infomediaries that are widening the use of B2B e-commerce. Forrester and Gartner, major research firms on online commerce estimated that B2B commerce is 10 to 15 times greater than B2C commerce. Firms are using B2B auction sites, spot exchanges, online product catalogues, and other online resources to obtain better prices.

Consumer-to-Consumer (C2C)

In this type of e-commerce consumers sells to other consumers with the help of an online market maker, such as the auction site eBay. In C2C e-commerce, the consumer prepares the product for market, places the product for auction or sale, and relies on the market maker to provide catalog, search engine, and transaction-clearing capabilities so that products can be easily displayed, discovered, and paid for. The size of the market is estimate over $5 billion and is growing rapidly.

AOL boasts some 14000 chat rooms covering such topics as healthy eating, caring for your Bonsai tree, and exchanging views about latest soap opera happenings.

Peer-to-Peer e-commerce (P2P)

Peer-to-peer technology enables internet users to share files and computer resources directly without having to go through a central Web server. In this e-commerce no intermediary is required.

Examples:

1. Gnutella is a peer-to-peer freeware software application that permits users to directly exchange musical tracks, typically without any charge.
2. Napster.com established to aid internet users in finding and sharing online music files known as MP3 files.

M-commerce

Mobile commerce or m-commerce refers to the use of wireless digital devices to enable transactions on the Web. It utilizes wireless networks to connect call phones and handheld devices such as the PalmVIIx to the Web. Once it is connected the mobile consumers can conduct many types of transactions, including stock trades, in-store price comparisons, banking, travel reservations, and more. It is most widely used in Japan and Europe where cell phones are more prevalent than in the United States but it is expected to grow more rapidly.

Marketing in New Globalised Economy

Today's Companies need fresh thinking about how to operate and compete in the new economy. Today's economy is made up of old and new elements and is essentially a hybrid. We want to emphasize new elements such as the following:

- Companies are increasingly subcontracting activities to outsourcing firms. Their principle is to outsource those activities that others can do cheaper and better but retain core activities.
- Companies are increasingly benchmarking their performance against best-of-class companies anywhere in the world.
- Companies are deepening their partnering arrangements with key suppliers and distributors.
- Companies are emphasizing interdepartmental teamwork to manage Key processes rather than relying on traditional departmental systems.
- Companies are recognizing that, much of their market value comes from intangible assets, particularly their brands, customer base, employees, distributor and supplier relations, and intellectual capital.
- Companies are making substantial investments in information systems as the key to lower their costs and gain a competitive edge.

Many standard marketing practices like mass media advertising, sales promotion, sales force calls were part of the old economy. They will continue to be important, but today's businesses will have to answer such questions as:

1. "Is too much money being spent on mass advertising and not enough on one-to-one customer relationship management?
2. "Will companies need as many salespeople as before in an information-rich economy?"
3. "Should companies reduce their huge sales promotion expenditures and move to everyday low prices?"

The Major Driver's of the New Economy

Many forces play a major role in reshaping the world economy, among them technology, globalization and market deregulation play a major role. Here we will describe four specific drivers that strengthen the new economy:

1. Digitalization and connectivity
2. Disintermediation and re-intermediation
3. Customization and customerization
4. Industry convergence.

Digitalization and Connectivity

Today most appliances and systems operate with digital information, which convert text data, sound, and images into a stream of zeroes and ones that can be combined into bits and transmitted from appliance to appliance. Software is essentially digital instructions for operating systems, games, storage, and other applications.

But bits will not reside in separate appliance unless connectivity is established. For bits to flow from one appliance and location to another, a wired or wireless communication network is necessary. The Internet, the "information highway," can dispatch bits at incredible speeds from one location to another. Much of today's business is carried over networks connecting people and companies. When they connect people within a company to one another and to the company mainframe these networks are called Intranets. Extranets when they connect a company with its suppliers and distributors; and the Internet when they connect users to a large worldwide "information repository." Connectivity is further enhanced by wireless communication. Consumers and business people no longer need to be near a computer to send and receive information. All they need is a cellular phone or personal digital assistant (PDA, such as a Palm). While they are on the move, they can connect with the internet to check stock prices, the weather, sports scores, or send and receive email messages. They can place online orders by simply using a phone or a PDA.

Disintermediation and Reinterpretation

The new technological capabilities have led thousands of entrepreneurs to launch a dotcom in the hope of striking gold. The amazing success of early online dot-coms such as AOL, Amazon, and yahoo struck terror in the hearts of many established manufacturers and retailers. For example, Compaq had its hands tied because it sold its computers through retailers, whereas Dell Computer grew faster by choosing to sell online. Established store-based retailers-notably bookstores, music stores, travel agents, stockbrokers and car dealers – began to doubt their future as more businesses went into direct online marketing. They feared, and rightly so, being disintermediated by the new e-tailers.

But disintermediation was only half the story. Re-intermediation took place on a grand scale. New online middlemen appeared such as mysimon.com, Priceline.com, lifeshopper.com, buy.com, compare.com.

As for the traditional "brick-only" firms – such as Compaq and Merrill Lynch started their own online sales channels becoming "brick-and-click" competitors.

Customization and Customerization

The old economy revolved around manufacturing companies whose main drive was to standardize production, products, and business processes. Through standardization and branding, manufacturers hoped to grow and take advantage of economies of scale. In contrast, the new economy is supported by information businesses. As companies grew proficient at gathering information about individual customers and business partners (suppliers, distributors, retailers), and as their factories were designed more flexibly, they increased their ability to individualize their market offerings, messages and media.

For example, Dell Computer invites customers to specify exactly what they want in a computer and delivers a custom-built one in a few days.

The combination of operational customization and marketing customization has been called customerization. A company is customerized when it is able to dialogue with individual customers and respond by customizing its products, services and messages on a one-to-one basis.

Customization is not for every company: There are several downsides.

(a) Customization can raise the cost of goods by more than the customer is willing to pay.

(b) Some customers do not know what they want until they see actual products.

(c) Customers cannot cancel the order after the company has started the work on the product.

(d) The product may be hard to repair and have little sales value.

In spite of this, customization has worked well for some products like laptop computers, apparel, skincare products, and vitamins and is an opportunity worth investigating.

Industry Convergence

Industry boundaries are blurring at an incredible rate. Film companies such as Kodak are also chemical companies, but they are moving into electronics to digitize their image-making capabilities. Disney is not only into cartoons and theme parks, but it makes major films, licenses characters, and manage retail stores, hotels, cruise ships, and educational facilities. In all these cases, companies are recognizing that new opportunities lie at the intersection of two or more industries.

How business practices are changing

(a) From organizing by product units to organizing by customer segments.

(b) From focusing on profitable transactions to focusing on customers lifetime value.

(c) From focusing on just the financial scorecard to focusing also on the marketing scorecard.

(d) From focusing on shareholders to focusing on stakeholders.

(e) From Marketing being the exclusive responsibility of the marketing department to marketing being every employee's responsibility.

(f) From building brands through advertising to building brand through performance.

(g) From focusing on customer acquisition to focusing on customer retention.

(h) From no customer satisfaction measurement to in-depth customer satisfaction measurement.

(i) From over-promise, under-deliver to under-promise, over-deliver.

(j) Today's marketplace is made up of traditional consumers (who do not buy online), cyber consumers (who mostly buy online), and hybrid consumers (who do both). Most consumers are hybrid. They shop in grocery stores but occasionally order from Peapod; they buy books in Barnes & Noble bookstores and sometimes order books from bn.com.

But people still like to squeeze the tomatoes, touch the fabric, smell the perfume, and interact with salespeople. Consumers are motivated by other needs than only shopping efficiency. Most companies will need a presence of both offline and online to cater to these hybrid consumers. Companies are adjusting their marketing practices to meet new conditions. Two newer practices that companies and their marketers are getting involved are:

1. E-business and
2. Customer relationship management.

How marketing practices are changing:

E-business

E-business describes the use of electronic means and platforms to conduct a company's business. The advent of the internet has greatly increased the ability of companies to conduct their business faster, more accurately, over a wide range of time and space, at reduced cost, and with the ability to customize and personalize customer offerings. Countless companies have set up websites to inform and promote their products and services. They have created Intranets to facilitate employees communicating with one another and to facilitate downloading and uploading information to and from the company's computers. Companies have also set up Extranets with major suppliers and distributors to facilitate information exchange, orders, transactions, and payments.

E-commerce is more specific than e-business; it means that in addition to providing information to visitors about the company, its history, policies products, and job opportunities, it also offers to transact or facilitate the selling of products and services online. Amazon.com, e-plasticsnet, e-steel are examples of e-commerce sites. E-commerce has given rise in turn to e-purchasing and e-marketing.

E-purchasing means companies decide to purchase goods, services, and information from various online suppliers. Smart e-purchasing has already saved companies millions of dollars.

E-marketing describes company efforts to inform, communicate, promote and sell its products and services over the Internet.

Customer Relationship Marketing

Customer relationship marketing (CRM) enables companies to provide excellent real-time customer service by developing a relationship with each valued customer through the effective use of individual account information. Based on what they know about each individual customer, companies can customize market offerings, services, programs, messages and media.

Examples for E-marketing

These are the examples/names of the companies and their products which sell their products through online.

Sony Company

The products of Sony Company are as under:

1. Sony cameras and optics
2. Sony digital cameras
3. Sony laptops and accessories
4. Sony TV and accessories
5. Sony LCD TV
6. Home Audio
7. Portable CD player
8. T.V. remote

9. Computer
10. Sony hardware
11. Sony mobile games
12. Walkman
13. In-car entertainment
14. Battery & charger.

IBM (International Business Machines)

The products of IBM Company are as under:

1. Punched card machinery
2. Time clock
3. Typewriters
4. Mainframe computers
5. Minicomputer
6. Softwares
7. Small business products
8. Medium business products
9. All IT services like, IT strategies, security and privacy services, integrated communication services, etc.
10. System and servers

Nike Company

1. Watches
2. Digital sports watch
3. Compass watch
4. Clothes (men & women)
5. Bags
6. Shoes
7. Spectacles
8. Sandals
9. Sports digital audio play
10. Jackets
11. Water shoes
12. Hiking shoes

Adidas

1. Basketballs
2. Golf

3. Tennis
4. Foot ball
5. Eyewear
6. Watches
7. Deo spray
8. Bags
9. Hats
10. Balls
11. Apparel for men and men
12. Gloves

Pros and Cons of Online Marketing

Pros

1. *Convenience:* Customers can order products 24 hours a day wherever they are.
2. *Information:* Customers can find reams of comparative information about company's products, competitors and prices without leaving their office or home.
3. *Fewer hassles:* Customers don't have to face sales people or open themselves up to persuasion and they don't have to wait in line.
4. *Lower costs:* On-line marketers avoid the expense of maintaining a store and the costs of rent, insurance and utilities.

Cons

1. *Limited Consumer exposure and buying:* Web users are doing more surfing than buying. Only an estimated 18% of surfers actually use the web regularly for shopping or to obtain commercial services such as travel information.
2. *Chaos and clutter:* The Internet offers millions of web sites and a staggering volume of information. Navigating the web can be frustrating. Many sites go unnoticed.
3. *Security:* Consumers worry that unscrupulous interlopers will intercept their credit-card numbers.
4. *Skewed user demographics and psychographics:* Online users are more upscale and technically oriented than the general population, making them ideal for computer, electronics and financial services but less so for mainstream products.

Case Study on Ultralase Advertising

Ultralase are a company offering laser eye treatment – a high value consumer service. In 2003 their market was characterised by intense competition with other suppliers such as Optimax, Optical Express and AccuVision. Ultralase had relatively low brand awareness and was struggling with a long sales cycle and relatively uninformed customers. The main communications disciplines used were:

* Press
* Direct Mail
* PR
* Brochures
* From 2004 onwards, they increased their digital expenditure and in 2006 at Ad Tech presented their achievements through their agency, Agency.com. These included:
* 10 Million site visits per year
* 3.7 billion ad impressions (Jan to Sept 2006)
* Reach between 18M and 22M unique users per month-Now the dominant online brand with a high brand awareness and a shorter sales cycle.

To achieve this, they introduced online media channels including:

* Affiliate marketing
* Paid search marketing
* Display advertising
* Email marketing based on permission-based lead generation through offers on their website.
* DVD's.

Ultralase case study from agency Advertising.com-they are one of the largest UK Internet advertisers.

Costly product – up to four thousand plans.

Laser eye surgery clinics – 100,000 UK customersIn 2003, relatively there was low brand awareness, long sales cycle, and low brand familiarity. Reassurance and education are important. Their advertising objectives with new agency were to improve these areas. Big Internet display ad campaign run by Agency.com more or less continuously-2006 to-date with 3.7 billion ad impressions generating 18 to 20m unique users per month. If we assume 1 visit per unique visitor I make that around 0.5% click through, so probably higher since more than one.

Ultralase use a direct response model – customers register for more information – pack and book a consultation by phone or by call-centre. All data is stored within E-CRM system. They track individual customers through their terms, e.g. Brand clicks e.g. Ultralase Generic only, e.g. Laser eye treatment When volumes highest, found increased searches on brand term, increased conversion rates on search and higher conversion rate from E-CRM/E-mail marketing activity. Shorter conversion from consultation to treatment.

Found two types of leads:

- Fast online lead – direct response – only works well over 25% of ad inventory
- Complex online lead – halo effect – longer period – works over more of network to increase leads – searches, etc. Ultralase have a deep site engages people through interactive consultation guides and consultation.

Nike Versus Adidas Case Study

Nike and Adidas are two primary footwear companies along with their competitors who have adopted an online e-commerce strategy to increase their sales and product awareness. Most importantly, companies like Nike and Adidas have invested heavily into online brand building and image development. Nike launched the nike.com web site in August 1996 primarily to provide information to its consumers.

In 1996, there were no e-commerce capabilities present, however the web site served as a brand building tool for the company. In 1999, Nike redesigned their web site with expanded e-commerce functionality. Adidas launched their web site in the spring of 2000, which was later integrated with e-commerce capabilities.

In order to maximize their market share, both Nike and Adidas have placed a great importance in developing their branding and marketing strategies on the net through web appearance and user friendly functionalities such as ease of purchase, speed, and navigation. Nike and Adidas have adopted a merchant model which encompassed three pillars of their e-commerce strategy: pure-play e-tailer, bricks and clicks, and their online store. The main purposes of acquiring relationships with pure-play e-tailers is to promote and market products; focus on the content to create new exposure and; gather, gain and transfer market knowledge to their business counterparts.

The Internet has proven to be a useful tool for firms such as Nike and Adidas by increasing sales and reducing cost.

But most importantly their web sites have provided them with an intangible asset such as market research and consumer buying behaviors. With the data retrieve from consumers, these firms are able to analyse and monitor the buying behaviors of their consumers. The data can also be used to exploit new marketing campaigns and promotions. Furthermore, the data collected can be used to produce innovative designs and improve their research capabilities.

Although, there are perceived benefits in conducting e-business over the Internet there are also potential barriers. The major barrier of e-commerce with respect to large firms such as Nike and Adidas is the technological barrier ranging from infrastructure to security. An ongoing battle the e-commerce industry faces is security. With time and additional research and resources, this problem will be mitigated. Meanwhile, both Nike and Adidas must minimize their technological risks.

While both Nike and Adidas currently have an essential advantage over their rivals, but there are chances that their advantages will not last forever.

Although, Nike and Adidas have engaged in e-commerce there are apparent gaps within their e-business strategy. E-commerce is only available in restricted regions such as the United States and the United Kingdom, therefore opportunities exists within the global market to expand.

A daring dream began in 1920 when Adi Dassler fashioned his first shoe in Herzogenaurach, Germany. In 1948, Adidas was founded along with its identifying trademark, the three stripes.

From its inception, Adidas has faithfully adhered to three guiding principles embedded deep into its DNA:

1. Produce the best shoe for the requirements of the sport,
2. Protect the athlete from injury, and
3. Make the product durable.

As time has passed, Adidas has evolved and is now one of the premier global leaders in sporting brands offering athletic footwear, apparel and accessories. This feat has been cultivated through continuous innovation and a broad product portfolio. With time, Adidas discovered that in order to continue to evolve further its strategy had to include the Internet. This led to the development of www.thestore.adidas.com, an e-commerce site focused on interactively profiling Adidas's extensive product offerings accompanied by detailed product information.

Initially, what started as Blue Ribbon Sports in 1962 became Nike Inc. in 1972, based in Beaverton, Oregon. Nike was named for the Greek winged goddess of victory. The founders were Bill Bowerman, a track & field coach and Phil Knight, a runner under Bowerman. From their modest start, Nike has grown to be a global leader in the sporting goods industry. It is recognized as the world's leading designer, marketer and distributor of athletic footwear, apparel, and accessories for a wide variety of sports and fitness activities. For Nike, an established and growing organization, a strong Internet presence felt like a natural extension to their already globally focused strategy. Today www.niketown.com, Nike's e-commerce site offers a unique experience, products and product information for its potential and existing customers.

Value Configuration The inputs to the e-commerce value configuration for both Nike and Adidas are:

1. Brand Image,
2. Price,
3. Web site design,
4. Service, and
5. Innovation.

In financial Analysis of Nike and Adidas

SWOT Analysis for Nike.com & Adidas.com

Strengths

1. First movers advantage in e-commerce
2. Diversity and variety in products offered on the web (footwear, apparel, sporting equipment, etc.)
3. Innovative designs in footwear enabling consumers to design their own shoes online
4. Diversity and variety in products offered on the web (footwear, apparel, sporting equipment, etc.) Adidas even offers items not available in its retail stores
5. Secondary web sites (i.e. soccerevolution.com to simply promote soccer, Adidas leads the market in this sport)

Weaknesses

1. E-commerce is limited to USA
2. The direct sale to consumers is creating conflicts with its own resellers

3. Currently available supply chain, manufacturing, and fulfillment technologies aren't easily integrated with online build-to-order not known for its research and development leading to innovative designssystems
4. The e-commerce is limited to USA, however, has planned to expand to Canada and international in the near future
5. Online customer service not "helpful" or easy to find.

Opportunities

1. Increasing demand in the industry for products available online
2. E-commerce will reduce the cost of goods sold thus improving the "bottom line"
3. New technology and innovation to stay on top of market needs
4. Expand e-commerce to global markets
5. Possibility of outsourcing the web development and e-commerce to a third party developer
6. E-commerce will reduce the cost of goods sold thus improving the "bottom line"
7. Expand e-commerce to global markets
8. Collaborate with other online retailers to offer Adidas products

Because of E-commerce

Nike's ability to realize the potential of the Internet has placed them in the e-commerce leadership position among other sporting goods companies. Both Adidas's and Nike's strategy seem to be well ahead of their competition contributing to their e-commerce success. No other athletic footwear company is able to outshine these two firms when it comes to e-commerce, at least for now and in the near future as this task would involve large infrastructure investment and more importantly thorough commitment.

Role of IT in Rural Marketing

In recent years, rural markets have acquired significance, as the overall growth of the economy has resulted into substantial increase in the purchasing power of the rural communities. Rural areas are evolving into strategic market for companies which include not only domestic but MNCs too. There is great potential that lies in rural market.

More and more stress is therefore being given on marketing products. It is very interesting to notice that the rural markets are at par with the urban markets. The credit for this scenario goes to the marketing policies.

ITC e-Choupal is the greatest example of information technology in rural marketing. Launched in June 2000, 'e-Choupal', has already become the largest initiative in all internet-based interventions in rural India. ITC followed a different media/communication strategy which is more elaborate and extensive in rural marketing so far, which benefits both the farmers and the organization.

The strategy use the Information Technology and bridge the information and service gap in rural India which gives an edge to market its products like seeds, fertilizers and pesticides and other products like consumer goods etc.

They use the e-Choupal to order seed, fertilizer, and other products such as consumer good from ITC or its partners, at prices lower than those available from village traders. In this Paper we discuss about the role of IT in rural market, e-Chou pal, different strategy, vision and planning behind the e-Chou pal.

Significance

In recent years, rural markets have acquired significance in countries like China and India, as the overall growth of the economy has resulted into substantial increase in the purchasing power of the rural communities. On account of the green revolution in India, the rural areas are consuming a large quantity of industrial and urban manufactured products. In this context, a special marketing strategy, namely, *rural marketing* has taken shape. Sometimes, *rural marketing* is confused with *agricultural marketing* – the later denotes marketing of produce of the rural areas to the urban consumers or industrial consumers, whereas rural marketing involves delivering manufactured or processed inputs or services to rural producers or consumers. Also, when we consider the scenario of India and China, there is a picture that comes out, huge market for the developed products as well as the labor support. This has led to the change in the mindset of the marketers to move to these parts of the world.

Also rural market is getting an importance because of the saturation of the urban market. As due to the competition in the urban market, the market is more or so saturated as most of the capacity of the purchasers have been targeted by the marketers. So the marketers are looking for extending their product categories to an unexplored market i.e. the rural market. This has also led to the CSR activities being done by the corporate to help the poor people attain some wealth to spend on their product categories. Here we can think of HLL (now, HUL) initiatives in the rural India.

One of such project is the Project Shakti, which is not only helping their company attain some revenue but also helping the poor women of the village to attain some money which is surely going to increase their purchasing power. Also this will increase their brand loyalty as well as recognition in that area. Similarly we can think of the ITC E-Chou pal, which is helping the poor farmers get all the information about the weather as well as the market price of the food grains they are producing. In other view these activities are also helping the companies increase their brand value. So as it is given above the significance of the rural market has increased due to the saturation of the urban market as well as in such conditions the company which will lead the way will be benefited as shown by the success of HUL and ITC initiatives.

Strategies

Dynamics of rural markets differ from other market types, and similarly rural marketing strategies are also significantly different from the marketing strategies aimed at an urban or industrial consumer. This, along with several other related issues, have been subject matter of intense discussions and debate in countries like India and China and focus of even international symposia organized in these countries.

Rural markets and rural marketing involve a number of strategies, which include:

- Client and location specific promotion
- Joint or cooperative promotion..
- Bundling of inputs
- Management of demand
- Developmental marketing
- Unique selling proposition (USP)
- Extension services
- Business ethics
- Partnership for sustainability.

Client and Location specific promotion-involves a strategy designed to be suitable to the location and the client. Joint or co-operative promotion-strategy involves participation between the marketing agencies and the client.

'Bundling of inputs'-denote a marketing strategy, in which several related items are sold to the target client, including arrangements of credit, after-sale service, and so on. Management of demand-Involves continuous market research of buyer's needs and problems at various levels so that continuous improvements and innovations can be undertaken for a sustainable market performance. Developmental marketing-refer to taking up marketing programmers keeping the development objective in mind and using various managerial and other inputs of marketing to achieve these objectives. Media-both traditional as well as the modern media, is used as a marketing strategy.

Unique Selling Propositions (USP)-involves presenting a theme with the product to attract the client to buy that particular product. For examples, some of famous Indian Farm equipment manufactures have coined catchy themes, which they display along with the products, to attract the target client that is the farmers. English version of some of such themes would read like:

- The heartbeats of rural India
- With new technique for a life time of company
- For the sake of progress and prosperity.

Extension Services-denote, in short, a system of attending to the missing links and providing the required know-how.

Ethics in Business-form, as usual, an important plank for rural markets and rural marketing.

Partnership for sustainability-involves laying and building a foundation for continuous and long lasting relationship.

"' Building sustainable market linkages for rural products: Industry's role, scope, opportunities and challenges'"

E-Chou Pal Concept

ITC Limited is one of India's leading diversified conglomerates. Traditionally a tobacco and cigarette producer, it has grown into a conglomerate dealing in hotels, packaging, agribusiness, information technology, and fast moving consumer goods (FMCGs). ITC initiated its e-Chou pal project in 2000 to streamline its dealings with Indian farmers.

This is a project on a massive scale that ultimately aims to cover every sixth Indian village. Each Chou pal covers around six villages and 36,000 villages have been covered to date in Madhya Pradesh, Uttar Pradesh, Maharashtra, Rajasthan, Karnataka, and Andhra Pradesh.

Objectives and Goals

E-Chou pal aims to provide Indian farmers ready access to crop-specific real-time information and customized knowledge in their native language. By doing so, ITC wants to improves the farmers' decision-making ability, thereby helping them to better align their farm output to the projected demand in Indian and international markets.

Technologies

Typically, the Chou pals use Pentium computers along with a dot matrix printer and a UPS (500VA). ITC had initially upgraded telephone exchanges by using RNS (RAX Network Synchronization) kits, but eventually in most of the e-Chou pals, wireless VSAT links have been installed by bypassing the exchanges. Even with these improvements, the bandwidth often remains limited. Hence, e-Chou pals have started compensating by caching static content locally. ITC also uses a specially designed template for managing data combined with new imaging techniques in order to speed up downloads and to optimize bandwidth use. To overcome the problem of sporadic electricity, several kiosk computers use back-up batteries recharged with solar panels

Conclusion

E-Chou pals deliver relevant technology in the hands of the farmers, which can improve the economic condition of the entire village. E-Chou pal is one of the very few ICT projects in India that has effectively utilized e-commerce transactions for poverty alleviation. One of the key lessons is that ICT can reduce the number of middlemen involved between agriculture commodity producers and final consumers. Another key factor is that very simple technology solutions are available to create networks in rural areas, which can function as virtual agricultural commodity market places.

Marketing in Transition

Marketing is the management process that identifies, anticipates and satisfies customer requirements profitably. In pre-modern economies, the predominance of small enterprise and there was monopoly and there was no recognition of marketing as a separate field of expertise. Marketing emerged as a separate technical field only in the late 19th century.

In the present scenario, the changing needs and wants or taste and preferences among the customers leads to paradigm shift in marketing. This is due to changing attitude and behaviour of the customers, globalization, increasing purchasing power and changing life style of the customers.

Causes for Marketing in Transition;

- Globalization – Globalization has brought changes in technology, quality, service, work culture and undoubtedly fierce competition.

- Emerging Middle-Class Consumers – the increasing Purchasing Power of the Middle-Class consumers creates the MNC's to seek opportunity in the emerging market.
- Changing Lifestyle and attitude of Consumers – since there is a change in the customers lifestyle due to western influence the customer's needs and expectations has increased.
- Increasing literacy rate
- Children influence in buying decision making
- Changing perspective of rural marketing in India
- Increasing penetration of mass media
- Consumer awareness
- Information revolution
- An Enormous growth in international business.

Formation of marketing concepts and practices;

- 1905-the University of Pennsylvania offered a course in "The Marketing of Products"
- 1908-Harvard Business School opens
- 1940s-electronic computers developed
- 1980s-emergence of relationship marketing
- 1984- introduction of guerilla marketing
- 1995-2001-the Dot-com bubble temporarily re-defines the future of marketing
- 1996- identification of viral marketing.

Emerging New Marketing Practices

Due to increased competition the companies had necessity to enhance additional features to their products to promote the sale of their products. Many companies followed different marketing practices to attract their customers.

Winning concepts and marketing practices are;

- Relationship marketing
- Co-branding
- Viral Marketing
- Sachet Marketing
- Green marketing
- Rural marketing
- Destination marketing

- Online marketing
- Cause related marketing.

A transition from a product oriented approach to a resource oriented approach;

	Transaction marketing	*Relationship marketing*
Focus on	Obtaining new customers	Customer retention
Orientation to	Service features	Customer benefits
Timescale	shorts	long
Customer service	Little emphasis	High emphasis
Customer commitment	Limited	High
Customer contact	Limited	High
Quality concern	Primarily an operations The concern to all	

Nowadays many companies are practicing the new marketing concepts and practices. Some of the examples are as follows.

Relationship marketing: The domain of relationship marketing extends into many areas of marketing and strategic decision making. In the phenomenon of cooperation and collaboration with customers becomes the dominant paradigm of marketing practices. Relationship marketing has the potential to emerge as the predominance perspective in the paradigm of marketing. In the fierce competitive market customer relationship management is emerging as the core marketing activity in companies. For that to maintain companies practices customer retention strategies and having good relation with the customers.

Example: HSBC bank sent greeting cards to the customers on their birthdays to have good relationship

Whirlpool do very good post sale service to the customers.

Sachet Marketing

In India, Unilever successfully markets Sunsil and Lux shampoo sachets sold in units of 2-4 dollar cents; Clinic All Clear anti-dandruff shampoo sachets at 2.5 rupees each; and 16 cent Rexona deodorant sticks. Idhayam gingili oil available for Rs. 4/-package.

Green Marketing

It refers to the process of selling products and/or services based on their environmental benefits. Such a product or service may be environmentally friendly in itself or produced and/or packaged in an environmentally friendly way.

Green marketing can be a very powerful marketing strategy though when it's done right. Nowadays all companies are trying to produce eco-friendly products. And many companies have got ISO 14001 awards and strive to get.

Examples are; ITC products, in the note books it is environment friendly notebook.

Changing Perspective of Rural Marketing in India

The great Indian rural market is characterized by huge untapped potential and opportunities. It is estimated that almost 70% of Indian consumers live in rural areas, which generate almost half of the national income. The number of middle income households in rural India is growing to above 111 million by 2007. There are almost twice as many lower middle income households in rural areas as in the urban areas. A large number of corporate are excited about tapping the potential of rural areas. The recent entry of some corporate like Bharti, ITC, DCM shriram consolidated, EID parry and Amul etc. proved their fascination towards this sector. These corporates tried to develop successful model of integrating information-technology in rural transformation in a profitable way.

The tamilnadu based EID parry has developed an agro-portal www.indiaagrline.com to cater the specific needs of the rural farming community. It is an endeavor to catalyze e-commerce in agricultural and non-farms products by offering a network of partnerships. The content is available in local Tamil language. The Anand, Gurajat based Amuls DISK dairy information system KIOSK project is yet another milestone of integrating corporate sector and information technology. These kiosk serve valuable information related to dairying, breeding and rearing cattle. ITC e-choupal has emerged as one of the most ambitious project integrating information technology and corporate sector for rural transformation. ITC e-choupal network has already covered approximately 3.1 million farmers through 5050 choupal in 29,500 villages.

The company has ambitious plan to reach 1,00,000 villages covering 10 million farmers by 2010 with whopping approximately 1,000 crore. It is opening 5-6 e-choupals everyday in six different states of India.

Pepsi Rural Marketing

Pepsi company India has entered into rural market by having joint programme with the Punjab agriculture university in ludiana and Punjab agro industries corporation in chandigarh. The programme focuses on evolving agricultural practices to help Punjab farmers produce crops that would make Indian products internationally competitive. To cultivate a range of sweet oranges for its Tropicana range. Apart from that, they have given advertisement to attract the rural people with the celebrity of Amitabh Bachchan and star cricketer Sachin Tendulkar.

Coca-cola Rural Marketing

With the help of Isha foundation coca-cola released the CD of the coca-cola Tamil CSR film "Nesa Karangal" and also acknowledged and appreciated coca-cola's efforts in promoting social cohesiveness and sportsmanship with an aim to transform rural lives,

Advertisements to attract the rural customers are maasa-actress Rani Mukherji acted in this advertisement and says "masti ka chataka", Satis shah's maaza ad is also based on village background. Aamir khan acted in the advertisement which showcases a beautiful village background with the punch line "thanda ka matlab cocacola" and also ad title "soni kudi" targeted the villagers.

Destination Marketing

Destination marketing is all about selling the experience. To sell the experience is far more difficult. In destination marketing media plays a major role. Word of mouth plays a vital role in destination marketing, people love to discuss their tour, infact they feel proud in telling their experiences,they bring gifts for their close ones they show their photographs and purchases to their relatives and neighbours e.g. Kerala has implemented the destination marketing very successfully and emerged as the most acclaimed tourist destination of the country in the recent past. Because of this destination marketing Kerala has achieved remarkable success in generating revenue and employment in state through tourism. It is estimated nearly $100 million which generate the employment opportunity in Kerala.

In the recent past all the successful stories of destination marketing that is Malaysia, Goa, Kerala, Singapore etc.

Emergence of theme parks such as ADHISAYAM, MGM, BLACK THUNDER – all are examples of destination marketing.

Transition from Kirana stores to modern organized retail outlets:

Modern retailing in India is growing rapidly. Although it commands just 3% of the overall retail market share, changing demographics and consumer taste are driving the growth of more than 30% of the modern retail formats. It is expected to grow another 9% in the year of 2010. India is more attractive than ever to global retailers.

Major Players in India are;

Pantaloon retail India limited or future group, RPG group, Tata group, K.Raheja Corp. group of companies, RRL (Reliance retail limited), A.B.Birla group, Gati, Calvin Klein, Murjani group, Disney artist stores, Vishal group (Vishal Megamart)

Foreign players in India are;

Wal-mart stores, Carrefour, Tesco, Rosy blue group, LVMH Group, Metro.

Transition in Segmentation

Transition from demographic based segmentation to psychographic based segmentation, since 1950's market segmentation has been referred to as a process of identifying groups of individuals who are similar in attitudes etc. and the segmentation is of demographic segmentation after 1970s it is psychographic segmentation, know about the customer taste and preferences and collect at the real time point of purchase data. And now it is need based segmentation is using for different marketing functions like advertising and new product development.

Cause Related Marketing

Cause related marketing is practiced on the rationale that consumers are human beings are kind hearted. The customer pay the amount with some satisfaction that the specific amount is to for relevant social cause.

Example

A sanitary napkin brand "whisper" announced a contribution o Re.1 on every pack of sales for blind relief society. This helps in improving whisper's market share. HLL announced a contribution of Rs. 0.50 on the sale of each of its brand of lifebuoy brand soap to a diarrhea project.

Co-branding

Co-branding is when two companies form an alliance to work together, creating marketing synergy. This co-branding is innovative in the marketing practices.

Examples:

- Andhra bank and ICFAI university are using the strategy of co-branding.
- Andhra bank and Hindustan petroleum also launched their co-branded card

- SBI card and LG electronics India launched the LG-SBI card. This is the country's first co-branded credit card for the consumer appliances industry and can be used at more than 2 lakh outlets in India.
- Idea cellular and HDFC Bank launched two co-branded cards providing multiple benefits to customers of both.
- Pillsbury Brownies with Nestle Chocolate
- Dell Computers with Intel Processors

Online Marketing

Internet marketing, also referred to as online marketing, Internet advertising, or eMarketing, is the marketing of products or services over the Internet. Internet marketing also includes management of digital customer data and electronic customer relationship management (E-CRM) systems.

Samsung Marketing Practices

Viral Marketing, Interactive Marketing: Samsung created its "Fun Club" as a way to engage with Samsung mobile phone owners to help them get the most from their phones. Samsung provides content such as games, ringers, and wallpapers that are designed specifically for Samsung mobile phone models. Hearing about new mobile content is one of the benefits of joining the "Fun Club." Samsung was looking for a new way to use rich multimedia to promote the game, Skipping Stone, to its customers. Samsung engaged Enpocket to create a mobile marketing campaign promoting Skipping Stone using the graphically rich MMS channel.

Conclusion

In the present competitive scenario, there should be transition in marketing practices in order to survive in the market. Since "change in the only thing which never change" in the world, companies have to adapt themselves according to the changing environment. The best emerging practices in the corporate world is win-win concept to be the leader in the market.

The Imperative of Internal Marketing

People are the very essence of an organization. All the technological up gradation, state of the art facilities, et al, can come to a naught if all the employees in the company are not performing optimally. It is important for employees to be engaged as much to be developed, so that their productivity is aligned with the organizational requirements.

Companies need to find out indigenous ways to challenge employees so as to keep them engaged.

The Internal Marketing concept was first proposed in the mid 1970's as a way of achieving service quality – a major problem in the services area. Its basic premise was 'to have satisfied customers, the firm must also have satisfied employs' and that this could be best achieved by treating employees as customers, i.e. by applying the principles of marketing to job design and employee motivation. Since then, the concept has seen a number of major developments and its application is no longer confined to the services area. It has been shown that any type of organization can use Internal Marketing to facilitate the implementation of it external marketing strategy or any other organizational strategies.

Despite the rapidly growing literature on Internal Marketing, relatively few organizations actually apply the concept in practice. One of the main problems contributing to this is that there does not exist, a single unified concept of what is meant by Internal Marketing. However, Internal Marketing can be holistically defined as "Internal marketing is a planned effort using a marketing-like approach directed at motivating employees, for implementing and integrating organizational strategies towards customer orientation".

Literature Review

Pete Naude opines that Internal Marketing orientation is an area within the broader market orientation that remains relatively under-researched.

The article by Tim R.V. Davis examines the impact of consultative and participative styles of management on internal marketing. It shows how general managers, department managers and individuals can use internal marketing to increase employee involvement in reaching decisions, making commitments and taking action.

David Ballantyne explores the structural relationships through which internal marketing can create value for an organisation, its customers and its employees. It is argued that internal marketing requires a relationship-mediated approach, where planned phases of learning activity in volunteer groups generate new internally valid knowledge critical to the improvement of external market performance.

Marelise Pitt, Johan Bruwer, Deon Nel and Paul Berthon state that internal marketing is a critical issue facing marketing professions, human resources and other executives. They argue that if poor service is provided between employees it is unlikely that good service will ultimately be provided to the external customer. Internal marketing (IM) focuses on acquiring and retaining customer-oriented employees. Critics of internal marketing claim that the term is simply a synonym for good human resources management. The concepts of internal marketing and human resource effectiveness (HRE), at both a strategic and technical level, are considered and suitable measures identified.

Gould states that when information is integrated with skills, understanding and experience, it becomes knowledge which the organization can use to its advantage. His research illustrates the importance of communication processes alongside business processes to achieve continuing improvement. He concludes that many businesses should give serious consideration to the idea that HR and marketing should be combined.

Nigel F. Piercy observes that while customer satisfaction measurement is currently one of the commonest prescriptions in both the marketing and management literatures, little attention has been paid to the effects of customer satisfaction measurement, particularly in terms of the impact on the internal market, i.e. the employees and managers inside the organization.

Gilbert D. Harrell & Matthew in their study, Marketing services to satisfy internal customers, conclude that staff unit managers in a range of disciplines who want to serve internal publics better can effectively market their services internally by understanding and responding to internal decision processes and expectations.

Walter E. Greene, Gary D. Walls& Larry J. Schrest in their article in Journal of Services Marketing, declare that the firms that do not or will not embrace the issues of internal marketing and incorporate those ingredients into their strategic marketing plan will see their market share and profit base erode.

The article titled, Building brand values through Internal Marketing, shows that quality of service is central to building brand differentiation within industries that do not produce tangible products. Internal marketing is an effective way of drawing attention to service, and encouraging staff in various ways to give the best of themselves.

A paper titled, Internal brand building and structuration: the role of leadership, by Christine Vallaster & Leslie de Chernatony provides empirical insights about how change is brought about during internal brand building.

Carmel Herington, Lester W. Johnson& Don Scott have found that competitive advantage can be attained through development of a relationship-building culture which includes building relationships inside the organization as well as customer relationships. In fact, successful customer relationships rely on successful internal relationships.

Timothy W. Aurand, Linda Gorchels & Terrence R. Bishop in the, Journal of Product & Brand Management, have found that employees seem to have a more positive attitude toward the brand and are more likely to incorporate this image into their work activities when there is some degree of HR involvement in the internal branding process.

Robert E. Morgan in their study Business agility and internal marketing, have found that fundamentally, the same principles which are used to market solutions to the organisation's external customers can be employed to better segment, target and position the Information Service solutions to the internal customer base.

Need For Further Research

- Many enterprises are continually in some form of transformation-mergers, alliances, downsizing and rightsizing generating the need for constant communication.
- Some enterprises may rename themselves as a result and this rebranding requires communication to all stakeholders including employees.
- More companies are empowering staff to take on increased focus in the customer relationship. This needs full involvement, immersion and training in brand values.
- There is less reciprocal loyalty between employer and employee; the employee's time becomes transactional.The "internal" brand can be a way to bind the two parties together with shared goals and values.
- New ways of working require organizations and staff to constantly learn new skills and sometimes these are acquired through alliances. Building a learning company will be an important future consideration. Internal brand values can be an umbrella for this effort.

However, to date, there has been a considerable knowledge gap about the components of Internal Marketing. To reinforce this point, a study by Intercommunic reported in Marketing week showed that 85% of companies did not even have a human resources or marketing budget for internal promotions.

It is commonly believed that sole role of marketing is to sell products and services outwardly to customers. In fact, the first and most urgent job of marketing is often to sell inwardly toward a company's people. For, it is only when the people of the company fully understand and are committed to the value proposition of the organization and its brands that external marketing can reach its full potential.

" Marketing is absolutely critical to being internally successful,"

Relationship Marketing-An Overview

Marketing is continually evolving in response to the changing environment. New strategies, techniques and tools for marketing managers are constantly being developed. Marketing has also moved away from the original idea of bringing about mutually satisfying benefits or exchanges. Consumers have responded to these changes and have become more sophisticated in their demand and expectations. Service marketing is a growing specialty, and concepts such as internal marketing have been developed with in the services sector, are now widely recognized to be highly relevant to all organizations.

Relationship marketing goes a step further. Organizations are urged to focus not only on their relationship with customers external and internal but with other elements within the industry and society. An emphasis to it is not on bringing about exchange processes but on building relationships. The traditional perspective of marketing fails to bring the three critical areas such as marketing orientation, customer service and quality into closer alignment. Thus the relationship-marketing concept emerged as a new paradigm integrating customer service and quality with a market orientation.

Relationship Marketing-Definition

Relationship marketing is nothing but an effort directed at creating loyal customers. Philip Kotler defined relationship marketing as." The process of creating, maintaining and enhancing value-laden relationship with valued customers, distributors, dealers and suppliers by promising and consistently delivering high quality products, good services and fair prices". Marketing is shifting from trying to maximize the profit on individual transactions rather than to building mutually beneficial relationship with consumers and other parties.

Evolution

The concept of relationship marketing was first introduced by Franklin Berry (1983) in a service context to describe a long-term approach to marketing. Since then it has attracted considerable attention from both the practitioners and researchers.

In the 1950's marketing interest was primarily focused on consumer goods. In the 1960's increased attention was placed on industrial markets, while in 1970's considerable academic effort was placed on the area of non profit or societal marketing. In the 1980's attention started to be directed at the services sector, an area of marketing that had received remarkably little attention in view of its importance in the overall economy. In the 1990's the marketing concept was shifted to relationship marketing.

Key Linkages in Relationship Marketing

Marketing orientation, quality and Customer service are the three basic elements in Relationship marketing. The linkage between these three factors will help to achieve a total customer satisfaction and long-term relationship.

As quality, customer service and market orientation are the three elements in relationship marketing, it is necessary to find the role of each factor in relationship marketing.

Role of Customer Service

Historically customer service has been seen from a narrow perspective where the primary role of the customer service is concerned with getting the right products at the right place at right time and the focus is much on distributors and logistics view points.

The new vision of customer service places it in a much broader context as a multi–dimensional issue with an impact on relationships with specific target groups across a broad range of company activities. It is concerned with building of financial bonds (in which marketers offer pricing as an incentive to encourage customers to do more and more business with the firm), social bonds (which offer personalized service delivery) and structural bonds (which emphasize provision of quality services that are valuable the clients and not readily available with competitors which helps the customers to resist the temptation from the competitors) with customers and the other markets or groups to ensure long term relationships of mutual advantage.

Role of Quality

The role of quality is also undergoing review. The typical approach of the quality is changing from one of final inspection of outputs to one of assessing whether critical processes are in control and giving guidance to others in the techniques involved.

Total Quality Management (TQM) programme is designed to constantly improve the quality of products, services and marketing processes. The idea of the total quality across all functions focuses the scope of quality on relationship between the firm and its customers, suppliers and other key elements on an ongoing basis.

Role of Marketing Orientation

Traditionally marketing has been seen as a process of perceiving, understanding, stimulating and satisfying the needs of specially selected target markets by channeling an organizations resources to meet those needs. It is concerned with the dynamic inter-relationship between a company's products and services, the customers need and want and the activities of the company. The marketing frame work mainly consists of marketing mix, market forces and the marketing process.

Relationship marketing places emphasis on building and maintaining a good workforce. Service quality depends to a very great extent on people, and developing long-term relationships with internal customers is just as important as building relationship with external ones.

Relationship Marketing-A Broader View

Traditionally marketing has been from the perspective of managing relationship with customer groups. However, a much broader viewpoint is appropriate in relationship marketing. Generally this can be done through two ways, viz,

1. By considering a wider range of markets; and
2. By expanding the marketing mix.

Chapter 3

Search Engine Marketing

Search engine marketing, or SEM, is a form of Internet marketing that seeks to promote websites by increasing their visibility in search engine result pages (SERPs) through the use of search engine optimization, paid placement, contextual advertising, and paid inclusion.. Usage of the term “search engine marketing” has been inconsistent. The trade association Search Engine Marketing Professional Organization (SEMPO) includes search engine optimization (SEO), and SEO is also included in the industry definitions of SEM by Forrester Research, eMarketer, Search Engine Watch, and industry expert Danny Sullivan.. However, the New York Times restricts the definition to ‘the practice of buying paid search listings’.

Market Structure

In 2008, North American advertisers spent US$13.5 billion on search engine marketing. The largest SEM vendors are Google AdWords, Yahoo! Search Marketing and Microsoft adCenter. As of 2006, SEM was growing much faster than traditional advertising and even other channels of online marketing. Because of the complex technology, a secondary “search marketing agency” market has evolved. Many marketers have difficulty understanding the intricacies of search engine marketing and choose to rely on third party agencies to manage their search marketing.

History

As the number of sites on the Web increased in the mid-to-late 90s, search engines started appearing to help people find information quickly. Search engines developed business models to finance their services, such as pay per click programs offered by Open Text in 1996 and then Goto.com in 1998. Goto.com later changed its name to Overture in 2001, and was purchased by Yahoo! in 2003, and now offers paid search opportunities for advertisers through Yahoo! Search Marketing. Google also began to offer advertisements on search results pages in 2000 through the Google AdWords program. By 2007, pay-per-click programs proved to be primary money-makers for search engines. In a market dominated by Google, in 2009 Yahoo! and Microsoft announced the intention to forge an alliance. The Yahoo! & Microsoft Search Alliance eventually received approval from regulators in the US and Europe in February 2010.

Search engine optimization consultants expanded their offerings to help businesses learn about and use the advertising opportunities offered by search engines, and new agencies focusing primarily upon marketing and advertising through search engines emerged. The term "Search Engine Marketing" was proposed by Danny Sullivan in 2001 to cover the spectrum of activities involved in performing SEO, managing paid listings at the search engines, submitting sites to directories, and developing online marketing strategies for businesses, organizations, and individuals.

Some of the latest theoretical advances include Search Engine Marketing Management (SEMM). SEMM relates to activities including SEO but focuses on return on investment (ROI) management instead of relevant traffic building (as is the case of mainstream SEO). SEMM also integrates organic SEO and PayPerClick SEO. For example some of the attention is placed on the web page layout design and how content and information is displayed to the website visitor.

Ethical Questions

Paid search advertising has not been without controversy, and the issue of how search engines present advertising on their search result pages has been the target of a series of studies and reports by Consumer Reports Web Watch. The Federal Trade Commission (FTC) also issued a letter in 2002 about the importance of disclosure of paid advertising on search engines, in response to a complaint from Commercial Alert, a consumer advocacy group with ties to Ralph Nader. Vested interests appear to use the expression *SEM* to mean exclusively *Pay per click advertising* to the extent that the wider advertising and marketing community have accepted this narrow definition. Such usage excludes the wider search marketing community that is engaged in other forms of SEM such as Search Engine Optimization and Search Retargeting.

Another ethical controversy associated with search marketing has been the issue of trademark infringement. The debate as to whether third parties should have the right to bid on their competitors' brand names has been underway for years. In 2009 Google changed their policy, which formerly prohibited these tactics, allowing 3rd parties to bid on branded terms as long as their landing page in fact provides information on the trademarked term. Though the policy has been changed this continues to be a source of heated debate.

Search Engine Optimization

Search engine optimization (SEO) is the process of improving the volume or quality of traffic to a web site or a web page (such as a blog) from search engines via "natural" or un-paid ("organic" or "algorithmic") search results as opposed to search engine marketing (SEM) which deals with paid inclusion. The theory is that the earlier (or higher) a site appears in the search results list, the more visitors it will receive from the search engine. SEO may target different kinds of search, including image search, local search, video search and industry-specific vertical search engines. This gives a web site web presence.

As an Internet marketing strategy, SEO considers how search engines work and what people search for. Optimizing a website primarily involves editing its content and HTML and associated coding to both increase its relevance to specific keywords and to remove barriers to the indexing activities of search engines.

The acronym "SEO" can refer to "search engine optimizers," a term adopted by an industry of consultants who carry out optimization projects on behalf of clients, and by employees who perform SEO services in-house. Search engine optimizers may offer SEO as a stand-alone service or as a part of a broader marketing campaign. Because effective SEO may require changes to the HTML source code of a site, SEO tactics may be incorporated into web site development and design. The term "search engine friendly" may be used to describe web site designs, menus, content management systems, images, videos, shopping carts, and other elements that have been optimized for the purpose of search engine exposure. Another class of techniques, known as black hat SEO or spamdexing, use methods such as link farms, keyword stuffing and article spinning that degrade both the relevance of search results and the user-experience of search engines. Search engines look for sites that employ these techniques in order to remove them from their indices.

History

Webmasters and content providers began optimizing sites for search engines in the mid-1990s, as the first search engines were cataloging the early Web. Initially, all a webmaster needed to do was submit the address of a page, or URL, to the various engines which would send a "spider" to "crawl" that page, extract links to other pages from it, and return information found on the page to be indexed. The process involves a search engine spider downloading a page and storing it on the search engine's own server, where a second program, known as an indexer, extracts various information about the page, such as the words it contains and where these are located, as well as any weight for specific words, and all links the page contains, which are then placed into a scheduler for crawling at a later date.

Site owners started to recognize the value of having their sites highly ranked and visible in search engine results, creating an opportunity for both white hat and black hat SEO practitioners. According to industry analyst Danny Sullivan, the phrase "search engine optimization" probably came into use in 1997.

Early versions of search algorithms relied on webmaster-provided information such as the keyword meta tag, or index files in engines like ALIWEB. Meta tags provide a guide to each page's content. Using meta data to index pages was found to be less than reliable, however, because the webmaster's choice of keywords in the meta tag could potentially be an inaccurate representation of the site's actual content. Inaccurate, incomplete, and inconsistent data in meta tags could and did cause pages to rank for irrelevant searches. Web content providers also manipulated a number of attributes within the HTML source of a page in an attempt to rank well in search engines.

By relying so much on factors such as keyword density which were exclusively within a webmaster's control, early search engines suffered from abuse and ranking manipulation. To provide better results to their users, search engines had to adapt to ensure their results pages showed the most relevant search results, rather than unrelated pages stuffed with numerous keywords by unscrupulous webmasters. Since the success and popularity of a search engine is determined by its ability to produce the most relevant results to any given search, allowing those results to be false would turn users to find other search sources. Search engines responded by developing more complex ranking algorithms, taking into account additional factors that were more difficult for webmasters to manipulate.

Graduate students at Stanford University, Larry Page and Sergey Brin, developed "backrub," a search engine that relied on a mathematical algorithm to rate the prominence of web pages. The number calculated by the algorithm, PageRank, is a function of the quantity and strength of inbound links. PageRank estimates the likelihood that a given page will be reached by a web user who randomly surfs the web, and follows links from one page to another. In effect, this means that some links are stronger than others, as a higher PageRank page is more likely to be reached by the random surfer.

Page and Brin founded Google in 1998. Google attracted a loyal following among the growing number of Internet users, who liked its simple design. Off-page factors (such as PageRank and hyperlink analysis) were considered as well as on-page factors (such as keyword frequency, meta tags, headings, links and site structure) to enable Google to avoid the kind of manipulation seen in search engines that only considered on-page factors for their rankings. Although PageRank was more difficult to game, webmasters had already developed link building tools and schemes to influence the Inktomi search engine, and these methods proved similarly applicable to gaming PageRank. Many sites focused on exchanging, buying, and selling links, often on a massive scale. Some of these schemes, or link farms, involved the creation of thousands of sites for the sole purpose of link spamming.

By 2004, search engines had incorporated a wide range of undisclosed factors in their ranking algorithms to reduce the impact of link manipulation. Google says it ranks sites using more than 200 different signals. The leading search engines, Google and Yahoo, do not disclose the algorithms they use to rank pages. Notable SEOs, such as Rand Fishkin, Barry Schwartz, Aaron Wall and Jill Whalen, have studied different approaches to search engine optimization, and have published their opinions in online forums and blogs. SEO practitioners may also study patents held by various search engines to gain insight into the algorithms.

In 2005 Google began personalizing search results for each user. Depending on their history of previous searches, Google crafted results for logged in users. In 2008, Bruce Clay said that "ranking is dead" because of personalized search. It would become meaningless to discuss how a website ranked, because its rank would potentially be different for each user and each search.

In 2007 Google announced a campaign against paid links that transfer PageRank. On June 15, 2009, Google disclosed that they had taken measures to mitigate the effects of PageRank sculpting by use of the nofollow attribute on links. Matt Cutts, a well-known software engineer at Google, announced that Google Bot would no longer treat nofollowed links in the same way, in order to prevent SEOs from using nofollow for PageRank sculpting. As a result of this change the usage of nofollow leads to evaporation of pagerank. In order to avoid the above, SEOs developed alternative techniques that replace nofollowed tags with obfuscated Javascript and thus permit PageRank sculpting. Additionally several solutions have been suggested that include the usage of iframes, Flash and Javascript.

In December 2009 Google announced it would be using the web search history of all its users in order to populate search results.

Real-time-search was introduced in late 2009 in an attempt to make search results more timely and relevant. Historically site administrators have spent months or even years optimizing a website to increase search rankings. With the growth in popularity of social media sites and blogs the leading engines made changes to their algorithms to allow fresh content to rank quickly within the search results. This new approach to search places importance on current, fresh and unique content.

Relationship with Search Engines

By 1997 search engines recognized that webmasters were making efforts to rank well in their search engines, and that some webmasters were even manipulating their rankings in search results by stuffing pages with excessive or irrelevant keywords. Early search engines, such as Infoseek, adjusted their algorithms in an effort to prevent webmasters from manipulating rankings.

Due to the high marketing value of targeted search results, there is potential for an adversarial relationship between search engines and SEOs. In 2005, an annual conference, AIRWeb, Adversarial Information Retrieval on the Web, was created to discuss and minimize the damaging effects of aggressive web content providers.

SEO companies that employ overly aggressive techniques can get their client websites banned from the search results. In 2005, the Wall Street Journal reported on a company, Traffic Power, which allegedly used high-risk techniques and failed to disclose those risks to its clients. Wired magazine reported that the same company sued blogger and SEO Aaron Wall for writing about the ban. Google's Matt Cutts later confirmed that Google did in fact ban Traffic Power and some of its clients.

Some search engines have also reached out to the SEO industry, and are frequent sponsors and guests at SEO conferences, chats, and seminars. In fact, with the advent of paid inclusion, some search engines now have a vested interest in the health of the optimization community. Major search engines provide information and guidelines to help with site optimization. Google has a Sitemaps program to help webmasters learn if Google is having any problems indexing their website and also provides data on Google traffic to the website. Google guidelines are a list of suggested practices Google has provided as guidance to webmasters. Yahoo! Site Explorer provides a way for webmasters to submit URLs, determine how many pages are in the Yahoo! index and view link information.

Methods

Getting Indexed

The leading search engines, such as Google and Yahoo!, use crawlers to find pages for their algorithmic search results. Pages that are linked from other search engine indexed pages do not need to be submitted because they are found automatically. Some search engines, notably Yahoo!, operate a paid submission service that guarantee crawling for either a set fee or cost per click. Such programs usually guarantee inclusion in the database, but do not guarantee specific ranking within the search results. Two major directories, the Yahoo Directory and the Open Directory Project both require manual submission and human editorial review. Google offers Google Webmaster Tools, for which an XML Sitemap feed can be created and submitted for free to ensure that all pages are found, especially pages that aren't discoverable by automatically following links.

Search engine crawlers may look at a number of different factors when crawling a site. Not every page is indexed by the search engines. Distance of pages from the root directory of a site may also be a factor in whether or not pages get crawled.

Preventing Crawling

To avoid undesirable content in the search indexes, webmasters can instruct spiders not to crawl certain files or directories through the standard robots.txt file in the root directory of the domain. Additionally, a page can be explicitly excluded from a search engine's database by using a meta tag specific to robots. When a search engine visits a site, the robots.txt located in the root directory is the first file crawled. The robots.txt file is then parsed, and will instruct the robot as to which pages are not to be crawled. As a search engine crawler may keep a cached copy of this file, it may on occasion crawl pages a webmaster does not wish crawled. Pages typically prevented from being crawled include login specific pages such as shopping carts and user-specific content such as search results from internal searches. In March 2007, Google warned webmasters that they should prevent indexing of internal search results because those pages are considered search spam.

Increasing Prominence

A variety of other methods are employed to get a webpage shown up at the search results. These include:

- Cross linking between pages of the same website. Giving more links to main pages of the website, to increase PageRank used by search engines. Linking from other websites, including link farming and comment spam. However, link spamming can also have a bad impact on your search result position.
- Writing content that includes frequently searched keyword phrase, so as to be relevant to a wide variety of search queries. Adding relevant keywords to a web page meta tags, including keyword stuffing.
- URL normalization of web pages accessible via multiplerurls, using the "canonical" meta tag.

White Hat Versus Black Hat

SEO techniques can be classified into two broad categories: techniques that search engines recommend as part of good design, and those techniques of which search engines do not approve. The search engines attempt to minimize the effect of the latter, among them spamdexing. Some industry commentators have classified these methods, and the practitioners who employ them, as either white hat SEO, or black hat SEO. White hats tend to produce results that last a long time, whereas black hats anticipate that their sites may eventually be banned either temporarily or permanently once the search engines discover what they are doing.

A search engine optimization technique is considered white hat SEO if it conforms to the search engines' guidelines and involves no deception. We can say the legal SEO is a white hat SEO. As the search engine guidelines are not written as a series of rules or commandments, this is an important distinction to note. White hat SEO is not just about following guidelines, but is about ensuring that the content a search engine indexes and subsequently ranks is the same content a user will see. White hat advice is generally summed up as creating content for users, not for search engines, and then making that content easily accessible to the spiders, rather than attempting to trick the algorithm from its intended purpose. White hat SEO is in many ways similar to web development that promotes accessibility, although the two are not identical.

Black hat SEO attempts to improve rankings in ways that are disapproved of by the search engines, or involve deception. One black hat technique uses text that is hidden, either as text coloured similar to the background, in an invisible div, or positioned off screen. Another method gives a different page depending on whether the page is being requested by a human visitor or a search engine, a technique known as cloaking. Invisible iframes are yet another black hat SEO technique, where a page you see is not necessarily from the company that is hosting that webpage. People create these types of pages in order to download software on your computer in the background without your knowledge.

Search engines may penalize sites they discover using black hat methods, either by reducing their rankings or eliminating their listings from their databases altogether. Such penalties can be applied either automatically by the search engines' algorithms, or by a manual site review. Infamous examples are the February 2006 Google removal of both BMW Germany and Ricoh Germany for use of deceptive practices and the April 2006 removal of the PPC Agency Big Mouth Media. All three companies, however, quickly apologized, fixed the offending pages, and were restored to Google's list.

As a Marketing Strategy

Eye tracking studies have shown that searchers scan a search results page from top to bottom and left to right (for left to right languages), looking for a relevant result. Placement at or near the top of the rankings therefore increases the number of searchers who will visit a site. However, more search engine referrals does not guarantee more sales. SEO is not necessarily an appropriate strategy for every website, and other Internet marketing strategies can be much more effective, depending on the site operator's goals. A successful Internet marketing campaign may drive organic traffic to web pages, but it also may involve the use of paid advertising on search engines and other pages, building high quality web pages to engage and persuade, addressing technical issues that may keep search engines from crawling and indexing those sites, setting up analytics programs to enable site owners to measure their successes, and improving a site's conversion rate.

SEO may generate a return on investment. However, search engines are not paid for organic search traffic, their algorithms change, and there are no guarantees of continued referrals. (Some trading sites such as eBay can be a special case for this, it will announce how and when the ranking algorithm will change a few months before changing the algorithm). Due to this lack of guarantees and certainty, a business that relies heavily on search engine traffic can suffer major losses if the search engines stop sending visitors. It is considered wise business practice for website operators to liberate themselves from dependence on search engine traffic. A top-ranked SEO blog Seomoz.org has suggested, "Search marketers, in a twist of irony, receive a very small share of their traffic from search engines.." Instead, their main sources of traffic are links from other websites.

International Markets

Optimization techniques are highly tuned to the dominant search engines in the target market. The search engines' market shares vary from market to market, as does competition. In 2003, Danny Sullivan stated that Google represented about 75% of all searches. In markets outside the United States, Google's share is often larger, and Google remains the dominant search engine worldwide as of 2007. As of 2006, Google had an 85-90% market share in Germany. While there were hundreds of SEO firms in the US at that time, there were only about five in Germany. As of June 2008, the marketshare of Google in the UK was close to 90% according to Hitwise. That market share is achieved in a number of countries.

As of 2009, there are only a few large markets where Google is not the leading search engine. In most cases, when Google is not leading in a given market, it is lagging behind a local player. The most notable markets where this is the case are China, Japan, South Korea, Russia and the Czech Republic where respectively Baidu, Yahoo! Japan, Naver, Yandex and Seznam are market leaders.

Successful search optimization for international markets may require professional translation of web pages, registration of a domain name with a top level domain in the target market, and web hosting that provides a local IP address. Otherwise, the fundamental elements of search optimization are essentially the same, regardless of language.

Legal Precedents

On October 17, 2002, Searching filed suit in the United States District Court, Western District of Oklahoma, against the search engine Google. Searching's claim was that Google's tactics to prevent spamdexing constituted a tortious interference with contractual relations. On May 27, 2003, the court granted Google's motion to dismiss the complaint because Searching "failed to state a claim upon which relief may be granted."

In March 2006, Kinder Start filed a lawsuit against Google over search engine rankings. Kinder Start's web site was removed from Google's index prior to the lawsuit and the amount of traffic to the site dropped by 70%. On March 16, 2007 the United States District Court for the Northern District of California (San Jose Division) dismissed Kinder Start's complaint without leave to amend, and partially granted Google's motion for Rule 11 sanctions against Kinder Start's attorney, requiring him to pay part of Google's legal expenses.

Sales Letter

A sales letter is a piece of direct mail which is designed to persuade the reader to purchase a particular product or service in the absence of a salesman. It has been defined as "A form of direct mail in which an advertiser sends a letter to a potential customer." It is distinct from other direct mail techniques, such as the distribution of leaflets and catalogues, as the sales letter typically sells a single product or product line, and further tends to be mainly textual as opposed to graphics-based. It is typically used for products or services which, due to their price, are a considered purchase at medium or high value (typically tens to thousands of dollars). A sales letter is often, but not exclusively, the last stage of the sales process before the customer places an order, and is designed to ensure that the prospect is committed to becoming a customer.

Since the advent of the internet, the sales letter has become an integral part of internet marketing, and typically takes the form of an email or webpage. Unsolicited sales emails are known as spam, although spam typically consists of emails which are much shorter than a normal sales letter. Offline, unsolicited sales letters are known as junk mail.

Components

The sales letter is split into several key sections. In addition, other sections may be used, such as sub-headlines.

Headline

The headline is the most prominent text on the sales letter, and is designed to be among the first item the reader attends to.

Body Copy

This section is typically quite long, with 4, 8 and 16 page letters being common formats. This section will typically contain testimonials from the firm's customers as well as pictures and information about the product. On the internet, the body copy may include embedded video or audio.

Call to Action

All sales letters include a call to action which is intended to get the customer to commit to purchasing the product or service, typically without any further intervention.

Graphic Design

The graphic design of a sales letter is an important part of the branding. The font, layout, line spacing, paragraph formatting, images, etc. all have an effect on the efficacy of the letter.

Development of Sales Letters

Because of the direct response nature of sales letters, they can be carefully tested on an ongoing basis to determine which version performs best in terms of converting readers to customers. Sales letters are typically developed incrementally, with split testing of various elements. This allows the marketeer or copywriter to confirm which headline, body text or graphic design converts best. On the internet, it is possible to track additional variables, such as the open rate of emails, the bounce rate, clickthrough to the checkout, etc.

Classic Letters

Some sales letters have become design classics in their own right, notably the letter by John Caples which sold a home study (also known as distance learning or correspondence course) in piano playing. This letter had the headline "They Laughed When I Sat Down At the Piano But When I Started to Play! —"

Spamvertising

Spamvertising is the practice of sending E-mail spam, advertising a website. The word is a portmanteau of the words "spam" and "advertising".

It also refers to vandalizing wikis, blogs and online forums with hyperlinks in order to get a higher search engine ranking for the vandal's website. Spamvertisers insert links to their websites (typically, sites purporting to sell some commercial product) and add keywords of common or related searches. The apparent goal is that a search engine will find the vandalized page full of links and improve the popularity rating of the pages to which they link. This is typically done by automated editing programs which look for editable text fields in web forms and automatically fill them in with web links. The links typically lead to pills, porn and poker sites.

Most legitimate website providers do not tolerate this practice, and will delete any site that has been spamvertised.

This practice has led to many editable online resources employing anti-spam countermeasures, including the use of captchas to prevent automated editing

New Media Marketing

New Media Marketing is a relatively new concept used by businesses in developing an online community, which allows satisfied customers to congregate and extol the virtues of a particular brand. In most cases, the online community includes mechanisms such as blogs, podcasts, message boards, and product reviews, all of which contribute to a transparent forum to post praises, criticisms, questions, and suggestions.

One of the primary arguments to promote New Media Marketing is the premise that traditional advertising is losing its influence on consumers. Backed by statistical evidence demonstrating a growing trend of consumers making purchasing decisions off Internet research and referrals. These advocates strongly adhere to the notion that consumers are more inclined to believe feedback from like-minded peers than corporate marketing verbiage dispersed through traditional television, radio, direct mail, or newspaper advertising.

Although businesses would be exposing certain weaknesses to the marketplace by allowing individuals, or even competitors, to post critical comments, responding with an honest and transparent answer designed around solving the issue at hand may mitigate potential risks. New Media Marketing is most effectively marketed by Internet-driven technology such as blogs, RSS, Web video productions, and podcasts

Social Marketing Intelligence

Social Marketing Intelligence is the method of extrapolating valuable information from social network interactions and large data flows that can enable companies for example; to launch new products and services into the market place at greater speed and at significantly lower cost. This is a very new area of research however, companies using social marketing intelligence have achieved drastic improvement in marketing campaigns.

Through Social Marketing Intelligence companies can identify the people that are the most influential within their communities. These are the most connecting and connected people within any given social network. According to Xtract these people, called the Alpha Users or Hubs, have considerable influence over the spread of information within their social network.

Alpha Users

Alpha Users are key elements of any social networks, who manage the connectivity of the core members of the community. Similar to how viruses spread in nature, there is an initial starting point to communications in social networks, and the originators of such communications are Alpha Users. They tend to be highly connected users with exceptional influence to the other thought-leaders of any social network.

Before digital communications, it was only possible to isolate the most influential members of any community by interviewing every member and tracing their full communication patterns within the social network. Traditional fixed landline telephone and internet use did not give enough accuracy to be able to pinpoint Alpha Users to a meaningful degree. With the advent of mobile phones, a personal digital communication channel was available to study. Early research by mathematicians at Xtract in Finland produced models that suggested mobile networks could indeed track the full communication and isolate the Alpha Users. Since then several companies including Xtract have launched commercial tools to detect Alpha Users, usually using mobile operator billing and telecoms traffic data.

Today modern Engagement Marketing campaigns attempt to use Alpha Users as spokespersons in marketing and advertising. The idea is that consumers will trust more the opinion of their friend or known contact from a social network, than the random marketing and advertising messages of companies and brands. The desire is to achieve viral marketing effects by which the Alpha Users would spread the messages further.

Alpha Users were first briefly discussed in public in the book *3G Marketing* by Ahonen, Kasper and Melkko in 2004. The first industry article about Alpha Users was by Ahonen and Ahvenainen in Total Telecom in February 2005. The first telecoms conference where Alpha Users were explained was the 3G Mobile World Congress in Tokyo in January 2005. The topic was part of the strategy keynote address at the 3GSM World Congress in Cannes in February 2005. The first book to discuss Alpha Users at length was *Communities Dominate Brands* by Ahonen and Moore in 2005.

Direct Text Marketing

Direct Text Marketing is the marketing efforts using today modern technologies (mobile phones, laptops, etc..). This includes using a medium which involves text messaging over a mobile device. A very high percentage of Americans today carry around with them a mobile phone. Some carry a PDA (personal data assistant) that has mobile phone capabilities. Direct text marketing uses the same style of direct marketing with the merger of text messaging technology into one viable marketing solution.

Companies and businesses can benefit from using this forum of modern marketing, by sending either promotional content, or discount coupons via text format directly to individuals via their personal mobile phones or PDAs. Since mobile phones or PDAs are very personal technologies, text spamming is usually out of the question. Services of sending promotional or coupon discounts are usually an opt-in service. Which means a business can not send any content to an individual's mobile device, unless otherwise requested by the individual who owns the mobile device.

Pay Per Click

Pay Per Click (PPC) is an Internet advertising model used on websites, in which advertisers pay their host only when their ad is clicked. With search engines, advertisers typically bid on keyword phrases relevant to their target market. Content sites commonly charge a fixed price per click rather than use a bidding system.

Cost per click (CPC) is the amount of money an advertiser pays search engines and other Internet publishers for a single click on its advertisement that brings one visitor to its website.

In contrast to the generalized portal, which seeks to drive a high volume of traffic to one site, PPC implements the so-called affiliate model, that provides purchase opportunities wherever people may be surfing. It does this by offering financial incentives (in the form of a percentage of revenue) to affiliated partner sites. The affiliates provide purchase-point click-through to the merchant. It is a pay-for-performance model: If an affiliate does not generate sales, it represents no cost to the merchant. Variations include banner exchange, pay-per-click, and revenue sharing programs.

Websites that utilize PPC ads will display an advertisement when a keyword query matches an advertiser's keyword list, or when a content site displays relevant content. Such advertisements are called *sponsored links* or *sponsored ads*, and appear adjacent to or above organic results on search engine results pages, or anywhere a web developer chooses on a content site.

Although many PPC providers exist, Google AdWords, Yahoo! Search Marketing, and Microsoft adCenter are the three largest network operators, and all three operate under a bid-based model. Cost per click (CPC) varies depending on the search engine and the level of competition for a particular keyword.

The PPC advertising model is open to abuse through click fraud, although Google and others have implemented automated systems to guard against abusive clicks by competitors or corrupt web developers.

Determining Cost Per Click

There are two primary models for determining cost per click: flat-rate and bid-based. In both cases the advertiser must consider the potential value of a click from a given source. This value is based on the type of individual the advertiser is expecting to receive as a visitor to his or her website, and what the advertiser can gain from that visit, usually revenue, both in the short term as well as in the long term. As with other forms of advertising targeting is key, and factors that often play into PPC campaigns include the target's interest (often defined by a search term they have entered into a search engine, or the content of a page that they are browsing), intent (e.g. to purchase or not), location (for geo targeting), and the day and time that they are browsing.

Flat-rate PPC

In the flat-rate model, the advertiser and publisher agree upon a fixed amount that will be paid for each click. In many cases the publisher has a rate card that lists the CPC within different areas of their website or network. These various amounts are often related to the content on pages, with content that generally attracts more valuable visitors having a higher CPC than content that attracts less valuable visitors. However, in many cases advertisers can negotiate lower rates, especially when committing to a long-term or high-value contract. The flat-rate model is particularly common to comparison shopping engines, which typically publish rate cards. However, these rates are sometimes minima, and advertisers can pay more for greater visibility. These sites are usually neatly compartmentalized into product or service categories, allowing a high degree of targeting by advertisers. In many cases, the entire core content of these sites is paid ads.

Bid-based PPC

In the bid-based model, the advertiser signs a contract that allows them to compete against other advertisers in a private auction hosted by a publisher or, more commonly, an advertising network. Each advertiser informs the host of the maximum amount that he or she is willing to pay for a given ad spot (often based on a keyword), usually using online tools to do so. The auction plays out in an automated fashion every time a visitor triggers the ad spot.

When the ad spot is part of a search engine results page (SERP), the automated auction takes place whenever a search for the keyword that is being bid upon occurs. All bids for the keyword that target the searcher's geo-location, the day and time of the search, etc. are then compared and the winner determined. In situations where there are multiple ad spots, a common occurrence on SERPs, there can be multiple winners whose positions on the page are influenced by the amount each has bid. The ad with the highest bid generally shows up first, though additional factors such as ad quality and relevance can sometimes come into play.

In addition to ad spots on SERPs, the major advertising networks allow for contextual ads to be placed on the properties of 3rd-parties with whom they have partnered. These publishers sign up to host ads on behalf of the network. In return, they receive a portion of the ad revenue that the network generates, which can be anywhere from 50% to over 80% of the gross revenue paid by advertisers. These properties are often referred to as a *content network* and the ads on them as *contextual ads* due to the fact that the ad spots are associated with keywords based on the context of the page on which they are found. In general, ads on content networks have a much lower click-through rate (CTR) and conversion rate (CR) than ads found on SERPs and consequently are less highly valued. Content network properties can include websites, newsletters, and e-mails.

Advertisers pay for each click they receive, with the actual amount paid based on the amount bid. It is common practice amongst auction hosts to charge a winning bidder just slightly more (e.g. one penny) than the next highest bidder or the actual amount bid, whichever is lower. This avoids situations where bidders are constantly adjusting their bids by very small amounts to see if they can still win the auction while paying just a little bit less per click.

To maximize success and achieve scale, automated bid management systems can be deployed. These systems can be used directly by the advertiser, though they are more commonly used by advertising agencies that offer PPC bid management as a service. These tools generally allow for bid management at scale, with thousands or even millions of PPC bids controlled by a highly automated system. The system generally sets each bid based on the goal that has been set for it, such as maximize profit, maximize traffic at breakeven, and so forth. The system is usually tied into the advertiser's website and fed the results of each click, which then allows it to set bids. The effectiveness of these systems is directly related to the quality and quantity of the performance data that they have to work with-low-traffic ads can lead to a scarcity of data problem that renders many bid management tools useless at worst, or inefficient at best.

History

In February 1998 Jeffrey Brewer of Goto.com, a 25-employee startup company (later Overture, now part of Yahoo!), presented a pay per click search engine proof-of-concept to the TED conference in California. This presentation and the events that followed created the PPC advertising system. Credit for the concept of the PPC model is generally given to Idealab and Goto.com founder, Bill Gross. Google started search engine advertising in December 1999. It was not until October 2000 that the AdWords system was introduced, allowing advertisers to create text ads for placement on the Google search engine. However, PPC was only introduced in 2002; until then, advertisements were charged at cost-per-thousand impressions

Although GoTo.com started PPC in 1998, Yahoo! did not start syndicating GoTo.com (later Overture) advertisers until November 2001. Prior to this, Yahoo's primary source of SERPS advertising included contextual IAB advertising units (mainly 468x60 display ads). When the syndication contract with Yahoo! was up for renewal in July 2003, Yahoo! announced intent to acquire Overture for $1.63 billion.

Marketing Plan

A marketing plan is a written document that details the necessary actions to achieve one or more marketing objectives. It can be for a product or service, a brand, or a product line. Marketing plans cover between one and five years. A marketing plan may be part of an overall business plan. Solid marketing strategy is the foundation of a well-written marketing plan. While a marketing plan contains a list of actions, a marketing plan without a sound strategic foundation is of little use.

The Marketing Planning Process

Marketing process be realised by the marketing mix in step 4. The last step in the process is the marketing controlling. In most organizations, "strategic planning" is an annual process, typically covering just the year ahead. Occasionally, a few organizations may look at a practical plan which stretches three or more years ahead.

To be most effective, the plan has to be formalized, usually in written form, as a formal "marketing plan." The essence of the process is that it moves from the general to the specific, from the overall objectives of the organization down to the individual action plan for a part of one marketing program. It is also an interactive process, so that the draft output of each stage is checked to see what impact it has on the earlier stages-and is amended.

Marketing Planning Aims and Objectives

Behind the corporate objectives, which in themselves offer the main context for the marketing plan, will lie the "corporate mission," which in turn provides the context for these corporate objectives. In a sales-oriented organization, the marketing planning function designs incentive pay plans to not only motivate and reward frontline staff fairly but also to align marketing activities with corporate mission. This "corporate mission" can be thought of as a definition of what the organization is, of what it does: "Our business is ...". This definition should not be too narrow, or it will constrict the development of the organization; a too rigorous concentration on the view that "We are in the business of making meat-scales," as IBM was during the early 1900s, might have limited its subsequent development into other areas. On the other hand, it should not be too wide or it will become meaningless; "We want to make a profit" is not too helpful in developing specific plans.

Abell suggested that the definition should cover three dimensions: "customer groups" to be served, "customer needs" to be served, and "technologies" to be utilized. Thus, the definition of IBM's "corporate mission" in the 1940s might well have been: "We are in the business of handling accounting information [customer need] for the larger US organizations [customer group] by means of punched cards [technology]."

Perhaps the most important factor in successful marketing is the "corporate vision." Surprisingly, it is largely neglected by marketing textbooks, although not by the popular exponents of corporate strategy-indeed, it was perhaps the main theme of the book by Peters and Waterman, in the form of their "Superordinate Goals." "In Search of Excellence" said: "Nothing drives progress like the imagination. The idea precedes the deed." If the organization in general, and its chief executive in particular, has a strong vision of where its future lies, then there is a good chance that the organization will achieve a strong position in its markets (and attain that future). This will be not least because its strategies will be consistent and will be supported by its staff at all levels. In this context, all of IBM's marketing activities were underpinned by its philosophy of "customer service," a vision originally promoted by the charismatic Watson dynasty. The emphasis at this stage is on obtaining a complete and accurate picture.

A "traditional"-albeit product-based-format for a "brand reference book" (or, indeed, a "marketing facts book") was suggested by Godley more than three decades ago:

1. Financial data—Facts for this section will come from management accounting, costing and finance sections.
2. Product data—From production, research and development.
3. Sales and distribution data-Sales, packaging, distribution sections.
4. Advertising, sales promotion, merchandising data-Information from these departments.
5. Market data and miscellany-From market research, who would in most cases act as a source for this information. His sources of data, however, assume the resources of a very large organization. In most organizations they would be obtained from a much smaller set of people (and not a few of them would be generated by the marketing manager alone).

It is apparent that a marketing audit can be a complex process, but the aim is simple: *"it is only to identify those existing (external and internal) factors which will have a significant impact on the future plans of the company."*

It is clear that the basic material to be input to the marketing audit should be comprehensive. Accordingly, the best approach is to accumulate this material continuously, as and when it becomes available; since this avoids the otherwise heavy workload involved in collecting it as part of the regular, typically annual, planning process itself-when time is usually at a premium.

Even so, the first task of this *annual* process should be to check that the material held in the current *facts book* or *facts files* actually *is* comprehensive and accurate, and can form a sound basis for the marketing audit itself.

The structure of the facts book will be designed to match the specific needs of the organization, but one simple format-suggested by Malcolm McDonald-may be applicable in many cases. This splits the material into three groups:

1. Review of the marketing environment. A study of the organization's markets, customers, competitors and the overall economic, political, cultural and technical environment; covering developing trends, as well as the current situation.
2. Review of the detailed marketing activity. A study of the company's marketing mix; in terms of the 7 Ps.

3. Review of the marketing system. A study of the marketing organization, marketing research systems and the current marketing objectives and strategies. The last of these is too frequently ignored. The marketing system itself needs to be regularly questioned, because the validity of the whole marketing plan is reliant upon the accuracy of the input from this system, and 'garbage in, garbage out' applies with a vengeance.
   - Portfolio planning. In addition, the coordinated planning of the individual products and services can contribute towards the balanced portfolio.
   - 80:20 rule. To achieve the maximum impact, the marketing plan must be clear, concise and simple. It needs to concentrate on the 20 percent of products or services, and on the 20 percent of customers, which will account for 80 percent of the volume and 80 percent of the profit.
   - 7 P's: Product, Place, Price and Promotion, Physical Environment, People, Process. The 7 P's can sometimes divert attention from the customer, but the framework they offer can be very useful in building the action plans.

It is only at this stage (of deciding the marketing objectives) that the active part of the marketing planning process begins. This next stage in marketing planning is indeed the key to the whole marketing process.

The "marketing objectives" state just where the company intends to be at some specific time in the future.

James Quinn succinctly defined objectives in general as: *Goals (or objectives) state what is to be achieved and when results are to be accomplished, but they do not state 'how' the results are to be achieved.* They typically relate to what products (or services) will be where in what markets (and must be realistically based on customer behavior in those markets). They are essentially about the match between those "products" and "markets." Objectives for pricing, distribution, advertising and so on are at a lower level, and should not be confused with marketing objectives. They are part of the marketing strategy needed to achieve marketing objectives. To be most effective, objectives should be capable of measurement and therefore "quantifiable." This measurement may be in terms of sales volume, money value, market share, percentage penetration of distribution outlets and so on. An example of such a measurable marketing objective might be "to enter the market with product Y and capture 10 percent of the market by value within one year." As it is quantified it can, within limits, be unequivocally monitored, and corrective action taken as necessary.

The marketing objectives must usually be based, above all, on the organization's financial objectives; converting these financial measurements into the related marketing measurements. He went on to explain his view of the role of "policies," with which strategy is most often confused: "Policies are rules or guidelines that express the 'limits' within which action should occur." Simplifying somewhat, marketing strategies can be seen as the means, or "game plan," by which marketing objectives will be achieved and, in the framework that we have chosen to use, are generally concerned with the 8 P's. Examples are:

1. Price-The amount of money needed to buy products
2. Product-The actual product
3. Promotion (advertising)-Getting the product known
4. Placement-Where the product is located
5. People-Represent the business
6. Physical environment-The ambiance, mood, or tone of the environment
7. Process-How do people obtain your product
8. Packaging-How the product will be protected

(Note: At GCSE the 4 P's are Place, Promotion, Product and Price and the "secret" 5th P is Packaging, but which applies only to physical products, not services usually, and mostly those sold to individual consumers)

In principle, these strategies describe how the objectives will be achieved. The 7 P's are a useful framework for deciding how the company's resources will be manipulated (strategically) to achieve the objectives. It should be noted, however, that they are not the only framework, and may divert attention from the real issues. The focus of the strategies must be the objectives to be achieved-not the process of planning itself. Only if it fits the needs of these objectives should you choose, as we have done, to use the framework of the 7 P's. The strategy statement can take the form of a purely verbal description of the strategic options which have been chosen. Alternatively, and perhaps more positively, it might include a structured list of the major options chosen.

One aspect of strategy which is often overlooked is that of "timing." Exactly when it is the best time for each element of the strategy to be implemented is often critical. Taking the right action at the wrong time can sometimes be almost as bad as taking the wrong action at the right time. Timing is, therefore, an essential part of any plan; and should normally appear as a schedule of planned activities. Having completed this crucial stage of the planning process, you will need to re-check the feasibility of your objectives and strategies in terms of the market share, sales, costs, profits and so on which these demand in practice. As in the rest of the marketing discipline, you will need to employ judgment, experience, market research or anything else which helps you to look at your conclusions from all possible angles.

Detailed Plans and Programs

At this stage, you will need to develop your overall marketing strategies into detailed plans and program. Although these detailed plans may cover each of the 7 P's, the focus will vary, depending upon your organization's specific strategies. A product-oriented company will focus its plans for the 7 P's around each of its products. A market or geographically oriented company will concentrate on each market or geographical area. Each will base its plans upon the detailed needs of its customers, and on the strategies chosen to satisfy these needs.

Again, the most important element is, indeed, that of the detailed plans, which spell out exactly what programs and individual activities will take place over the period of the plan (usually over the next year). Without these specified-and preferably quantified-activities the plan cannot be monitored, even in terms of success in meeting its objectives. It is these programs and activities which will then constitute the "marketing" of the organization over the period. As a result, these detailed marketing programs are the most important, practical outcome of the whole planning process. These plans must therefore be:

- Clear-They should be an unambiguous statement of 'exactly' what is to be done.
- Quantified-The predicted outcome of each activity should be, as far as possible, quantified, so that its performance can be monitored.
- Focused-The temptation to proliferate activities beyond the numbers which can be realistically controlled should be avoided. The 80:20 Rule applies in this context too.
- Realistic-They should be achievable.
- Agreed-Those who are to implement them should be committed to them, and agree that they are achievable. The resulting plans should become a working document which will guide the campaigns taking place throughout the organization over the period of the plan. If the marketing plan is to work, every exception to it (throughout the year) must be questioned; and the lessons learned, to be incorporated in the next year's planning.

Content of the Marketing Plan

A marketing plan for a small business typically includes Small Business Administration Description of competitors, including the level of demand for the product or service and the strengths and weaknesses of competitors

1. Description of the product or service, including special features
2. Marketing budget, including the advertising and promotional plan
3. Description of the business location, including advantages and disadvantages for marketing
4. Pricing strategy
5. Market Segmentation

Medium-sized and Large Organizations

The main contents of a marketing plan are:

1. Executive Summary
2. Situational Analysis
3. Opportunities/Issue Analysis-SWOT Analysis
4. Objectives
5. Strategy
6. Action Program (the operational marketing plan itself for the period under review)
7. Financial Forecast
8. Controls.

In detail, a complete marketing plan typically includes:

1. Title page
2. Executive Summary
3. Current Situation – Macroenvironment
   - economy
   - legal
   - government
   - technology
   - ecological
   - sociocultural
   - supply chain.
4. Current Situation-Market Analysis;
   - market definition

- o market size
- o market segmentation
- o industry structure and strategic groupings
- o Porter 5 forces analysis
- o competition and market share
- o competitors' strengths and weaknesses
- o market trends.

5. Current Situation-Consumer Analysis
   - o nature of the buying decision
   - o participants
   - o demographics
   - o psychographics
   - o buyer motivation and expectations
   - o loyalty segments.
6. Current Situation – Internal;
   - o company resources:
     - financial
     - people
     - time
     - skills.
   - o Objectives:
     - mission statement and vision statement
     - corporate objectives
     - financial objective
     - marketing objectives
     - long term objectives
     - description of the basic business philosophy.
   - o corporate culture.
7. Summary of Situation Analysis;
   - o external threats
   - o external opportunities
   - o internal strengths
   - o internal weaknesses
   - o Critical success factors in the industry
   - o our sustainable competitive advantage.

8. Marketing research;
   - o information requirements
   - o research methodology
   - o research results.
9. Marketing Strategy;
   - o product mix
   - o product strengths and weaknesses:
     - perceptual mapping.
   - o product life cycle management and new product development
   - o Brand name, brand image, and brand equity
   - o the augmented product
   - o product portfolio analysis:
     - B.C.G. Analysis
     - contribution margin analysis
     - G.E. Multi Factoral analysis
     - Quality Function Deployment.
10. Marketing Strategy-segmented marketing actions and market share objectives;
    - o by product,
    - o by customer segment,
    - o by geographical market,
    - o by distribution channel.
11. Marketing Strategy-Price
    - o pricing objectives
    - o pricing method (eg.: cost plus, demand based, or competitor indexing)
    - o pricing strategy (eg.: skimming, or penetration)
    - o discounts and allowances
    - o price elasticity and customer sensitivity
    - o price zoning
    - o break even analysis at various prices.
12. Marketing Strategy-promotion
    - o promotional goals
    - o promotional mix

- o advertising reach, frequency, flights, theme, and media
- o sales force requirements, techniques, and management
- o sales promotion
- o publicity and public relations
- o electronic promotion (eg.: Web, or telephone)
- o word of mouth marketing (buzz)
- o viral marketing.

13. Marketing Strategy-Distribution
    - o geographical coverage
    - o distribution channels
    - o physical distribution and logistics
    - o electronic distribution.
14. Implementation;
    - o personnel requirements:
        - assign responsibilities
        - give incentives
        - training on selling methods.
    - o financial requirements
    - o management information systems requirements
    - o month-by-month agenda
        - PERT or critical path analysis
    - o monitoring results and benchmarks
    - o adjustment mechanism
    - o contingencies (What if's).
15. Financial Summary:
    - o assumptions
    - o pro-forma monthly income statement
    - o contribution margin analysis
    - o breakeven analysis
    - o Monte Carlo method
    - o ISI: Internet Strategic Intelligence.
16. Scenarios;
    - o Prediction of Future Scenarios
    - o Plan of Action for each Scenario.

17. Appendix;
    - o pictures and specifications of the new product
    - o results from research already completed.

Measurement of Progress

The final stage of any marketing planning process is to establish targets (or standards) so that progress can be monitored. Accordingly, it is important to put both quantities and timescales into the marketing objectives (for example, to capture 20 percent by value of the market within two years) and into the corresponding strategies.

Changes in the environment mean that the forecasts often have to be changed. Along with these, the related plans may well also need to be changed. Continuous monitoring of performance, against predetermined targets, represents a most important aspect of this.

However, perhaps even more important is the enforced discipline of a regular formal review. Again, as with forecasts, in many cases the best (most realistic) planning cycle will revolve around a quarterly review. Best of all, at least in terms of the quantifiable aspects of the plans, if not the wealth of backing detail, is probably a quarterly rolling review-planning one full year ahead each new quarter. Of course, this does absorb more planning resource; but it also ensures that the plans embody the latest information, and-with attention focused on them so regularly-forces both the plans and their implementation to be realistic.

Plans only have validity if they are actually used to control the progress of a company: their success lies in their implementation, not in the writing'.

Performance Analysis

The most important elements of marketing performance, which are normally tracked, are:

Sales Analysis

Most organizations track their sales results; or, in non-profit organizations for example, the number of clients. The more sophisticated track them in terms of 'sales variance'-the deviation from the target figures-which allows a more immediate picture of deviations to become evident.

'Micro-analysis', which is a nicely pseudo-scientific term for the normal management process of investigating detailed problems, then investigates the individual elements (individual products, sales territories, customers and so on) which are failing to meet targets.

Market Share Analysis

Few organizations track market share though it is often an important metric. Though absolute sales might grow in an expanding market, a firm's share of the market can d

ecrease which bodes ill for future sales when the market starts to drop. Where such market share is tracked, there may be a number of aspects which will be followed:

- overall market share
- segment share-that in the specific, targeted segment
- relative share-in relation to the market leaders
- annual fluctuation rate of market share.

Expense Analysis

The key ratio to watch in this area is usually the 'marketing expense to sales ratio'; although this may be broken down into other elements (advertising to sales, sales administration to sales, and so on).

Financial Analysis

The "bottom line" of marketing activities should at least in theory, be the net profit (for all except non-profit organizations, where the comparable emphasis may be on remaining within budgeted costs). There are a number of separate performance figures and key ratios which need to be tracked:

- gross contribution<>net profit
- gross profit<>return on investment
- net contribution<>profit on sales.

There can be considerable benefit in comparing these figures with those achieved by other organizations (especially those in the same industry); using, for instance, the figures which can be obtained (in the UK) from 'The Centre for Interfirm Comparison'. The most sophisticated use of this approach, however, is typically by those making use of PIMS (Profit Impact of Management Strategies), initiated by the General Electric Company and then developed by Harvard Business School, but now run by the Strategic Planning Institute.

The above performance analyses concentrate on the quantitative measures which are directly related to short-term performance. But there are a number of indirect measures, essentially tracking customer attitudes, which can also indicate the organization's performance in terms of its longer-term marketing strengths and may accordingly be even more important indicators. Some useful measures are:

- market research-including customer panels (which are used to track changes over time)
- lost business-the orders which were lost because, for example, the stock was not available or the product did not meet the customer's exact requirements
- customer complaints-how many customers complain about the products or services, or the organization itself, and about what.

Use of Marketing Plans

A formal, written marketing plan is essential; in that it provides an unambiguous reference point for activities throughout the planning period. However, perhaps the most important benefit of these plans is the planning process itself. This typically offers a unique opportunity, a forum, for information-rich and productively focused discussions between the various managers involved. The plan, together with the associated discussions, then provides an agreed context for their subsequent management activities, even for those not described in the plan itself.

Budgets as Managerial Tools

The classic quantification of a marketing plan appears in the form of budgets. Because these are so rigorously quantified, they are particularly important. They should, thus, represent an unequivocal projection of actions and expected results. What is more, they should be capable of being monitored accurately; and, indeed, performance against budget is the main (regular) management review process.

The purpose of a marketing budget is, thus, to pull together all the revenues and costs involved in marketing into one comprehensive document. It is a managerial tool that balances what is needed to be spent against what can be afforded, and helps make choices about priorities. It is then used in monitoring performance in practice.

The marketing budget is usually the most powerful tool by which you think through the relationship between desired results and available means. Its starting point should be the marketing strategies and plans, which have already been formulated in the marketing plan itself; although, in practice, the two will run in parallel and will interact. At the very least, the rigorous, highly quantified, budgets may cause a rethink of some of the more optimistic elements of the plans.

Marketing Management

Marketing management is a business discipline which is focused on the practical application of marketing techniques and the management of a firm's marketing resources and activities. Rapidly emerging forces of globalization have compelled firms to market beyond the borders of their home country making International Marketing highly significant and an integral part of a firm's marketing strategy. Marketing managers are often responsible for influencing the level, timing, and composition of customer demand accepted definition of the term. In part, this is because the role of a marketing manager can vary significantly based on a business' size, corporate culture, and industry context. For example, in a large consumer products company, the marketing manager may act as the overall general manager of his or her assigned product

From this perspect, it consists of 5 steps, beginning with the market & environment research. After fixing the targets and setting the strategies, they will be realised by the marketing mix in step 4. The last step in the process is the marketing controlling. Marketing management strategy and design effective, cost-efficient implementation programs, firms must possess a detailed, objective understanding of their own business and the market in which they operate. In analysing these issues, the discipline of marketing management often overlaps with the related discipline of strategic planning.

Traditionally, marketing analysis was structured into three areas: Customer analysis, Company analysis, and Competitor analysis (so-called "3Cs" analysis). More recently, it has become fashionable in some marketing circles to divide these further into certain five "Cs": Customer analysis, Company analysis, Collaborator analysis, Competitor analysis, and analysis of the industry Context.

Department analysis is to develop a schematic diagram for market segmentation, breaking down the market into various constituent groups of customers, which are called customer segments or market segmentations. Marketing managers work to develop detailed profiles of each segment, focusing on any number of variables that may differ among the segments: demographic, psychographic, geographic, behavioural, needs-benefit, and other factors may all be examined. Marketers also attempt to track these segments' perceptions of the various products in the market using tools such as perceptual mapping.

In company analysis, marketers focus on understanding the company's cost structure and cost position relative to competitors, as well as working to identify a firm's core competencies and other competitively distinct company resources. Marketing managers may also work with the accounting department to analyse the profits the firm is generating from various product lines and customer accounts.

The company may also conduct periodic brand audits to assess the strength of its brands and sources of brand equity.

The firm's collaborators may also be profiled, which may include various suppliers, distributors and other channel partners, joint venture partners, and others. An analysis of complementary products may also be performed if such products exist. Marketing management employs various tools from economics and competitive strategy to analyse the industry context in which the firm operates. These include Porter's five forces, analysis of strategic groups of competitors, value chain analysis and others. Depending on the industry, the regulatory context may also be important to examine in detail.

In Competitor analysis, marketers build detailed profiles of each competitor in the market, focusing especially on their relative competitive strengths and weaknesses using SWOT analysis. Marketing managers will examine each competitor's cost structure, sources of profits, resources and competencies, competitive positioning and product differentiation, degree of vertical integration, historical responses to industry developments, and other factors.

Marketing management often finds it necessary to invest in research to collect the data required to perform accurate marketing analysis. As such, they often conduct market research (alternately marketing research) to obtain this information. Marketers employ a variety of techniques to conduct market research, but some of the more common include:

- Qualitative marketing research, such as focus groups
- Quantitative marketing research, such as statistical surveys
- Experimental techniques such as test markets
- Observational techniques such as ethnographic (on-site) observation.

Marketing managers may also design and oversee various environmental scanning and competitive intelligence processes to help identify trends and inform the company's marketing analysis.

Marketing Strategy

Once the company has obtained an adequate understanding of the customer base and its own competitive position in the industry, marketing managers are able to make key strategic decisions and develop a marketing strategy designed to maximize the revenues and profits of the firm. The selected strategy may aim for any of a variety of specific objectives, including optimizing short-term unit margins, revenue growth, market share, long-term profitability, or other goals.

To achieve the desired objectives, marketers typically identify one or more target customer segments which they intend to pursue. Customer segments are often selected as targets because they score highly on two dimensions: 1) The segment is attractive to serve because it is large, growing, makes frequent purchases, is not price sensitive (i.e. is willing to pay high prices), or other factors; and 2) The company has the resources and capabilities to compete for the segment's business, can meet their needs better than the competition, and can do so profitably. In fact, a commonly cited definition of marketing is simply "meeting needs profitably."

The implication of selecting target segments is that the business will subsequently allocate more resources to acquire and retain customers in the target segment(s) than it will for other, non-targeted customers. In some cases, the firm may go so far as to turn away customers that are not in its target segment. The doorman at a swanky nightclub, for example, may deny entry to unfashionably dressed individuals because the business has made a strategic decision to target the "high fashion" segment of nightclub patrons.

In conjunction with targeting decisions, marketing managers will identify the desired positioning they want the company, product, or brand to occupy in the target customer's mind. This positioning is often an encapsulation of a key benefit the company's product or service offers that is differentiated and superior to the benefits offered by competitive products. For example, Volvo has traditionally positioned its products in the automobile market in North America in order to be perceived as the leader in "safety", whereas BMW has traditionally positioned its brand to be perceived as the leader in "performance."

Ideally, a firm's positioning can be maintained over a long period of time because the company possesses, or can develop, some form of sustainable competitive advantage. The positioning should also be sufficiently relevant to the target segment such that it will drive the purchasing behavior of target customers.

Implementation Planning

The Marketing Metrics Continuum provides a framework for how to categorize metrics from the tactical to strategic.

After the firm's strategic objectives have been identified, the target market selected, and the desired positioning for the company, product or brand has been determined, marketing managers focus on how to best implement the chosen strategy. Traditionally, this has involved implementation planning across the "4Ps" of marketing: Product management, Pricing, Place (i.e. sales and distribution channels), and Promotion.

Taken together, the company's implementation choices across the 4Ps are often described as the marketing mix, meaning the mix of elements the business will employ to "go to market" and execute the marketing strategy. The overall goal for the marketing mix is to consistently deliver a compelling value proposition that reinforces the firm's chosen positioning, builds customer loyalty and brand equity among target customers, and achieves the firm's marketing and financial objectives. In many cases, marketing management will develop a marketing plan to specify how the company will execute the chosen strategy and achieve the business' objectives. The content of marketing plans varies from firm to firm, but commonly includes:

- An executive summary
- Situation analysis to summarize facts and insights gained from market research and marketing analysis
- The company's mission statement or long-term strategic vision
- A statement of the company's key objectives, often subdivided into marketing objectives and financial objectives
- The marketing strategy the business has chosen, specifying the target segments to be pursued and the competitive positioning to be achieved
- Implementation choices for each element of the marketing mix (the 4Ps).

Project, Process, and Vendor Management

Once the key implementation initiatives have been identified, marketing managers work to oversee the execution of the marketing plan. Marketing executives may therefore manage any number of specific projects, such as sales force management initiatives, product development efforts, channel marketing programs and the execution of public relations and advertising campaigns. Marketers use a variety of project management techniques to ensure projects achieve their objectives while keeping to established schedules and budgets.

More broadly, marketing managers work to design and improve the effectiveness of core marketing processes, such as new product development, brand management, marketing communications, and pricing. Marketers may employ the tools of business process reengineering to ensure these processes are properly designed, and use a variety of process management techniques to keep them operating smoothly.

Effective execution may require management of both internal resources and a variety of external vendors and service providers, such as the firm's advertising agency. Marketers may therefore coordinate with the company's Purchasing department on the procurement of these services.

Organizational Management and Leadership

Marketing management may spend a fair amount of time building or maintaining a marketing orientation for the business. Achieving a market orientation, also known as "customer focus" or the "marketing concept", requires building consensus at the senior management level and then driving customer focus down into the organization. Cultural barriers may exist in a given business unit or functional area that the marketing manager must address in order to achieve this goal. Additionally, marketing executives often act as a "brand champion" and work to enforce corporate identity standards across the enterprise.

In larger organizations, especially those with multiple business units, top marketing managers may need to coordinate across several marketing departments and also resources from finance, research and development, engineering, operations, manufacturing, or other functional areas to implement the marketing plan. In order to effectively manage these resources, marketing executives may need to spend much of their time focused on political issues and inte-departmental negotiations.

The effectiveness of a marketing manager may therefore depend on his or her ability to make the internal "sale" of various marketing programs equally as much as the external customer's reaction to such programs.

Reporting, Measurement, Feedback and Control Systems

Marketing management employs a variety of metrics to measure progress against objectives. It is the responsibility of marketing managers – in the marketing department or elsewhere – to ensure that the execution of marketing programs achieves the desired objectives and does so in a cost-efficient manner.

Marketing management therefore often makes use of various organizational control systems, such as sales forecasts, sales force and reseller incentive programs, sales force management systems, and customer relationship management tools (CRM). Recently, some software vendors have begun using the term "marketing operations management" or "marketing resource management" to describe systems that facilitate an integrated approach for controlling marketing resources. In some cases, these efforts may be linked to various supply chain management systems, such as enterprise resource planning (ERP), material requirements planning (MRP), efficient consumer response (ECR), and inventory management systems.

Measuring the return on investment (ROI) of and marketing effectiveness various marketing initiatives is a significant problem for marketing management. Various market research, accounting and financial tools are used to help estimate the ROI of marketing investments. Brand valuation, for example, attempts to identify the percentage of a company's market value that is generated by the company's brands, and thereby estimate the financial value of specific investments in brand equity. Another technique, integrated marketing communications (IMC), is a CRM database-driven approach that attempts to estimate the value of marketing mix executions based on the changes in customer behavior these executions generate.

Free Website Promotion Tutorial

Welcome to A Promotion Guide. If this is your first visit, you might want to take the time to read through this page. It contains a free step-by-step website promotion tutorial that also serves as a "User's Guide" to the site. Reading it will give you a good idea on what you need to do, when you need to do it and how the articles on this site will help you. This tutorial is split into three phases that each have two, three or four steps. It is highly recommended that you start from the first phase and move forwards only after you have completed all of the steps in it.

We'll begin with the assumption that your site is brand new and that you haven't done any website promotion work yet. However, that doesn't mean that you can't use the tutorial if you have submitted to a few search engines or registered your site with a couple of directories. If you notice that there are some things you have already done, feel free to simply skip over them.

Promoting your site takes a lot of time and may involve waiting several weeks or even months to get into certain directories and search engines. Thus, it might be wise to bookmark this page so that you can return to it later and continue the tutorial from where you left off.

Website Promotion, Phase One-Directories

You should start your website promotion efforts by listing your site at the most popular Internet directories. Because they can send you substantial amounts of traffic and affect your ranking in various search engines, it is wise to make sure that your site is present in all of the major directories before doing anything else.

Step One-General Information

Submitting to directories is easy and doesn't require much effort. It's ensuring that your submission will be accepted that makes this task a hard one.

1. First, read "Boost your traffic with website directories" to get a basic idea on what directories are and how to submit to them.
2. Examine the article about web page design to get some tips on how to improve your site and reduce the chances of it being rejected.

Step Two-The Open Directory Project

Start with the Open Directory Project. While your site has to offer good, unique content to be accepted to the ODP, its editors usually review sites quickly and won't reject them without a good reason for doing so. This, along with the fact that submitting to the ODP is free of charge, makes it a perfect starting point. Completing this step successfully will also provide you with experience that will prove to be very valuable later on.

1. Read my thoughts on how Google's ranking algorithm works and notice how an ODP listing seems to affect your ranking at Google. Keep this information in mind when you submit.
2. Take a look at the advice on submitting your website to the ODP.
3. Finally, submit your site to the ODP.
4. If your submission isn't successful, consider becoming an editor at the Open Directory and listing your own site.

Step Three-Yahoo

After securing a listing at ODP, your next task is to get the folks at Yahoo to notice that your site exists and is worth a place in their directory.

This might cost you a fair amount of money if you are running a commercial site, but is usually worth it. Non-commercial sites can get in for free, but might require several submissions and a lot of patience before they are accepted.

1. Check out the Yahoo-specific guidelines and hints and the article about how Yahoo's search feature ranks sites.
2. Bite the bullet and submit your site to Yahoo.

Website Promotion, Phase Two-Search Engines

Now that your site has been included in ODP and Yahoo, you should already be receiving clearly more traffic than before. The next task is to get to know search engines and use them to bring even more people to your pages. Because you have completed phase one, you have established a good foundation for making your site perform well in the search engines.

Step One-Search Engine Optimization, Basics

In order to gain good rankings, you'll need to learn the basics of search engine algorithms (ranking systems) and adjust your pages to meet their criteria as well as possible. This will take some time and effort, but doing some work now will save you from a lot of trouble in the future.

1. First, try to make the design of your site as search engine friendly as possible. To read more about the subject, take a look at my article about website optimization.
2. Next, you'll need to do some keyword optimization. Sounds frightening, but in plain English it simply means choosing the correct keywords for your pages. Using the wrong words is perhaps the most common reason why people don't get satisfying results from their search engine optimization work.
3. Continue by reading these search engine optimization tips.
4. Read the article about META tags and add them to all of your pages. The META keywords tag isn't absolutely necessary, but the META description tag is very important.
5. Learn what link popularity is and how search engines use it to rank your pages.
6. Unless you have already done so, read about Google's algorithm. Google is among the most popular search services of today, so it is wise to take its requirements into account.
7. Use all of this information to optimize your pages for the search engines.

Step Two-Search Engine Optimization, Advanced

Your site is now adequately prepared to really start bringing in traffic from search engines. But if you want to widen your knowledge about them and increase your chances of success, you still have some work to do.

On the other hand, if you're totally exhausted and just want to get this thing over with, you'll be delighted to know that this step isn't absolutely necessary.

1. Study some of the more advanced things related to search engine optimization. Among them are cloaking, css tricks, doorway pages, themes and how to improve your search engine ranking with click popularity.
2. Read about the things you should avoid doing from this article that outlines common web site promotion mistakes.

Step Three-Submitting to Search Engines?

Now is the time to make sure that your site has a presence in the indexes of major search engines. Fortunately, they are quite good at finding your site on their own. There are things you can do to help them, though..

1. Get to know how search engine submission works and how the search engines determine which sites to list.
2. Read the article "Targeting your search engine marketing" to see which engines are the most popular ones.
3. If you are running a commercial site, you might also want to consider paying for search engine placement. Take a look at how you can use PPC search engine advertising to buy your way to the top.

Website Promotion, Phase Three-More Techniques

After being accepted into the largest directories and having pages of your site come up in answer to searches done at the major search engines, the long hours that you've spent on website promotion have begun to pay off and your daily visitor count is starting to look good. But there is still plenty you can do to help your site attract even more traffic.

In phase three, we'll examine different promotion methods that you might want to try. However, in order to prevent you from wasting your time on things that don't work, we'll also go over a few techniques that have proven to be less than spectacular when I experimented with them.

Step One-Keep these in Mind

First, let's take a look at the good stuff. The articles introduced in this step are about the website promotion methods that are at least partially effective. Some of them work better than others, but if used correctly, all of them can produce results that will be worth your while. Of course, most of the articles include advice on what you need to do to obtain the best possible results with the method discussed.

1. If you sell something on your site, you might want to try banner ads. Usually banner campaigns are seen as expensive and ineffective, but it is partially because advertisers don't know how to design good banners.
2. Read the article on how to increase traffic with return visitors. Getting people to come back is the secret to why some sites get amazingly many hits per day.
3. Learn what reciprocal links are and how to get them, then put that knowledge into use. In addition to sending you visitors, reciprocal links will also increase your link popularity and help your site rank higher in the search engines.
4. Start using E-mail signatures. They might not produce thousands of visitors, but are a great way to promote your site a bit without having to actually do anything.
5. Evaluate whether your site could benefit from joining a topsite list. These lists have their good and bad sides, but might be at least worth a try.
6. Consider trying to build traffic with Usenet advertising. It can give you a nice traffic boost and help spread the word about your site, but only if done properly. Read the article to learn why Usenet promotion should only be done with great care.
7. Writing newsletter articles often works well and can send you large amounts of targeted traffic in a short period of time, for free.

Step Two-Forget these

As said, everything just doesn't always work the way it should in the world of promotion. In step two, our attention is focused on website promotion methods that are more trouble than they are worth.

They might not be entirely useless, but your time would be better spent on improving your site or spreading the word about your site in other ways.

1. Click exchange programs are easy, fast, free and will get you a lot of visitors. That's why it might be a surprise to hear that they really aren't good website promotion tools.
2. A lot has been written about FFA pages and for the past few years, most of it has been negative. The only thing they are good for is increasing the flow of spam to your E-mail address.

3. Winning website awards can occasionally be useful, especially if the awards are well-known. However, sometimes the winner of the award is not the real winner.

Final Words

Congratulate yourself for being persistent, bright and hard-working. Most get frustrated and quit before this point, which is why most sites never become anything. After all, the secret to having a successful site is working hard in both promoting and creating it. You just might have what it takes.

After going through those three phases, you've read just about everything this site has to offer. While there is more to website promotion than what we have discussed here, you now know quite a lot about the subject. If you still desire more information, don't forget to come back to this site every now and then. This tutorial is always incomplete, because I continuously notice things that I want to write about.

I hope that A Promotion Guide has been able to help you to make your site more popular and thus given you the chance to spread your ideas and thoughts to a larger audience. And remember, if you have achieved good results, it's not because I showed you how to do it-it's because you did it.

The Future of Internet Marketing

Internet marketers by and large are utilized for selling and marketing to, a predominantly western audience. Today's web sites, mailing lists, payment processing systems, and overall way of doing business have evolved around the needs and wants of target markets in the western world. And any experienced marketer knows it can be difficult. Despite popular notions that you can start an Internet business and watch the money roll in, the reality is that there is a lot of competition from other webmasters, regardless of the market or type of products you promote.

Looking ahead, have you considered the impact of even more competition-lots more? In Asia, in particular China and India, large, well-educated populations, a lower cost of living with much-improved standards, and more widely available Internet access may combine in the near future to create a lot more Internet marketers. Many are well-versed in technical aspects of the Internet, including programming and site development. In fact, if you've ever used any of the various freelance sites to outsource technical projects, you've seen that many of the bidders are from Asia.

With populations of one billion people and more in those two countries alone, the current generation is certainly well-attuned to the Internet, and being avid surfers, are no doubt aware of the commercial opportunities and worldwide reach available only on the net. It's likely only a matter of time before they begin marketing to western audiences themselves. Whether through affiliate marketing, or by developing new products to sell on their own behalf, the prospect of increased competition for current Internet marketers is very real, and likely very near. The biggest hurdles will be language and market understanding. After all, it's difficult enough to write effective sales letters in ones native language, even if addressed to a market and culture you understand. Over time, even those barriers will fall-face it, just as programming can be outsourced, so can marketing and language assistance.

The potential competition can sound ominous. And depending on your outlook, it can be. For every new product that pays affiliate commissions, there soon could be lots more marketers trying to promote it to the same audience. And for every new product of your own you develop, similar products with more features and selling for a lower price could appear. That already happens now to an extent. What will it be like with even more marketers and developers competing?

But change can also be good news. You as an individual marketer can either complain about the unfairness of it all, or you can choose to adapt your business to the inevitable and prosper. As new marketers, and surfers in general, from China, India, and elsewhere come online, they will also create entirely new markets to sell to, markets that weren't there just a short time ago. After all, as marketers they will need the same types of products and services that western marketers need. And as surfers and eventual online buyers, their consumers will want not only western, but also regional and cultural goods, just as online shoppers in the western world do now. Of course, marketers in those regions will also compete in their local markets, as well as western ones.

The globalization of Internet marketing will continue rapidly, no doubt about it. To stay in the game, North American Marketers would be well-advised to begin their strategic planning for this trend now. New markets and new opportunities are emerging!

A look forward at how things could change in the world of internet marketing.

With every day that passes more and more people are tuning in to the huge possibilities that the internet offers for making an income of their own-one that isn't dependent on an employer. As the internet gets more crowded with people trying to earn a living from their own homes there is the prospect of existing marketers fending off more competition on a worldwide basis. More and more countries are becoming ?internet savvy' and with the advent of Web 2.0 it's clear that it's becoming even easier to jump into internet marketing and make a mark with no money necessary to get you started.

The development of social networking and bookmarking sites has also led to a new avenue for promoting goods and services online in a more personal way. Many internet marketers have recognized this and have already jumped on the bandwagon to get their profiles established in order to start attracting friends and potential customers from these very sources.

Web 2.0 has introduced a more interactive internet for marketers to get to grips with, and it may be that the people who can do this the most successfully will be the ones to grab the lion's share of sales in the next few years. Only time will tell whether this becomes a reality. Whatever happens it's important to keep improving our own services and products to help ward off the competition otherwise we may find ourselves left in the dust. Never has the need to keep pushing for more improvements in our own businesses been so important.

It's also possible that the trend for promoting your wares through videos posted on sites like YouTube will become more pronounced. This technique has been latched onto by a lot of internet marketers with mixed results, but when it's done properly it can add a whole new dimension to promotions. Instead of merely reading about how wonderful a product is (where we know its shortcomings can be more easily masked by clever copywriting) we can see it for ourselves and are better able to make an informed decision about whether to buy it or not.

As the internet marches steadily on into the 21st century however it will become even more essential to learn the basics of internet marketing in as fast a time as possible. In the recent past it seemed to be enough to learn as we went along, making mistakes here and there but turning them around to work in our favour and building on the new knowledge it gave us.

But it's becoming increasingly important to learn on our feet now, if we want to build an internet business worth having. This trend of running to keep up looks set to continue and pick up pace as the internet makes even more progress and reaches into even more parts of the world. But it's not all negative. This same fact means that you have a chance to make yourself indispensable. If you can learn the necessary skills to become a successful internet marketer in the 21st century, you can teach those skills to others and make a small fortune in the process. It's all a question of focus. If you can remain focused on the benefits that the ever developing internet can offer you, your business will flourish and rise above the competition.

Social Media Marketing

Social media marketing is a term that describes use of social networks, online communities, blogs, wikis or any other online collaborative media for marketing, sales, public relations and customer service. Common social media marketing tools include Twitter, LinkedIn, Facebook, Flickr, Wikipedia, Orkut and YouTube.

In the context of internet marketing, social media refers to a collective group of web properties whose content is primarily published by users, not direct employees of the property (e.g., the vast majority of video on YouTube is published by non-YouTube employees).

Concept

Social media marketing has three important aspects:

1. Creating buzz or newsworthy events, videos, tweets, or blog entries that attract attention, and become viral in nature. Buzz is what makes social media marketing work. It replicates a message through user to user contact, rather than the traditional method of purchasing of an ad or promoting a press release. The message does not necessarily have to be about the product. Many successful viral campaigns have gathered steam through an amusing or compelling message, with the company logo or tagline included incidentally.
2. Building ways that enable fans of a brand or company to promote a message themselves in multiple online social media venues. Fan pages in Twitter, MySpace of Facebook follow this model.
3. It is based around online conversations. Social media marketing is not controlled by the organization. Instead it encourages user participation and dialogue. A badly designed social media marketing campaign can potentially backfire on the organization that created it. To be successful SMM campaigns must fully engage and respect the users.

According to Lloyd Salmons, first chairman of the Internet Advertising Bureau social media council "Social media isn't just about big networks like Facebook and MySpace, it's about brands having conversations.".

Social Network Marketing

Social network marketing or social level marketing, is an advertising method that makes use of social network service and to increase their web presence. This ranges from simply advertising directly on social networking sites, viral marketing that spreads throughout the web, email, and word of mouth, or providing niche social networking sites focused around the item being advertised.

Many sites include features where companies can create profiles. For example, on Facebook companies can create "pages" where users can become fans of this company, product, service, individual, etc. Many companies create MySpace pages for themselves. Companies sometimes invest in internet presence management, which can include social network marketing.

E-Marketing Mix

Traditionally the marketing mix is co-ordinated so efficient product, price, promotion and place strategies are developed for products purchased over the counter. The internet is changing the way we sell our products and services. That's a fact. Consumers now use the internet to research and purchase products/services online. Organisation now need online strategies to attract and retain customers. The e-marketing mix considers the elements of presenting the marketing mix online. Lets look at it in more detail.

E-product Strategies

We walk into a shop and see a product we like, we can assess it, touch it. Online, this immediate tangibility disappears. But, is that a disadvantage? Within the uk e-commerce sales are increasing at extremely high rates. Why? What does buying products online offer over one to one sales? Firstly there are clear online facts about the product you are purchasing.

The buyer knows immediately about product features, the facts, not a sales persons assumptions. www.comet.co.uk a UK electrical store offers clear information on products and their specification, consumers know what they get if not there is a customer service number where they can find out more. The buying process is also customised for returning visitors, making repeat purchases easier. Organisations can also offer immediately ancillary products along with the main purchase. For example, the chance to buy extra printer cartridges along with your purchase of your printer online. The product can also be customised to consumers needs. www.nike.com offer customised trainers to users online. Users can design and see their trainers online before they order!

E-price Strategies

As mentioned in our marketing mix section, pricing is always difficult to do and must take into account many considerations. Traditionally pricing was about finding about your costs, discovering how much consumers are willing to pay, taking account competition pricing then setting your price. The internet has made pricing very competitive. Many costs i.e. store costs, staff cost have disappeared for complete online stores, placing price pressures on traditional retailers.

The internet gives consumers the power to shop around for the best deal at a click of a button. Website such www.kelkoo.com compare products from different websites informing consumers of where the best deal is. Such easy access to information helps to maintain prices within the online world.

The growth of online auctions also helps consumers to dictate price. The online auction company www.ebay.com has grown in popularity with thousands of buyers and seller bidding daily.

E-pricing can also easily reward loyal customers. Technology allows repeat visitors to be tracked, easily allowing loyalty incentives to be targeted towards them. Payment is also easy, paypals, or online credit cards use allows for easy payments. However the downside to this is internet fraud, which is growing rapidly around the world.

E-place Strategies

One of the biggest changes to the marketing mix is online purchasing. Consumers can purchase direct from manufacturers cutting out retailers totally. The challenge for online retailers is to ensure that the product is delivered to the consumer within a reasonable time. Location is important within our place strategy. Online location can refer to where links are placed on other websites. Placing a link on www.google.com home page would generate high consumer traffic for you. Knowing your customer and knowing where they visit should help you understand where to place your online links and advertisements.

E-promotion Strategies

Promoting products and service online is concerned with a number of issues. Having a recognisable domain name is first stage towards e-promotion. Organisation such as egg.com have successfully positioned the brand on the online world as an online bank.

Most organisations today have some form of webpage used in most if not all advertisements. Placing banner advertisements on other webpages is a common form of e-promotion. Banner ads must be placed where potential customers browse. Web public relations (WPR) is another approach to promoting online. News worthy stories based on product or service launches can be placed on the companies webpage, or WPR articles sent to review sites for consumers to read. Hopefully this form of online promotion will pull the consumer in. Direct email is a popular and common form of e-promotions, although slowly becoming the most hated my many consumers. Organisations can send e-leaflets to hundreds and thousands of respondents, hoping a small percentage will reply. The problem is that for every 100 emails sent the response rate will be 1-2!. Direct emailing is also known as SPAM which stands for Sending Persistent Annoying eMail. (SPAM). To summaries e-promotion includes:

- Banner promotions
- Web public relations (WPR)
- E-leaflets
- Having a domain name.

The e-marketing mix must work together and support each other if the company is to have a successful online marketing strategy.

Relationship Marketing and the Internet

Relationship marketing is all about keeping the customer for the long-term. The life time value the customer has to offer. Traditionally the firm would develop a number of strategies to try to get the customer coming back to their stores. These strategies have evolved for the online world, and it is has become a challenge to try to make customers visit and purchase products from their websites regularly. Some strategies used to develop relationship with customers online include:

Customisation: Customer can customise their products online to give them a unique experience. Shoe manufacturer Nike and car manufacturer Mini Cooper allow their customers to customise their products when visiting their website. Giving users an interactive experience online.

Online questionnaires: Many retail websites are asking customers to feedback their experience of using the website almost instantly after they complete using their site. The information has the advantage of being analysed very quickly so the firm can offer what users need.

E-vouchers: Regular customers are often sent e-vouchers that give them discounts off their next purchase. Vouchers can be targeted around what the customer frequently buys. Firms may calculate that this particular customer has not purchased from them for a while and send a voucher enticing them back, to try and re-establish this online relationship.

Online chat: To recreate the shopping environment some websites are offering the ability to chat via webcam or chat window. This gives the opportunity for user to talk to sales persons via the web. Dell offer this facility online, where user can query computer specifications. By trying to recreate this interactivity customers may shift or secure their loyalty to a particular online firm.

Customer Service and Contact: A key to maintaining online relationships is how the customer is looked after, after the sale is complete, the post-transactional strategy. If a product is faulty, is it easy for the customer to return it? Some online electrical firms allow the customer to log the fault, print a returns number, and a date for pick up from their home. This is quite straight forward. If the customer feels that the process for returning and liaison with the online retailer is rather long, the chances are loyalties would shift. With technology changing at a very fast rate the experience of the user will become more interactive and this interactivity maybe the key to secure long-term online relationships.

Internet Marketing and Objectives

Every business needs to have objectives which should be SMART. Whether you are an online business or a combined clicks and mortar business, you need to have targets to aim for.

Objects of an Online Business (Clicks Business)

If your business is solely based online your objectives could be:

1. To inform users of your web presence and the benefit your website offers over its competitors.
2. To persuade users to use the services of the firm. This could be done by offering a discount for a limited time.
3. To make sure the business is listed in all the most popular search engines and directories.
4. Keep customers updated of any new products or changes to business services.
5. Make sure that customer have a pleasant website experience by continuously improving the navigation of the site.

6. To aim for sales of x amount and net profit of x amount in a given period.

Objectives of a Clicks and Mortar Business

If a business has a clicks and mortar strategy their objective maybe:

- To reduce costs by moving some of their operations online.
- To integrate online and offline strategies to maintain and improve relationships with customers. This could be by offering reserve online and pick up in store strategies like some retailers do.
- The company's strategy should support the overall marketing objectives of the firm this maybe to increase overall market share or profit.
- To promote both online and offline activities.

Market Research and the Internet

The internet is a great tool to help the organisation conduct research. Secondary data can easily be collected online, and primary data can be collected via clever use of online surveys. Market and Marketing research is essential for the company to stay ahead of its competitors and for the firm to provide what customers need. Technology is advancing and the way firms conduct their research is changing. The internet can be used to conduct research in a number of ways.

Cookies

Each time a user visits a website small text files called cookies are left on the computer, these files give an indication to the web companies what pages you have visited, and if you log into your account you have a customised view all the time.

In terms of research cookies tell the website owner what pages you visit frequently, how long you spend on that page and how you navigate around the website.

This information can help the firm develop a better customised experience for the user and help them develop a website which becomes more user friendly over time.

Competitor Analysis

The internet allows the company to research a competitor to analyse their marketing mix strategy online, their financial information, by looking at annual report of accounts or financial analysis done by independent websites. Also any rumours of product launches can be investigated online.

Usage Analysis

Businesses need to know how popular the internet is, and how long users spend online and what purchase patterns are like online. There are many websites that will give you this information. A quick Google search will give you a list of websites that will offer you that data to buy. The trend in the UK is towards more users spending time online not only for online shopping but also for social interaction via the use of Facebook and MSN.

Online Pestle Analysis

Every business needs to conduct an environmental analysis. The internet enables an organisation to monitor the external environment quite easily. RSS feeds from news websites can keep companies updated, as with newsletters, forums and posts. All Pestle factors can be monitored easily online.

Online Questionnaires

A simple form of primary research online is the use of online questionnaires. When the user visits a website they are asked to complete an online questionnaire. The data is usually analysed fairly quickly, with the results being used to improve online experiences.

Validity of Data

The internet is becoming saturated with lots of data and information. When a company uses this data online they must make sure that the data is accurate and valid. Sources should be checked, the date of publication should also be checked to makes sure it is valid.

Marketing Opportunities with Smartphones

The internet is becoming mobile, that is a fact. Smartphones like Apples iPhone have made access to the internet on the move a reality.

Within the UK according to Nielson research smartphone users increased from 5.6 to 6.2 million in 2009. According to BBC Click online 33% of all mobile sales within the UK 2010 will be from smartphones, this will increase to 40% of sales in 2013.

Many content based websites are now designing websites for smartphones. Users who visit BBC.co.uk are automatically referred to the mobile version of the website. One of the greatest use of smartphones is for social networking use, especially amongst the young. Firms can tap into this by advertising on social networking sites, or setting up a business profile on social networking sites, on Facebook users can then become 'fans' of that particular business.

The iPhone has grabbed the market share for smartphone users and there has been a rush by developers to provide 'apps' for users. Banks are taking advantage of this and providing iPhone apps for online banking, increasing their smartphone penetration. Currently various applications are being written for smartphones, and firms are making money developing these applications.

As a marketing medium, it is early days for the smartphone, as penetration and usage increases, we will see opportunities for advertisers to shift some of their advertising spend to smartphones.

Benefits of Internet Marketing for the Customer

Customers have gained immensely from the use of the internet. As the number of users of the internet increase more and more will shop online. Listed below are some of the benefits of the internet for the customer.

Customers Stay Updated

Customers are kept updated with product information either via the website or emails. With the internet now becoming mobile, through 3G technology and Wi-Fi, customers can be kept updated almost in real time.

Customers can Compare Online

One of the greatest advantages for the customer is that they can compare products or services they wish to purchase from the comfort of their own homes. Instead of visiting a number of different retail outlets, the user simply has to open different window tabs to compare prices or features of the product/service they wish to purchase.

Many retailing websites offer the facility where different products they sell can now be easily compared. There is also price comparison websites that customers can use to get the best possible price for their products.

Clear Product Information for the Customer

Websites offer clear product information on the product or service. There is little chance of misinterpretation or mishearing what the sales person said.

Transparent Pricing

Pricing online is very clear and transparent for the customer. Customers can take advantages of pricing that may change regularly or take advantages of special offers that last for a limited period.

Track Your Purchase

Consumers have to pay for their product/service before they receive it. It is important that consumers feel reassured when this happens. Many webistes allow consumers to track their purchase from order, dispatch to transportation before delivery to their home address. Again this reassures the consumer and makes them feel that they are obtaining a good service online.

Chapter 4

Business Models

Internet marketing is associated with several business models:

e-commerce — this is where goods are sold directly to consumers (B2C) or businesses (B2B).

Publishing — this is the sale of advertising.

Lead-based websites — this is an organization that generates value by acquiring sales leads from its website.

Affiliate marketing — this is the process in which a product or service developed by one person is sold by other active sellers for a share of profits. The owner of the product normally provide some marketing material (sales letter, affiliate link, tracking facility).

Local internet marketing-this is the process of a locally based company traditionally selling belly to belly and utilizing the Internet to find and nurture relationships, later to take those relationships offline.

Blackhat marketing-this is a form of internet marketing which employs deceptive, abusive, or less than truthful methods to drive web traffic to a website or affiliate marketing offer. This method sometimes includes spam, cloaking within search engine result pages, or routing users to pages they didn't initially request.

There are many other business models based on the specific needs of each person or the business that launches an Internet marketing campaign.

One-to-one Approach

The targeted user is typically browsing the Internet alone therefore the marketing messages can reach them personally. This approach is used in search marketing, where the advertisements are based on search engine keywords entered by the users.

Appeal to Specific Interests

Internet marketing and geo marketing places an emphasis on marketing that appeals to a specific behaviour or interest, rather than reaching out to a broadly-defined demographic. "On-and Off-line" marketers typically segment their markets according to age group, gender, geography, and other general factors. Marketers have the luxury of targeting by activity and geolocation. For example, a kayak company can post advertisements on kayaking and canoeing websites with the full knowledge that the audience has a related interest.

Internet marketing differs from magazine advertisements, where the goal is to appeal to the projected demographic of the periodical, but rather the advertiser has knowledge of the target audience—people who engage in certain activities (e.g., uploading pictures, contributing to blogs)— so the company does not rely on the expectation that a certain group of people will be interested in its new product or service.

Geo Targeting

Geo targeting (in internet marketing) and geo marketing are the methods of determining the geolocation (the physical location) of a website visitor with geolocation software, and delivering different content to that visitor based on his or her location, such as country, region/state, city, metro code/zip code, organization, Internet Protocol (IP) address, ISP or other criteria.

Different Content by Choice

A typical example for different content by choice in geo targeting is the FedEx website at FedEx.com where users have the choice to select their country location first and are then presented with a different site or article content depending on their selection.

Automated Different Content

With automated different content in Internet marketing and geomarketing, the delivery of different content based on the geographical geolocation and other personal information is automated.

Advantages

Internet marketing is relatively inexpensive when compared to the ratio of cost against the reach of the target audience. Companies can reach a wide audience for a small fraction of traditional advertising budgets. The nature of the medium allows consumers to research and purchase products and services at their own convenience. Therefore, businesses have the advantage of appealing to consumers in a medium that can bring results quickly. The strategy and overall effectiveness of marketing campaigns depend on business goals and cost-volume-profit (CVP) analysis.

Internet marketers also have the advantage of measuring statistics easily and inexpensively. Nearly all aspects of an Internet marketing campaign can be traced, measured, and tested. The advertisers can use a variety of methods: pay per impression, pay per click, pay per play, or pay per action.

Therefore, marketers can determine which messages or offerings are more appealing to the audience. The results of campaigns can be measured and tracked immediately because online marketing initiatives usually require users to click on an advertisement, visit a website, and perform a targeted action. Such measurement cannot be achieved through billboard advertising, where an individual will at best be interested, then decide to obtain more information at a later time..

Because exposure, response, and overall efficiency of Internet media are easier to track than traditional off-line media—through the use of web analytics for instance—Internet marketing can offer a greater sense of accountability for advertisers. Marketers and their clients are becoming aware of the need to measure the collaborative effects of marketing (i.e., how the Internet affects in-store sales) rather than siloing each advertising medium. The effects of multichannel marketing can be difficult to determine, but are an important part of ascertaining the value of media campaigns.

Limitations

Internet marketing requires customers to use newer technologies rather than traditional media. Low-speed Internet connections are another barrier. If companies build large or overly-complicated websites, individuals connected to the Internet via dial-up connections or mobile devices experience significant delays in content delivery.

From the buyer's perspective, the inability of shoppers to touch, smell, taste or "try on" tangible goods before making an online purchase can be limiting. However, there is an industry standard for e-commerce vendors to reassure customers by having liberal return policies as well as providing in-store pick-up services.

A survey of 410 marketing executives listed the following barriers to entry for large companies looking to market online: insufficient ability to measure impact, lack of internal capability, and difficulty convincing senior management.

Security Concerns

Information security is important both to companies and consumers that participate in online business. Many consumers are hesitant to purchase items over the Internet because they do not trust that their personal information will remain private.

Recently some companies that do business online have been caught giving away or selling information about their customers. Several of these companies provide guarantees on their websites, claiming that customer information will remain private. Some companies that purchase customer information offer the option for individuals to have their information removed from the database, also known as opting out. However, many customers are unaware if and when their information is being shared, and are unable to stop the transfer of their information between companies if such activity occurs.

Another major security concern that consumers have with e-commerce merchants is whether or not they will receive exactly what they purchase. Online merchants have attempted to address this concern by investing in and building strong consumer brands (e.g., Amazon.com, eBay, Overstock.com), and by leveraging merchant/ feedback rating systems and e-commerce bonding solutions. All of these solutions attempt to assure consumers that their transactions will be free of problems because the merchants can be trusted to provide reliable products and services. Additionally, the major online payment mechanisms (credit cards, PayPal, Google Checkout, etc.) have also provided back-end buyer protection systems to address problems if they actually do occur.

Broadband-induced Trends

Online advertising techniques have been dramatically affected by technological advancements in the telecommunications industry. In fact, many firms are embracing a new paradigm that is shifting the focus of online advertising from simple text ads to rich multimedia experiences. As a result, advertisers can more effectively engage in and manage online branding campaigns, which seek to shape consumer attitudes and feelings towards specific products. The critical technological development fueling this paradigm shift is Broadband.

In March 2005, roughly half of all American homes were equipped with broadband technology. By May 2008, broadband technologies had spread to more than 90% of all residential Internet connections in the United States. When one considers a Nielsen's study conducted in June 2008, which estimated the number of U.S. Internet users as 220,141,969, one can calculate that there are presently about 199 million people in the United States utilizing broadband technologies to surf the Web.

As a result, all 199 million members of this burgeoning market have the ability to view TV-like advertisements with the click of a mouse. And to be sure, online advertisers are working feverishly to design rich multimedia content that will engender a "warm-fuzzy" feeling when viewed by their target audience. As connection speeds continue to increase, so will the frequency of online branding campaigns.

Effects on Industries

The number of banks offering the ability to perform banking tasks over the internet has also increased. Online banking appeals to customers because it is often faster and considered more convenient than visiting bank branches. Currently over 150 million U.S. adults now bank online, with increasing Internet connection speed being the primary reason for fast growth in the online banking industry. Of those individuals who use the Internet, 44 percent now perform banking activities over the Internet.

Internet auctions have become a multi-billion dollar business. Unique items that could only previously be found at flea markets are now being sold on Internet auction websites such as eBay. Specialized e-stores sell an almost endless amount of items ranging from antiques, movie props, clothing, gadgets and much more. As the premier online reselling platform, eBay is often used as a price-basis for specialized items. Buyers and sellers often look at prices on the website before going to flea markets; the price shown on eBay often becomes the item's selling price. It is increasingly common for flea market vendors to place a targeted advertisement on the Internet for each item they are selling online, all while running their business out of their homes.

In addition to the major effect internet marketing has had on the technology industry, the effect on the advertising industry itself has been profound. In just a few years, online advertising has grown to be worth tens of billions of dollars annually. Pricewaterhouse Coopers reported that US$16.9 billion was spent on Internet marketing in the U.S. in 2006.

This has had a growing impact on the electoral process. In 2008 candidates for President heavily utilized Internet marketing strategies to reach constituents. During the 2007 primaries candidates added, on average, over 500 social network supporters per day to help spread their message. President Barack Obama raised over US$1 million in a single day during his extensive Democratic candidacy campaign, largely due to online donors.

Electronic Commerce

Electronic commerce, commonly known as (electronic marketing) e-commerce or eCommerce, consists of the buying and selling of products or services over electronic systems such as the Internet and other computer networks. The amount of trade conducted electronically has grown extraordinarily with widespread Internet usage. The use of commerce is conducted in this way, spurring and drawing on innovations in electronic funds transfer, supply chain management, Internet marketing, online transaction processing, electronic data interchange (EDI), inventory management systems, and automated data collection systems. Modern electronic commerce typically uses the World Wide Web at least at some point in the transaction's lifecycle, although it can encompass a wider range of technologies such as e-mail as well.

A large percentage of electronic commerce is conducted entirely electronically for virtual items such as access to premium content on a website, but most electronic commerce involves the transportation of physical items in some way. Online retailers are sometimes known as e-tailers and online retail is sometimes known as e-tail. Almost all big retailers have electronic commerce presence on the World Wide Web. Electronic commerce that is conducted between businesses is referred to as business-to-business or B2B. B2B can be open to all interested parties (e.g. commodity exchange) or limited to specific, pre-qualified participants (private electronic market). Electronic commerce that is conducted between businesses and consumers, on the other hand, is referred to as business-to-consumer or B2C. This is the type of electronic commerce conducted by companies such as Amazon.com.

Electronic commerce is generally considered to be the sales aspect of e-business. It also consists of the exchange of data to facilitate the financing and payment aspects of the business transactions.

History

The meaning of electronic commerce has changed over the last 30 years. Originally, electronic commerce meant the facilitation of commercial transactions electronically, using technology such as Electronic Data Interchange (EDI) and Electronic Funds Transfer

(EFT). These were both introduced in the late 1970s, allowing businesses to send commercial documents like purchase orders or invoices electronically. The growth and acceptance of credit cards, automated teller machines (ATM) and telephone banking in the 1980s were also forms of electronic commerce. Another form of e-commerce was the airline reservation system typified by Sabre in the USA and Travicom in the UK.

Online shopping is an important component of electronic commerce. From the 1990s onwards, electronic commerce would additionally include enterprise resource planning systems (ERP), data mining and data warehousing.

An early example of many-to-many electronic commerce in physical goods was the Boston Computer Exchange, a marketplace for used computers launched in 1982. An early online information marketplace, including online consulting, was the American Information Exchange, another pre Internet online system introduced in 1991. In 1990 Tim Berners-Lee invented the World Wide Web browser and transformed an academic telecommunication network into a worldwide everyman everyday communication system called internet/www. Commercial enterprise on the Internet was strictly prohibited until 1991.

Although the Internet became popular worldwide around 1994 when the first internet online shopping started, it took about five years to introduce security protocols and DSL allowing continual connection to the Internet. By the end of 2000, many European and American business companies offered their services through the World Wide Web. Since then people began to associate a word "ecommerce" with the ability of purchasing various goods through the Internet using secure protocols and electronic payment services.

Timeline

- 1982: Minitel was introduced nationwide in France by France Telecom and used for online ordering.
- 1987: Swreg begins to provide software and shareware authors means to sell their products online through an electronic Merchant account.
- 1990: Tim Berners-Lee writes the first web browser, World Wide Web, using a NeXT computer.
- 1992: J.H. Snider and Terra Ziporyn publish Future Shop: How New Technologies Will Change the Way We Shop and What We Buy. St. Martin's Press. ISBN 0312063598.

- 1994: Netscape releases the Navigator browser in October under the code name Mozilla. Pizza Hut offers online ordering on its Web page. The first online bank opens. Attempts to offer flower delivery and magazine subscriptions online. Adult materials also become commercially available, as do cars and bikes. Netscape 1.0 is introduced in late 1994 SSL encryption that made transactions secure.
- 1995: Jeff Bezos launches Amazon.com and the first commercial-free 24 hour, internet-only radio stations, Radio HK and Net Radio start broadcasting. Dell and Cisco begin to aggressively use Internet for commercial transactions. eBay is founded by computer programmer Pierre Omidyar as Auction Web.
- 1998: Electronic postal stamps can be purchased and downloaded for printing from the Web.
- 1999: Business.com sold for US $7.5 million to eCompanies, which was purchased in 1997 for US $149,000. The peer-to-peer filesharing software Napster launches. ATG Stores launches to sell decorative items for the home online.
- 2000: The dot-com bust.
- 2002: eBay acquires PayPal for $1.5 billion. Niche retail companies CSN Stores and NetShops are founded with the concept of selling products through several targeted domains, rather than a central portal.
- 2003: Amazon.com posts first yearly profit.
- 2007: Business.com acquired by R.H. Donnelley for $345 million.
- 2008: US eCommerce and Online Retail sales projected to have reached $204 billion, an increase of 17 percent over 2007.

Business Applications

Some common applications related to electronic commerce are the following:

- Email
- Enterprise content management
- Instant messaging
- Newsgroups
- Online shopping and order tracking
- Online banking
- Online office suites

- Domestic and international payment systems
- Shopping cart software
- Teleconferencing
- Electronic tickets.

Government Regulations

In the United States, some electronic commerce activities are regulated by the Federal Trade Commission (FTC). These activities include the use of commercial e-mails, online advertising and consumer privacy. The CAN-SPAM Act of 2003 establishes national standards for direct marketing over e-mail.

The Federal Trade Commission Act regulates all forms of advertising, including online advertising, and states that advertising must be truthful and non-deceptive. Using its authority under Section 5 of the FTC Act, which prohibits unfair or deceptive practices, the FTC has brought a number of cases to enforce the promises in corporate privacy statements, including promises about the security of consumers' personal information. As result, any corporate privacy policy related to e-commerce activity may be subject to enforcement by the FTC.

The Ryan Haight Online Pharmacy Consumer Protection Act of 2008, which came into law in 2008, amends the Controlled Substances Act to address online pharmacies.

Forms

Contemporary electronic commerce involves everything from ordering "digital" content for immediate online consumption, to ordering conventional goods and services, to "meta" services to facilitate other types of electronic commerce.

On the consumer level, electronic commerce is mostly conducted on the World Wide Web. An individual can go online to purchase anything from books or groceries, to expensive items like real estate. Another example would be online banking, i.e. online bill payments, buying stocks, transferring funds from one account to another, and initiating wire payment to another country. All of these activities can be done with a few strokes of the keyboard.

On the institutional level, big corporations and financial institutions use the internet to exchange financial data to facilitate domestic and international business.

Data integrity and security are very hot and pressing issues for electronic commerce today.

E-mail Marketing

E-mail marketing is a form of direct marketing which uses electronic mail as a means of communicating commercial or fundraising messages to an audience. In its broadest sense, every e-mail sent to a potential or current customer could be considered e-mail marketing. However, the term is usually used to refer to:

- sending e-mails with the purpose of enhancing the relationship of a merchant with its current or previous customers and to encourage customer loyalty and repeat business,
- sending e-mails with the purpose of acquiring new customers or convincing current customers to purchase something immediately,
- adding advertisements to e-mails sent by other companies to their customers, and
- sending e-mails over the Internet, as e-mail did and does exist outside the Internet (e.g., network e-mail and FIDO).

Researchers estimate that United States firms alone spent US$400 million on e-mail marketing in 2006.

Comparison to Traditional Mail

There are advantages and disadvantages to using traditional advertising mail in comparison to e-mail.

Advantages

E-mail marketing (on the Internet) is popular with companies for several reasons:

- A mailing list provides the ability to distribute information to a wide range of specific, potential customers at a relatively low cost.
- Compared to other media investments such as direct mail or printed newsletters e-mail is less expensive.
- An exact return on investment can be tracked ("track to basket") and has proven to be high when done properly. E-mail marketing is often reported as second only to search marketing as the most effective online marketing tactic.
- The delivery time for an e-mail message is short (i.e., seconds or minutes) as compared to a mailed advertisement (i.e., one or more days).
- An advertiser is able to "push" the message to its audience, as opposed to website-based advertising, which relies on a customer to visit that website.

- E-mail messages are easy to track. An advertiser can track users via autoresponders, web bugs, bounce messages, unsubscribe requests, read receipts, click-throughs, etc. These mechanisms can be used to measure open rates, positive or negative responses, and to correlate sales with marketing.
- Advertisers can generate repeat business affordably and automatically.
- Advertisers can reach substantial numbers of e-mail subscribers who have opted in (i.e., consented) to receive e-mail communications on subjects of interest to them.
- Over half of Internet users check or send e-mail on a typical day.
- Specific types of interaction with messages can trigger (1) other messages to be delivered automatically, or (2) other events, such as updating the profile of the recipient to indicate a specific interest category.
- E-mail marketing is paper-free (i.e., "green").
- Tracking and response metrics enables tuning and optimisation of the E-mail marketing channel by a process of testing different variants and calculation of statistically significant results.
- E-mail is popular with digital marketers, rising an estimated 15% in 2009 to £292m in the UK.

Disadvantages

Many companies use e-mail marketing to communicate with existing customers, but many other companies send unsolicited bulk e-mail, also known as *spam*.

Internet system administrators have always considered themselves responsible for dealing with "abuse of the net", but not "abuse *on* the net". That is, they will act quite vigorously against spam, but will leave issues such as libel or trademark infringement to the legal system. Most administrators possess a passionate dislike for spam, which they define as *any* unsolicited e-mail. Draconian measures—such as taking down a corporate website, with or without warning—are entirely normal responses to spamming. Typically, the terms of service in Internet companies' contracts permit such actions; therefore, the spammer often has no recourse. Illicit e-mail marketing predates legitimate e-mail marketing. On the early Internet (i.e., Arpanet), it was not permitted to use the medium for commercial purposes. As a result, marketers attempting to establish themselves as legitimate businesses in e-mail marketing have had an uphill battle, hampered also by criminal spam operations billing themselves as legitimate ones.

It is frequently difficult for observers to distinguish between legitimate and spam e-mail marketing. First, spammers attempt to represent themselves as legitimate operators. Second, direct-marketing political groups such as the United States Direct Marketing Association (DMA) have pressured legislatures to legalize activities that some Internet operators consider to be spamming, such as the sending of "opt-out" unsolicited commercial e-mail. Third, the sheer volume of spam has led some users to mistake legitimate commercial e-mail for spam. This situation arises when a user receives e-mail from a mailing list to which he/she subscribes. Additional confusion arises when both legitimate and spam messages have a similar appearance, as when messages include HTML and graphics.

One effective technique used by established email marketing companies is to require what is known as the "double opt-in" method of requiring a potential recipient to manually confirm their request for information by clicking a unique link which includes a unique identification code to confirm that the owner of the recipient email address has indeed requested the information. Responsible e-mail marketing and autoresponder companies use this double opt-in method to confirm each request before any information is sent out.

A report issued by the e-mail services company Return Path, as of mid-2008 e-mail deliverability is still an issue for legitimate marketers. According to the report, legitimate e-mail servers averaged a delivery rate of 56%; twenty percent of the messages were rejected, and eight percent were filtered.

Due to the volume of spam e-mail on the Internet, spam filters are essential to most users. Some marketers report that legitimate commercial e-mail messages frequently get caught and hidden by filters; however, it is somewhat less common for e-mail users to complain that spam filters block legitimate mail.

Companies considering the use of an e-mail marketing program must make sure that their program does not violate spam laws such as the United States' Controlling the Assault of Non-Solicited Pornography and Marketing Act, the European Privacy and Electronic Communications Regulations 2003, or their Internet service provider's acceptable use policy. Even if a company adheres to the applicable laws, it can be blacklisted (e.g., on SPEWS) if Internet e-mail administrators determine that the company is sending spam.

Opt-in e-mail Advertising

Opt-in e-mail advertising, or permission marketing, is a method of advertising via e-mail whereby the recipient of the advertisement has consented to receive it. This method is one of several developed by marketers to eliminate the disadvantages of e-mail marketing.

Opt-in e-mail marketing may evolve into a technology that uses a handshake protocol between the sender and receiver. This system is intended to eventually result in a high degree of satisfaction between consumers and marketers. If opt-in e-mail advertising is used, the material that is e-mailed to consumers will be "anticipated". It is assumed that the consumer wants to receive it, which makes it unlike unsolicited advertisements sent to the consumer. Ideally, opt-in e-mail advertisements will be more personal and relevant to the consumer than untargeted advertisements.

A common example of permission marketing is a newsletter sent to an advertising firm's customers. Such newsletters inform customers of upcoming events or promotions, or new products. In this type of advertising, a company that wants to send a newsletter to their customers may ask them at the point of purchase if they would like to receive the newsletter.

With a foundation of opted-in contact information stored in their database, marketers can send out promotional materials automatically. They can also segment their promotions to specific market segments.

Legal Requirements

In 2002 the European Union introduced the Directive on Privacy and Electronic Communications. Article 13 of the Directive prohibits the use of email addresses for marketing purposes. The Directive establishes the opt-in regime, where unsolicited emails may be sent only with prior agreement of the recipient.

The directive has since been incorporated into the laws of member states. In the UK it is covered under the Privacy and Electronic Communications (EC Directive) Regulations 2003 and applies to all organisations that send out marketing by some form of electronic communication.

The CAN-SPAM Act of 2003 authorizes a US$11,000 penalty per violation for spamming each individual recipient. Therefore, many commercial e-mail marketers within the United States utilize a service or special software to ensure compliance with the Act. A variety of older systems exist that do not ensure compliance with the Act. To comply with the Act's regulation of commercial e-mail, services typically require users to authenticate their return address and include a valid physical address, provide a one-click unsubscribe feature, and prohibit importing lists of purchased addresses that may not have given valid permission. In addition to satisfying legal requirements, e-mail service providers began to help customers establish and manage their own e-mail marketing campaigns. The service providers supply e-mail templates and general best practices, as well as methods for handling subscriptions and cancellations automatically. They also provide statistics pertaining to the number of messages received and opened, and whether the recipients clicked on any links within the messages.

Digital Marketing

Digital Marketing is the promoting of brands using the Internet, mobile and other interactive channels. Digital Marketing is the practice of promoting products and services using digital distribution channels to reach consumers in a timely, relevant, personal and cost-effective manner. Whilst digital marketing does include many of the techniques and practices contained within the category of Internet Marketing, it extends beyond this by including other channels with which to reach people that do not require the use of The Internet. As a result of this non-reliance on the Internet, the field of digital marketing includes a whole host of elements such as mobile phones, sms/mms, display/banner ads and digital outdoor.

Previously seen as a stand-alone service in its own right, it is frequently being seen as a domain that can and does cover most, if not all, of the more traditional marketing areas such as Direct Marketing by providing the same method of communicating with an audience but in a digital fashion. Digital is now being broadened to support the "servicing" and "engagement" of customers.

Digital Marketing – Pull vs. Push

There are 2 different forms of digital marketing, each of which has its pros and cons.

Pull

Pull digital marketing technologies involve the user having to seek out and directly grab (or pull) the content via web search. Web site/ blogs and streaming media (audio and video) are good examples of this. In each of these examples, users have a specific link (URL) to view the content.

Pros:

- No restrictions in terms of type of content or size as the user determines what they want.
- No technology required to send the content, only to store/display it.
- No regulations or opt-in process required.

Cons:

- Considerable marketing effort required for users to find the message/content.
- Limited tracking capabilities – only total downloads, page views, etc.
- No personalization – content is received and viewed the same across all audiences.

Push

Push digital marketing technologies involve both the marketer (creator of the message) as well as the recipients (the user). Email, SMS, RSS are examples of push digital marketing.

In each of these examples, the marketer has to send (push) the messages to the users (subscribers) in order for the message to be received.

Pros;

- Can be personalized — messages received can be highly targeted and specific to selected criteria – like a special offer for females, 21 years old or over and living in California.
- Detailed tracking and reporting – marketers can see not only how many people saw their message but also specific information about each user such as their name as well as demographic and psychographic data.
- High Return on Investment (ROI) possible – if executed the right way, push messaging can help drive new revenue as well as brand reinforcement.

Cons;

- Compliance issue – each push messaging technology has its own set of regulations, from minor (RSS) to heavily controlled (email and text messaging)
- Requires mechanism to deliver content – the marketer has to use an application to send the message, from an email marketing system to RSS feeders.
- Delivery can be blocked – if the marketer does not follow the regulations set forth by each push message type, the content can be refused or rejected before getting to the intended recipient.

Digital Marketing and Multi-Channel Communications

While digital marketing is effective using one message type, it is much more successful when a marketer combines multiple channels in the message campaigns. For example, if a company is trying to promote a new product release, they could send out an email message or text campaign individually. This, if properly executed, could yield positive results. However, this same campaign could be exponentially improved if multiple message types are implemented.

An email could be sent to a list of potential customers with a special offer for those that also include their cell phone number. A couple of days later, a follow up campaign would be sent via text message (SMS) with the special offer.

Push and pull message technologies can also be used in conjunction with each other. For example, an email campaign can include a banner ad or link to a content download. This enables a marketer to have the best of both worlds in terms of their marketing method.

Digital Marketing Terms

Banner Ad

An advertisement that appears on a Web page, most commonly at the top (header) or bottom (footer) of the page.

Blacklisted

A blacklisted notice means that the message may not have been delivered due to be flagged on one of the major lists that keep tabs of known spammers. Different ISPs use different blacklists to block mailings from being delivered to their clients. It can be a temporary ban or a permanent one, depending upon the list.

Blocked

A blocked notice means that the message did not get through due to being considered spam by the subscriber's ISP. This may be due to being on a blacklist or because the message contains a domain that is already being blocked.

Blog

Shortened from "web log" a blog is a user-generated Web site where entries are made in journal style and displayed in a reverse chronological order.

Campaign

A campaign is a specific message being sent to a specific group of recipients. The CAN SPAM ACT is a series of federal laws that must be followed by all email marketers. Those found in violation of the laws can be subjected to major penalties.

Click Through

The number of times people clicked on the links in your message. This is often referred to as. Note: you must have enabled click through tracking in the campaign in order for this to be recorded.

Digital Brand Engagement

Brand and consumer interaction through the Internet. This includes all aspects of dialogue through the social web and on the brand's own website.

DMA Market

DMA stands for Designated Market Area, which is often associated with the entertainment industry. DMAs are usually counties (or sometimes split counties) that contain a large population that can be targeted, such as New York City, Los Angeles or Chicago.

Email Service Provider (ESP)

Outside companies like mobile Storm that send bulk emails on behalf of their clients to prevent their messages as being labeled as spam or blocked entirely.

False Positives

Legitimate messages being labeled as "spam" Can cost companies potentially millions in potential lost revenue if not dealt with correctly.

GPRL

The Global Permanent Removal List consists of records that are automatically removed from a particular database. Almost all email service providers (ESP) or multi-channel messaging companies maintain these lists for their clients.

Instant Messaging

Instant messaging (often shortened to IM) is a type of communications service that enables you to create a kind of private chat room with another individual in order to communicate in real time over the Internet.

Keywords

Used in conjunction with SMS messages. A user types a short code and matching keyword in order to be added to a mobile club or database.

Microsite

A mini Web site design to promote a specific portion or brand from a larger corporate site. Used often with contests or as a landing page for a specific promotion.

Open Rate

This is a ratio determined by the number of people who opened your email against the total number of people to whom you sent the message. Typically, this number will be low for large campaigns and higher for more targeted campaigns.

Opt-In List

Email marketers have databases of subscribers to their newsletters, featuring these subscribers' email addresses and names. Such a list is known as an opt-in list (and is thus CAN-SPAM compliant; see above for info on the CAN-SPAM act) because users choose to receive the emails. This is in contrast to spam email, which is unsolicited.

Personalization

Personalization gives you the ability to create a customized message for each person in your database. Can be addressed by first/ last name, city, state, zip, etc.

RSS

RSS or Real Simple Syndication is technology designed to allow users to subscribe to a specific content feed and be automatically alerted when new updates are available.

RSS Reader

Application used to subscribe and monitor selected RSS content feeds.

Short Code

A short code is a 5 digit number that is used to send and respond to text messages. They can either be a random set of numbers or a "vanity" number tied to a specific brand or number pattern.

SMS

SMS (Short Message Service) is a one-way text message sent via a cell phone. It is usually received via the subscribers' text message inbox on their cell phone and can be a maximum of 160 characters per message.

Social Bookmarking

Social Bookmarking is a popular way to store, classify, share and search links that are combined into a single site for easy access.

Spam

An email message that is unwanted by the recipient. Legitimate emails can sometimes be incorrectly identified as spam and is a growing problem.

Streaming Technologies

Communication channel such as video and audio that is accessed online. Can be a pre-stored clip to access as well as a live feed that is streamed like an online broadcast.

Subscriber

A person who signs up to receive messages from a particular company or entity.

Targeting

Targeting allows you to send a message to people based on specific criteria from your subscriber database.

Voice Broadcast

Sending a pre-recorded voice messages to a large set of phone numbers at the time same. Can either be a voice call (meaning the recipient must answer the call for the message to play) or voice mail (meaning the message will play only if the recipient doesn't answer).

Widget

A small graphical device that does a highly focused, often single, specific task. Web widgets can be embedded in web pages or run on the desktop of a PC (Windows or Mac) using software such as Apple's Dashboard software or Yahoo! Widgets Engine

Advantages of Marketing an Online Business

The biggest advantage of online marketing or marketing an online business is its very reasonable cost. Unlike an expensive advertisement on TV or in a magazine, much online marketing costs next to nothing. The website owner only needs to create a headline that will catch the attention of someone who is surfing the internet. With online marketing the website owner has total control over the content on the website. Thus the website owner has greater control over the information that is provided to potential customers. Moreover, it is easy to watch for customer feedback and to change any of the information posted on the website.

Disadvantages of Online Marketing

Online marketing, like all forms of marketing, has one big disadvantage. The marketer must make a good first impression. The first impression of the potential customer can seldom be erased, and it will mold the customer's response to any marketing efforts. Fortunately, this disadvantage can be largely overcome by using the fact that the internet does not have space limitations. Attention to the fact that the internet does not have space limitations is one of the important online marketing strategies. It demonstrates an understanding of why people use the internet. They turn to the internet for information.

The wise website owner finds a way to give the potential customer lots of information. Internet marketing online follows a very simple formula. More information means more copy on the website. The longer the amount of copy is on a website, the greater the chances that an internet user will stay on that website and read. The longer an internet user stays on a website, the greater the chances that some product or service might be purchased from that website.

Such formulas need to be incorporated into any planned online marketing strategies. The user of such formulas must also take into account the keys to holding the interest of the website viewer. Strong advertising copy, copy that includes action verbs and emotion laden messages, will hold a reader's interest. That is why strong advertising copy has been listed among the important online marketing strategies.

Strategies

Part One: Three Step Formula

Developing a successful internet marketing strategy is an essential part of your online success. In order to succeed, you must develop and implement a strategic plan that includes all of the following:

- A great product
- A web site specifically designed to sell
- A killer marketing strategy.

Each step plays an important role in your overall strategy and must be developed to its fullest potential. If even one step fails, your chances of success will be minimal.

Developing Your Product

Your first step will be to develop a great product. You're probably thinking that's easier said than done, but it's really not. The absolute best product is one that you can develop yourself and deliver over the Internet. With today's technology, there is absolutely no reason why you can't create your own product. The knowledge you have within your own mind is extremely valuable. Everybody is good at something, has a special talent or some specialized knowledge. Use this knowledge to create a product.

The key to developing a great product is exclusiveness. Your product should be unique and not be in competition with hundreds of other similar products. You must give your potential customers exactly what they want. Develop a high-quality product that fills a void to increase your chance of success.

Another consideration of great importance is your target market. Keep in mind, the Internet is a global marketplace. Develop a product with a large geographic target and a wide appeal. A great product will fulfill a need or desire and provide instant gratification.

Here are a few of the top sellers:

- Software
- Information
- Private sites
- Internet services.

Before you develop your product, do some research — find out exactly what people want and develop your product accordingly.

The most important consideration when developing your product is quality. Your product should not only deliver what you promise, but should go above and beyond the expected and overdeliver. Your customers satisfaction is of the utmost importance.

Developing Your Web Site

Once you've developed a great product, your next step will be to develop a great web site. Your web site must be specifically designed to sell your product.

Everything within your web site should have one purpose — getting your visitor to take action. Words are the most powerful marketing tool you have. The right words will turn your visitors into customers. The wrong words will cause them to click away and never return.

Your words are the entire foundation of your business. Your product, your web site and your marketing strategies all depend upon your words. Fancy graphics don't make sales — words do.

Every word, sentence and headline should have one specific purpose — to lead your potential customer to your order page. Write your web site copy as if you are talking to just one person. Identify a problem and validate that one visitor's need for a solution. Continue to write and explain why your product is the solution to their problem. Tell them exactly what your product will do for them — why it will solve their problems and how. Pack your copy with benefits and more benefits. Write to persuade — that's the bottom line.

Developing Your Marketing Strategies

Your marketing strategy is the final process of your plan. Your plan must include both short-term and long-term strategies in order to succeed. Short term marketing strategies are those that bring you a temporary boost in traffic. Although these techniques are very important to your over-all plan, they are only a temporary traffic source and must not be solely relied upon.

Short term marketing strategies include:

- Purchasing Advertising
- Participating in Forums
- Search Engines
- etc.

Long term marketing strategies are those that bring you a steady stream of targeted traffic over time. These strategies will continue to produce results even years down the road.

Long term marketing strategies include:

- Opt-in Lists
- Blogging
- Social Networking Sites
- Social Bookmarking Sites
- Giving Away Freebies
- Article Marketing.

By creating and implementing a balanced marketing strategy, using both short-term and long-term strategies, you will drive a steady stream of targeted traffic to your web site.

If you use this simple formula when creating your Internet marketing strategy and excel at all three, you can literally guarantee your success.

Sidebar

Brad Callen has just released a new search engine optimization book that teaches you how to get long lasting, #1 Google rankings using his ultra powerful internet marketing strategies. I highly suggest checking it out, as it's completely free!

Product Development

Developing a product to market on the Internet isn't as difficult as you may think. Today's technology has opened a whole New World of opportunity for even the smallest homebased business owner. The knowledge you have within your own mind is all you'll need to develop a successful product.

Everybody is good at something. You don't have to be a Rocket Scientist in order to create your own product. If that were the case, most of us would fail. Maybe you have a special talent or some specialized knowledge. Use this knowledge to create a product.

Researching Your Product Development

Before you begin developing your product, make sure you've done your homework. Research the market to determine exactly what people want and develop your product accordingly. If your product doesn't have a market, it won't be successful.

Your product should not only fill a void, but should also be unique. The less competition you have, the better. If you enter a market in which you're competing against hundreds of other products similar to yours, your chance of success will be minimal. Develop a high-quality product that fills a void and provides people with exactly what they want.

Another consideration of great importance is your product's delivery method. The best form of product delivery on the Internet is automated. Internet users want the product they order as soon as their purchase is complete. This can be accomplished in a number of ways depending upon the type of product. For example, if your product is software or information, it can reside on your server and be instantly downloaded via a link. If your product is a private site, you can provide instant access as soon as your customer's payment has been processed.

Not only does instant product delivery benefit your customer, but it will also benefit you. By completely automating your product's ordering and delivery process, you can spend your time performing more important tasks, such as making more sales.

Brain Storming Your Product Development

The most difficult part of creating your own product is deciding upon the product itself. First of all, you'll need to decide what type of product you would like to develop.

Some of the top Internet sellers include:

- Software
- Information
- Private sites
- Internet services.

Once you have determined the type, then you can focus your attention on the subject matter.

If you would like to develop a software program, but aren't capable of writing it yourself, consider hiring a professional. If you would be interested in developing a desktop software program, simply visit a Search Engine and search for "software developers." If you would like to develop a software that resides on a server, search for "scripting services." Although this type of product will be the most expensive to develop, it can be very profitable.

Information is a big seller on the Internet and is also the most inexpensive to develop. Your information can be in the form of a report, an ebook or even a private site.

Internet users are starving for information, as that is what the Internet is all about. They have a sincere desire to learn and will search for the information they desire. The best form of information is "how-to" information that teaches or informs in regard to a specific subject. Even if the subject is very unique, the Internet is a great market for even the most niche products.

If you'd like to develop a product that is very inexpensive to create and has a great profit margin, then an informational product is your best bet. Most informational products are compiled into a downloadable file better known as an ebook. In order to compile your files into an ebook, you'll need to purchase a compiler. Prices start at around $25.

Here are a few subjects to give you some ideas:

- Recipes
- Cooking
- Sewing Tips
- Gardening
- Canning
- Makeup and Skin Care
- Weight Loss
- Self Improvement
- Health and Fitness
- Child Development
- Teenagers
- Romance
- Dating

- Relationships
- Divorce
- Single Mothers
- Single Fathers
- Teenage Mothers
- Teenage Fathers
- Home Decorating
- Home Remodeling
- Home Maintenance
- Plumbing
- Carpentry
- Small Appliance Repair
- Home Buying
- Auto Mechanics
- Auto Buying
- Home Finances
- Home Business
- Computers
- Internet.

Internet services are also very profitable. However, this type of product requires more of your time. In addition, you must be an expert in a given field in order to provide a quality service.

Here are a few popular Internet services:

- Web/Graphics Design
- Copywriting
- Software Development
- Marketing Consultant
- Publicist
- Search Engine Optimization/Submissions.

Alternative Products

If you'd rather not develop your own product, you may want to consider selling someone else's product. You can find hundreds of great affiliate programs here:

If you would be interested in selling some of the top name brand items, the following web site will provide you with hundreds of legitimate drop shippers. These companies will allow you to sell their products on your web site and even ship them to your customers.

Product Development Summary

Developing your own product is an essential part of your online success. Take your time and make sure you do your homework before you begin. No matter what product you develop, quality is of the utmost importance. Provide your customers with exactly what you promise and more — over-deliver.

If you develop a quality product that fills a void and provides Internet users with exactly what they want, your product will be a success.

Internet Marketing Strategies

Internet marketing can attract more people to your website, increase customers for your business, and enhance branding of your company and products. If you are just beginning your online marketing strategy the top 10 list below will get you started on a plan that has worked for many.

1. Start with a web promotion plan and an effective web design and development strategy.
2. Get ranked at the top in major search engines, and practice good Search Optimization Techniques.
3. Learn to use Email Marketing Effectively.
4. Dominate your marketing niche with affiliate, reseller, and associate programs.
5. Request an analysis from an Internet marketing coach or Internet marketing consultant.
6. Build a responsive opt-in email list.
7. Publish articles or get listed in news stories.
8. Write and publish online press releases.
9. Facilitate and run contests and giveaways via your web site.
10. Blog and interact with your visitors.

By following the above tips you'll be on your way to creating a concrete internet marketing strategy that could boost your business substantially.

Strategic Internet Marketing

How much of your marketing strategy should be handled online, which Internet marketing elements you use, and the importance you should give to your website, depends on the nature of your business, your budget, and, to some extent, your personal traits. All of these considerations are part of strategic Internet marketing decisions that help develop Internet marketing strategies for a business.

Using Offline Elements with Internet Marketing Strategies

Unless you transact business only online, for example if you are an eBay reseller, you will probably want to include some traditional offline marketing elements in your overall marketing strategy in addition to the elements in your Internet strategy in your marketing mix. Even those who conduct business only online might consider placing traditional ads in newspapers or magazines to bring prospects to their website to transact business online. Perfect examples of including offline elements as part of Internet marketing strategies are Expedia, Travelocity and Monster.com. While they are online businesses, they invest heavily in traditional advertising, including radio and TV advertising, to draw traffic to their sites where the actual business is conducted.

Develop Internet Marketing Strategies You Like

If you have a personal distaste for "spam", which most of us do, you may not want to include email marketing in your strategic Internet marketing plan. However, email marketing doesn't have to mean just sending out unsolicited messages to every email address you can gather. If you include a visitor registration form on your website, for example, or if you exhibit at trade shows, you have the vehicles needed to collect email addresses of interested prospects. You might consider creating a newsletter and sending it to these prospects on a regular basis as part of your strategic Internet marketing plan. Or, you might just set up a schedule where you periodically send an email to your interested prospects to see how they're doing, if you can be of assistance to them, or if their needs have changed since you last talked. So even if you don't incorporate email marketing into your Internet marketing strategy, per se, you are still using email as a tool to promote your business.

Your Budget and Your Internet Marketing Strategy

Of course, your budget will also determine the components you use in any of the Internet marketing strategies you might develop. A website will require you to choose a domain name and register it and to purchase web hosting services for your website. Both items are deeply discounted, in fact I recently saw an offer for domain name registration for only $1.99 per year-provided you also purchase other services, like hosting, which is now also available for less than $10 per month.

Once that's done, you'll need a design and content for your website, which you'll either need to provide yourself or pay to have a web content professional and/or web designer handle it for you.

Once your content and design are in place, you'll want your site to be found, so you'll want to learn about search engine optimization (SEO), which is an important part of strategic Internet marketing, whether you do it yourself of pay someone else to do it for you.

Ideally, if you pay to have web content written for you, that content should be optimized for search engines when it's written. Likewise, you or your web designer should know something about SEO because how your site is designed can enhance or limit your site traffic, and in the vast majority of cases, SEO should be a significant part of your Internet marketing strategy. In both cases, you may pay a bit more, but you'll save time in the long run.

Once your website is up and running, you'll either need to maintain it yourself or outsource the duties to an independent Webmaster to do it for you.

Pay-per-click advertising (PPC), like Google AdWords can be easy on your budget because you can specify how much you're willing to pay when someone clicks your ad and how much you're willing to pay per day. You can also specify whether you want to include your ad only on search pages or on other websites related to your keywords. You can set geographic and time of the day restrictions on when and where your ads run. Plus, PPC ads are fairly easy to activate and suspend whenever you need to do so, they're easy to update and they provide near real time tracking benefits you won't get with most other elements in your Internet marketing strategy. You can also use images and/or videos with PPC advertising, which may be more cost effective than placing banner ads on other websites.

On the other side of the coin, you can use pay per click ads to make money with your website, through programs like Google AdSense, Yahoo Publisher or Microsoft AdCenter.

Tracking the Results of Internet Marketing Strategies

Let's face it: the average home business operator is not awash in cash. If you're going to be spending money on strategic Internet marketing initiatives, you'll need to track how effective they are. As you do so, you'll discover which Internet marketing strategies work for your business and which do not. And, you can learn from the mistakes you make in your Internet advertising campaign to improve your skills and enhance your success. Knowing what's worth spending money on and what isn't is very helpful in developing Internet marketing strategies as your business matures.

Strategic Internet Marketing Needs to be Flexible

Keep in mind, in most cases, patience is a true virtue when it comes to tracking the success of a strategic Internet marketing campaign. Search engines aren't likely to find you overnight and your strategies may not generate revenues right away. Because you'll have literally millions of competitors who are also engaging in strategic Internet marketing, it will behoove you to keep on your toes and be ready to make necessary adjustments in your Internet marketing strategies when appropriate. However, some knowledge, some capable assistance, and a well-managed strategic Internet marketing plan can increase your chances for success.

Search Engine Marketing

Search engine marketing is the practice of marketing or advertising your web site through search engines, like Google, Yahoo or MSN. Search engine marketing (SEM) may consist of one or more of the following components:

- Organic Search Engine Optimization (SEO)-Search engine optimization is the practice of applying techniques to maximize your ranking in organic, or natural search results. Organic search results are the rankings of Web pages returned by a search engine when you search for a specific word or phrase-a "keyword" or "keyword phrase".
- Pay Per Click Advertising (PPC)-Ads you place for your website with a search engine, such as Google or Yahoo. You bid the amount you are willing to pay per click. The more you bid, the higher your ad will appear in the search engine results. Google AdWords has implemented an additional factor in where your ads rank that is based on the relevancy or importance that Google places on your site, which is very difficult to manipulate. You can also use pay per click advertising to your advantage on your own site. For example, you can make money with Google AdSense and other similar programs.
- Pay For Inclusion (PFI)-In addition to search engines, like Google, Yahoo and MSN search, numerous directories also exist on the web. These directories may be general in nature or related to a specific topic. You can get free listings in some online directories, like DMOZ but most directories now charge for a listing. Verizon's Super Pages is an example of a PFI directory.

Another example of a major directory is again, Yahoo. Yahoo Directory, which is separate from Yahoo search, is described in Yahoo's own words as: Subject-based directory listing websites in a wide range of topics, from arts, entertainment, and society and culture, to science, education, and health.

Why is Search Engine Marketing Important?

You may or may not decide to make search engine marketing part of your marketing and advertising strategy. If you don't have a Web site for your business and don't plan to ever have one, you certainly wouldn't need search engine marketing. However, in today's business climate, nearly all business are expected to have a website and most do.

Search engine marketing is used as a way to get traffic to your website, which in turn should ideally lead to getting new customers and adding to your home business revenues. Compared to other means of marketing and advertising, search engine marketing can be very cost effective. For example, you could implement some search engine optimization techniques on your own. Organic search rankings are free, so if you can move yourself up in the rankings, your traffic should increase, which, in turn, should increase your home business revenues. Similarly, Pay Per Click Advertising can be very inexpensive. Since you can set limits on how much you'll pay per click and how much you'll pay per day, it's fairly easy to keep your costs in line. Likewise, some Web directories-like DMOZ-allow free listings, and others can cost as little as $30 per year.

How do I Measure SEM Effectiveness?

How you measure the effectiveness of your search engine marketing program depends on what your objectives were when you started. If your intent was merely to increase the number of visitors to your Web site, you would determine if your SEM efforts were successful by comparing your Web traffic statistics before and after you implemented search engine marketing.

Be patient though, search engine marketing efforts may take considerable time to boost your traffic. Although you can instantly get your PPC ads running, if you are aiming at improving traffic through SEO, it can be several months before you see solid results-especially through Google. Likewise, if you request a directory listing from DMOZ, your listing may not appear for 6 months to a year. DMOZ is staffed by volunteers and, because DMOZ listings can have a positive affect on your organic search rankings, it is arguably the most popular and valuable free Web directory listing to get.

In addition to site traffic, you need to track your conversion rates. For example, if, as a result of your search engine marketing efforts, your traffic doubles from 250 to 500 visitors per month, how many new customers did you acquire from the additional 250 visitors to your site. Do you now have twice as many customers as you did before? Probably not. If you picked up 5 customers your conversion rate would be 2 percent of the new traffic (5 divided by 250) and 1 percent (5 of 500) overall.

Find ways to increase the number of visitors to your website, and then find ways to increase the conversion rates of those visitors, and you'll know exactly what it takes to make your search engine marketing program successful.

Search Engine Marketing is Just One Piece of the Puzzle

Search engine marketing (SEM) is just one of the many tools available to home businesses when it comes to online marketing.

Web Banner

A web banner or banner ad is a form of advertising on the World Wide Web. This form of online advertising entails embedding an advertisement into a web page. It is intended to attract traffic to a website by linking to the website of the advertiser. The advertisement is constructed from an image (GIF, JPEG, PNG), Java Script program or multimedia object employing technologies such as Java, Shockwave or Flash, often employing animation, sound, or video to maximize presence. Images are usually in a high-aspect ratio shape (i.e. either wide and short, or tall and narrow) hence the reference to banners. These images are usually placed on web pages that have interesting content, such as a newspaper article or an opinion piece. Affiliates earn money usually on a CPC (cost per click) basis, for every unique user click on the ad, the affiliate earns money.

Typical Web Banner, Sized 468×60 Pixels

The web banner is displayed when a web page that references the banner is loaded into a web browser. This event is known as an "impression". When the viewer clicks on the banner, the viewer is directed to the website advertised in the banner. This event is known as a "click through". In many cases, banners are delivered by a central ad server.

When the advertiser scans their logfiles and detects that a web user has visited the advertiser's site from the content site by clicking on the banner ad, the advertiser sends the content provider some small amount of money (usually around five to ten US cents). This payback system is often how the content provider is able to pay for the Internet access to supply the content in the first place. Usually though, advertisers use ad networks to serve their advertisements, resulting in a revshare system and higher quality ad placement.

Web banners function the same way as traditional advertisements are intended to function: notifying consumers of the product or service and presenting reasons why the consumer should choose the product in question, although web banners differ in that the results for advertisement campaigns may be monitored real-time and may be targeted to the viewer's interests. Behaviour is often tracked through the use of a click tag.

Many web surfers regard these advertisements as highly annoying because they distract from a web page's actual content or waste bandwidth. (Of course, the purpose of the banner ad is to attract attention and many advertisers try to get attention to the advert by making them annoying.

Without attracting attention it would provide no revenue for the advertiser or for the content provider.) Newer web browsers often include options to disable pop-ups or block images from selected websites. Another way of avoiding banners is to use a proxy server that blocks them, such as Privoxy.

History

The pioneer of online advertising was Prodigy, a company owned by IBM and Sears at the time. Prodigy used online advertising first to promote Sears products in the 1980s, and then other advertisers. Curiously, one of the advertisers on Prodigy in early 90s was AOL, one of Prodigy's competitors. Incidentally, Prodigy was first in online shopping, banking, stock trading as well. Prodigy was unable to capitalize on any of its first mover advantages, including online advertising.

The first clickable web ad (which later came to be known by the term "banner ad") was sold by Global Network Navigator (GNN) in 1993 to Heller, Ehrman, White and McAuliffe, a now defunct law firm with a Silicon Valley office. GNN was the first commercially supported web publication and one of the very first web sites ever.

HotWired was the first web site to sell banner ads in large quantities to a wide range of major corporate advertisers. Andrew Anker was HotWired's first CEO. Rick Boyce, a former media buyer with San Francisco advertising agency Hal Riney & Partners, spearheaded the sales effort for the company.

HotWired coined the term "banner ad" and was the first company to provide click through rate reports to its customers. The first web banner sold by HotWired was paid for by AT&T, and was put online on October 25, 1994. Another source also credits Hotwired and October 1994, but has Coors' "Zima" campaign as the first web banner.

In May 1994, Ken McCarthy mentored Boyce in his transition from traditional to online advertising, and first introduced the concept of a clickable/trackable ad. He stated that he believed that only a direct response model—in which the return on investment of individual ads was measured—would prove sustainable over the long run for online advertising. In spite of this prediction, banner ads were valued and sold based on the number of impressions they generated. This approach to banner ad sales proved successful and provided the economic foundation for the web industry from the period of 1994 to 2000 until the market for banner ads "crashed" and there was a radical revaluation of their value. The new online advertising model that emerged in the early years of the 21st century, introduced by GoTo.com (later Overture, then Yahoo and mass marketed by Google's AdWords program), relies heavily on tracking ad response rather than impressions.

Interactive Advertising

Interactive advertising uses online or offline interactive media to communicate with consumers and to promote products, brands, services, and public service announcements, corporate or political groups.

In the inaugural issue of the Journal of Interactive Advertising [1], editors Li and Leckenby (2000) defined Interactive Advertising as the "paid and unpaid presentation and promotion of products, services and ideas by an identified sponsor through mediated means involving mutual action between consumers and producers." This is most commonly performed through the Internet; often using video content as a delivery medium.

Interactive Advertising Objectives

The goals of interactive advertising are usually akin to the traditional objectives of advertising, i.e. to sell a product. This in turn means that many of the traditional elements of advertising impact and effectiveness remain relevant, even within the scope of interactive media.

However, according to the *Journal of Interactive Advertising* 2001, interactive advertising also has some properties that expand the range of potential objectives and that improve advertising effectiveness. Interactive advertising also has the potential to decrease the losses associated with poorly coordinated advertising, to reduce the difficulties commonly encountered in clearly communicating an advertising message and to help overcome new product hurdles, such as a consumer rejection.

Elements of Interactive Advertising

There are many different facets to Interactive Advertising, including varying methods and types. Using many different types of cognitive tools and advert presentations, organizations can enhance the impact of their campaigns with this type of advertising. According to Thorson (1996), all advertisements can be classified into one of five basic categories, including: product/service, public service announcement, issue, corporate and political. Advert types also interact with the user's motives to influence outcomes, or consumer responses, reinforcing the need for Interactive Advertising as a means of persuading potential consumers and target audiences.

Using the Internet as the main medium for Interactive Advertising to study the methods, types and outcomes, we can then sound out the different user or advertiser controlled aspects.

User Generated/Controlled Aspects

Functions, Internet motives and mode are the main factors of user controlled aspects. In fact, a number of researchers and practitioners argue that consumers have more control on the Internet than do advertisers. Some have gone so far as to argue that interactive marketing and advertising techniques will not work unless practitioners "step into the shoes" of and approach the Internet from the consumer's vantage point.

Advertiser Controlled Aspects

Internet aspects that are under the control of the advertiser. Most of these variables include structural elements, such as ad types, formats and features. This does not mean that consumers never control the structure of the interactive ads. Banner Ads, pop-up ads, sponsorship, hyperlinks and non-carrier websites are examples of Advertiser controlled Interactive Advertising.

Cost Per Impression

Cost per impression, often abbreviated to CPI or CPM for Cost per thousand impressions, is a phrase often used in online advertising and marketing related to web traffic. It is used for measuring the worth and cost of a specific e-marketing campaign. This technique is applied with web banners, text links, e-mail spam, and opt-in e-mail advertising, although opt-in e-mail advertising is more commonly charged on a cost per action (CPA) basis although sometimes CPM is used.

An online advertisement impression is a single appearance of an advertisement on a web page. Each time an advertisement loads onto a user's screen, the ad server may count that loading as one impression. However, the ad server may be programmed to exclude from the count certain nonqualifying activity such as a reload, internal user actions, and other events that the advertiser and ad serving company agreed to not count. For online advertising, the numbers of views can be a lot more precise. When a user requests a web page, the originating server creates a log entry. Also, a third party tracker can be placed in the web page to verify how many accesses that page had. There are other advertising pricing structures, which are generally referred to as Cost Per Action (CPA) :

- CPC-Cost per click Through
- CPL-Cost per lead (lead usually meaning a free registration)
- CPS-Cost per sale
- dCPM-Dynamic CPM.

CPI and/or Flat rate advertising deals are sometimes preferred by the publisher/webmaster because they will receive a more consistent fee proportional to the amount of traffic.

Today, it is very common for large publishers to charge for most of their advertising inventory on a *CPM* or CPT basis. A related term, effective cost per mille (CPM), is used to measure the effectiveness of advertising inventory sold (by the publisher) via a CPC, CPA, or CPT basis. This type of advertising arrangement closely resembles television and print advertising methods for speculating the cost of an advertisement. Often, industry agreed approximates are used. With television, the Nielsen ratings are used; print is based on the circulation a publication has.

Cost Per Thousand

CPM is frequently used in advertising to represent cost per thousand (where M is the roman numeral for 1000). When used in advertising it relates to the cost per thousand page impressions.

For sites earning revenue for advertising impressions, the related abbreviation RPM (revenue per thousand impressions) may be used.

It is important to remember that when someone says something like, "our CPM is $5," this means that the *cost per impression* is $0.005.

Affiliate Marketing

Affiliate Marketing is an Internet-based marketing practice in which a business rewards one or more affiliates for each visitor or customer brought about by the affiliate's marketing efforts. It is an application of crowdsourcing. Examples include rewards sites, where users are rewarded with cash or gifts, for the completion of an offer, and the referral of others to the site. The industry has four core players: the merchant (also known as 'retailer' or 'brand'), the network, the publisher (also known as 'the affiliate') and the customer. The market has grown in complexity to warrant a secondary tier of players, including affiliate management agencies, super-affiliates and specialized third parties vendors.

Affiliate marketing overlaps with other Internet marketing methods to some degree, because affiliates often use regular advertising methods. Those methods include organic search engine optimization, paid search engine marketing, e-mail marketing, and in some sense display advertising. On the other hand, affiliates sometimes use less orthodox techniques, such as publishing reviews of products or services offered by a partner.

Affiliate marketing—using one website to drive traffic to another—is a form of online marketing, which is frequently overlooked by advertisers. While search engines, e-mail, and website syndication capture much of the attention of online retailers, affiliate marketing carries a much lower profile. Still, affiliates continue to play a significant role in e-retailers' marketing strategies.

History

The concept of revenue sharing—paying commission for referred business—predates affiliate marketing and the Internet. The translation of the revenue share principles to mainstream e-commerce happened almost four years after the origination of the World Wide Web in November 1994.

The consensus of marketers and adult industry insiders is that Cybererotica was either the first or among the early innovators in affiliate marketing with a cost per click program.

During November 1994, CDNOW launched its Buy Web program. With this program CDNOW was the first non-adult website to introduce the concept of an affiliate or associate program with its idea of click-through purchasing. CDNOW had the idea that music-oriented websites could review or list albums on their pages that their visitors may be interested in purchasing. These websites could also offer a link that would take the visitor directly to CDNOW to purchase the albums. The idea for remote purchasing originally arose because of conversations with music label Geffen Records in the fall of 1994. The management at Geffen wanted to sell its artists' CDs directly from its website, but did not want to implement this capability itself. Geffen asked CDNOW if it could design a program where CDNOW would handle the order fulfillment. Geffen realized that CDNOW could link directly from the artist on its website to Geffen's website, bypassing the CDNOW home page and going directly to an artist's music page.

Amazon.com (Amazon) launched its associate program in July 1996. Amazon associates could place banner or text links on their site for individual books, or link directly to the Amazon home page.

When visitors clicked from the associate's website through to Amazon and purchased a book, the associate received a commission. Amazon was not the first merchant to offer an affiliate program, but its program was the first to become widely-known and serve as a model for subsequent programs.

In February 2000, Amazon announced that it had been granted a patent on all the essential components of an affiliate program. The patent application was submitted in June 1997, which predates most affiliate programs, but not PC Flowers & Gifts.com (October 1994), Auto Web.com (October 1995), Kbkids.com/BrainPlay.com (January 1996), EPage (April 1996), and several others.

Historic Development

Affiliate marketing has grown quickly since its inception. The e-commerce website, viewed as a marketing toy in the early days of the Internet, became an integrated part of the overall business plan and in some cases grew to a bigger business than the existing offline business. According to one report, the total sales amount generated through affiliate networks in 2006 was £2.16 billion in the United Kingdom alone. The estimates were £1.35 billion in sales in 2005. Marketing Sherpa's research team estimated that, in 2006, affiliates worldwide earned US$6.5 billion in bounty and commissions from a variety of sources in retail, personal finance, gaming and gambling, travel, telecom, education, publishing, and forms of lead generation other than contextual advertising programs.

Currently the most active sectors for affiliate marketing are the adult, gambling, and retail industries. The three sectors expected to experience the greatest growth are the mobile phone, finance, and travel sectors. Soon after these sectors came the entertainment (particularly gaming) and Internet-related services (particularly broadband) sectors. Also several of the affiliate solution providers expect to see increased interest from business-to-business marketers and advertisers in using affiliate marketing as part of their mix.

Web 2.0

Websites and services based on Web 2.0 concepts—blogging and interactive online communities, for example—have impacted the affiliate marketing world as well. The new media allowed merchants to become closer to their affiliates and improved the communication between them.

Compensation Methods

Predominant Compensation Methods

Eighty percent of affiliate programs today use revenue sharing or cost per sale (CPS) as a compensation method, nineteen percent use cost per action (CPA), and the remaining programs use other methods such as cost per click (CPC) or cost per mille (CPM).

Diminished Compensation Methods

Within more mature markets, less than one percent of traditional affiliate marketing programs today use cost per click and cost per mille. However, these compensation methods are used heavily in display advertising and paid search.

Cost per mille requires only that the publisher make the advertising available on his website and display it to his visitors in order to receive a commission. Pay per click requires one additional step in the conversion process to generate revenue for the publisher: A visitor must not only be made aware of the advertisement, but must also click on the advertisement to visit the advertiser's website.

Cost per click was more common in the early days of affiliate marketing, but has diminished in use over time due to click fraud issues very similar to the click fraud issues modern search engines are facing today. Contextual advertising programs are not considered in the statistic pertaining to diminished use of cost per click, as it is uncertain if contextual advertising can be considered affiliate marketing. While these models have diminished in mature e-commerce and online advertising markets they are still prevalent in some more nascent industries. China is one example where Affiliate Marketing does not overtly resemble the same model in the West. With many affiliates being paid a flat "Cost Per Day" with some networks offering Cost Per Click or CPM.

Performance Marketing

In the case of cost per mille/click, the publisher is not concerned about a visitor being a member of the audience that the advertiser tries to attract and is able to convert, because at this point the publisher has already earned his commission. This leaves the greater, and, in case of cost per mille, the full risk and loss (if the visitor can not be converted) to the advertiser.

Cost per action/sale methods require that referred visitors do more than visit the advertiser's website before the affiliate receives commission. The advertiser must convert that visitor first. It is in the best interest for the affiliate to send the most closely-targeted traffic to the advertiser as possible to increase the chance of a conversion. The risk and loss is shared between the affiliate and the advertiser.

Affiliate marketing is also called "performance marketing", in reference to how sales employees are typically being compensated. Such employees are typically paid a commission for each sale they close, and sometimes are paid performance incentives for exceeding targeted baselines. Affiliates are not employed by the advertiser whose products or services they promote, but the compensation models applied to affiliate marketing are very similar to the ones used for people in the advertisers' internal sales department.

The phrase, "Affiliates are an extended sales force for your business", which is often used to explain affiliate marketing, is not completely accurate. The primary difference between the two is that affiliate marketers provide little if any influence on a possible prospect in the conversion process once that prospect is directed to the advertiser's website. The sales team of the advertiser, however, does have the control and influence up to the point where the prospect signs the contract or completes the purchase.

Multi-tier Programs

Some advertisers offer multi-tier programs that distribute commission into a hierarchical referral network of sign-ups and sub-partners. In practical terms, publisher "A" signs up to the program with an advertiser and gets rewarded for the agreed activity conducted by a referred visitor. If publisher "A" attracts publishers "B" and "C" to sign up for the same program using his sign-up code, all future activities performed by publishers "B" and "C" will result in additional commission (at a lower rate) for publisher "A".

Two-tier programs exist in the minority of affiliate programs; most are simply one-tier. Referral programs beyond two-tier resemble multi-level marketing (MLM) or network marketing but are different. Multi-level marketing (MLM) or network marketing have more requirements/ qualifications to get paid a commission. Whereas affiliate programs do not.

From the Advertiser Perspective

Pros and Cons

Merchants favour affiliate marketing because in most cases it uses a "pay for performance" model, meaning that the merchant does not incur a marketing expense unless results are accrued (excluding any initial setup cost). Some businesses owe much of their success to this marketing technique, a notable example being Amazon.com. Unlike display advertising, however, affiliate marketing is not easily scalable.

Implementation Options

Some merchants run their own (i.e., in-house) affiliate programs using popular software while others use third-party services provided by intermediaries to track traffic or sales that are referred from affiliates. Merchants can choose from two different types of affiliate management solutions: standalone software or hosted services, typically called affiliate networks. Payouts to affiliates or publishers are either made by the networks on behalf of the merchant, by the network, consolidated across all merchants where the publisher has a relationship with and earned commissions or directly by the merchant itself.

Affiliate Management and Program Management Outsourcing

Successful affiliate programs require significant work and maintenance. Having a successful affiliate program is more difficult than when such programs were just emerging. With the exception of some vertical markets, it is rare for an affiliate program to generate considerable revenue with poor management or no management (i.e., "auto-drive"). Uncontrolled affiliate programs did—and continue to do so today—aid rogue affiliates, who use spamming, trademark infringement, false advertising, "cookie cutting", typosquatting, and other unethical methods that have given affiliate marketing a negative reputation. The increased number of Internet businesses and the increased number of people that trust the current technology enough to shop and do business online allows further maturation of affiliate marketing. The opportunity to generate a considerable amount of profit combined with a crowded marketplace filled with competitors of equal quality and size makes it more difficult for merchants to be noticed. In this environment, however, being noticed can yield greater rewards.

Recently, the Internet marketing industry has become more advanced. In some areas online media has been rising to the sophistication of offline media, in which advertising has been largely professional and competitive. There are significantly more requirements that merchants must meet to be successful, and those requirements are becoming too burdensome for the merchant to manage successfully in-house. An increasing number of merchants are seeking alternative options found in relatively new outsourced (affiliate) program management (OPM) companies, which are often founded by veteran affiliate managers and network program managers. OPM companies perform affiliate program management for the merchants as a service, similar to advertising agencies promoting a brand or product as done in offline marketing.

Types of Affiliate Websites

Affiliate websites are often categorized by merchants (i.e., advertisers) and affiliate networks. There are currently no industry-wide accepted standards for the categorization. The following types of websites are generic, yet are commonly understood and used by affiliate marketers.

- Search affiliates that utilize pay per click search engines to promote the advertisers' offers (i.e., search arbitrage)
- Comparison shopping websites and directories
- Loyalty websites, typically characterized by providing a reward system for purchases via points back, cash back
- CRM sites that offer charitable donations
- Coupon and rebate websites that focus on sales promotions
- Content and niche market websites, including product review sites
- Personal websites (This type of website was the reason for the birth of affiliate marketing; however, such websites are almost reduced to complete irrelevance compared to the other types of affiliate websites.)
- Weblogs and website syndication feeds
- E-mail list affiliates (i.e., owners of large opt-in-mail lists that typically employ e-mail drip marketing) and newsletter list affiliates, which are typically more content-heavy
- Registration path or co-registration affiliates who include offers from other merchants during the registration process on their own website

- Shopping directories that list merchants by categories without providing coupons, price comparisons, or other features based on information that changes frequently, thus requiring continual updates
- Cost per action networks (i.e., top-tier affiliates) that expose offers from the advertiser with which they are affiliated to their own network of affiliates
- Websites using adbars (e.g. Adsense) to display context-sensitive, highly-relevant ads for products on the site
- Virtual Currency: a new type of publisher that utilizes the social media space to couple an advertiser's offer with a handout of "virtual currency" in a game or virtual platform.

Publisher Recruitment

Affiliate networks that already have several advertisers typically also have a large pool of publishers. These publishers could be potentially recruited, and there is also an increased chance that publishers in the network apply to the program on their own, without the need for recruitment efforts by the advertiser.

Relevant websites that attract the same target audiences as the advertiser but without competing with it are potential affiliate partners as well. Vendors or existing customers can also become recruits if doing so makes sense and does not violate any laws or regulations.

Almost any website could be recruited as an affiliate publisher, although high-traffic websites are more likely interested in (for their own sake) low-risk cost per mille or medium-risk cost per click deals rather than higher-risk cost per action or revenue share deals.

Locating Affiliate Programs

There are three primary ways to locate affiliate programs for a target website:

1. Affiliate program directories,
2. Large affiliate networks that provide the platform for dozens or even hundreds of advertisers, and
3. The target website itself. (Websites that offer an affiliate program often have a link titled "affiliate program", "affiliates", "referral program", or "webmasters"—usually in the footer or "About" section of the website.)

If the above locations do not yield information pertaining to affiliates, it may be the case that there exists a non-public affiliate program. The most definitive method for finding this information is to contact the website owner directly.

Past and Current Issues

Since the emergence of affiliate marketing, there has been little control over affiliate activity. Unscrupulous affiliates have used spam, false advertising, forced clicks (to get tracking cookies set on users' computers), adware, and other methods to drive traffic to their sponsors. Although many affiliate programs have terms of service that contain rules against spam, this marketing method has historically proven to attract abuse from spammers.

E-mail Spam

In the infancy of affiliate marketing, many Internet users held negative opinions due to the tendency of affiliates to use spam to promote the programs in which they were enrolled. As affiliate marketing matured, many affiliate merchants have refined their terms and conditions to prohibit affiliates from spamming.

Search Engine Spam

As search engines have become more prominent, some affiliate marketers have shifted from sending e-mail spam to creating automatically-generated webpages that often contain product data feeds provided by merchants.

The goal of such webpages is to manipulate the relevancy or prominence of resources indexed by a search engine, also known as *spamdexing*. Each page can be targeted to a different niche market through the use of specific keywords, with the result being a skewed form of search engine optimization.

Spam is the biggest threat to organic search engines, whose goal is to provide quality search results for keywords or phrases entered by their users. Google's Page Rank algorithm update ("Big Daddy") in February 2006—the final stage of Google's major update ("Jagger") that began in mid-summer 2005—specifically targeted spamdexing with great success.

This update thus enabled Google to remove a large amount of mostly computer-generated duplicate content from its index.

Websites consisting mostly of affiliate links have previously held a negative reputation for under delivering quality content. In 2005 there were active changes made by Google, where certain websites were labeled as "thin affiliates".

Such websites were either removed from Google's index or were relocated within the results page (i.e., moved from the topmost results to a lower position). To avoid this categorization, affiliate marketer webmasters must create quality content on their websites that distinguishes their work from the work of spammers or banner farms, which only contain links leading to merchant sites.

Some commentators originally suggested that Affiliate links work best in the context of the information contained within the website itself. For instance, if a website contains information pertaining to publishing a website, an affiliate link leading to a merchant's Internet service provider (ISP) within that website's content would be appropriate.

If a website contains information pertaining to sports, an affiliate link leading to a sporting goods website may work well within the context of the articles and information about sports.

The goal in this case is to publish quality information within the website and provide context-oriented links to related merchant's websites.

However, more recent examples exist of "thin" Affiliate sites which are using the Affiliate Marketing model to create value for Consumers by offering them a service. These thin content service Affiliate fall into three categories:

- Price comparison
- Cause related marketing
- Time saving.

Adware

Although it differs from spyware, adware often uses the same methods and technologies.

Merchants initially were uninformed about adware, what impact it had, and how it could damage their brands. Affiliate marketers became aware of the issue much more quickly, especially because they noticed that adware often overwrites tracking cookies, thus resulting in a decline of commissions.

Affiliates not employing adware felt that it was stealing commission from them. Adware often has no valuable purpose and rarely provides any useful content to the user, who is typically unaware that such software is installed on his/her computer.

Affiliates discussed the issues in Internet forums and began to organize their efforts.

They believed that the best way to address the problem was to discourage merchants from advertising via adware. Merchants that were either indifferent to or supportive of adware were exposed by affiliates, thus damaging those merchants' reputations and tarnishing their affiliate marketing efforts.

Many affiliates either terminated the use of such merchants or switched to a competitor's affiliate program. Eventually, affiliate networks were also forced by merchants and affiliates to take a stand and ban certain adware publishers from their network.

The result was Code of Conduct by Commission Junction/before and Performance, Link Share's Anti-Predatory Advertising Addendum, and Share Sale's complete ban of software applications as a medium for affiliates to promote advertiser offers. Regardless of the progress made, adware continues to be an issue, as demonstrated by the class action lawsuit against Value Click and its daughter company Commission Junction filed on April 20, 2007.

Trademark Bidding

Affiliates were among the earliest adopters of pay per click advertising when the first pay-per-click search engines emerged during the end of the 1990s. Later in 2000 Google launched its pay per click service, Google AdWords, which is responsible for the widespread use and acceptance of pay per click as an advertising channel.

An increasing number of merchants engaged in pay per click advertising, either directly or via a search marketing agency, and realized that this space was already well-occupied by their affiliates. Although this situation alone created advertising channel conflicts and debates between advertisers and affiliates, the largest issue concerned affiliates bidding on advertisers names, brands, and trademarks.

Several advertisers began to adjust their affiliate program terms to prohibit their affiliates from bidding on those type of keywords.

Some advertisers, however, did and still do embrace this behavior, going so far as to allow, or even encourage, affiliates to bid on any term, including the advertiser's trademarks.

Lack of Self-regulation and Collaboration

Affiliate marketing is driven by entrepreneurs who are working at the edge of Internet marketing. Affiliates are often the first to take advantage of emerging trends and technologies. The "trial and error" approach is probably the best way to describe the operation methods for affiliate marketers.

This risky approach is one of the reasons why most affiliates fail or give up before they become successful "super affiliates", capable of generating US$10,000 or more per month in commission.

This "frontier" life combined with the attitude found in such communities is likely the main reason why the affiliate marketing industry is unable to self-regulate beyond individual contracts between advertisers and affiliates. Affiliate marketing has experienced numerous failed attempts to create an industry organization or association of some kind that could be the initiator of regulations, standards, and guidelines for the industry. Some examples of failed regulation efforts are the Affiliate Union and iAfma.

Online forums and industry trade shows are the only means for the different members from the industry—affiliates/publishers, merchants/advertisers, affiliate networks, third-party vendors, and service providers such as outsourced program managers—to congregate at one location. Online forums are free, enable small affiliates to have a larger say, and provide anonymity. Trade shows are cost-prohibitive to small affiliates because of the high price for event passes. Larger affiliates may even be sponsored by an advertiser they promote.

Because of the anonymity of online forums, the quantitative majority of industry members are unable to create any form of legally binding rule or regulation that must be followed throughout the industry.

Online forums have had very few successes as representing the majority of the affiliate marketing industry. The most recent example of such a success was the halt of the "Commission Junction Link Management Initiative" (CJ LMI) in June/July 2006, when a single network tried to impose the use of a Javascript tracking code as a replacement for common HTML links on its affiliates.

Lack of Industry Standards

Certification and Training

Affiliate marketing currently lacks industry standards for training and certification.

There are some training courses and seminars that result in certifications; however, the acceptance of such certifications is mostly due to the reputation of the individual or company issuing the certification.

Affiliate marketing is not commonly taught in universities, and only a few college instructors work with Internet marketers to introduce the subject to students majoring in marketing. Education occurs most often in "real life" by becoming involved and learning the details as time progresses. Although there are several books on the topic, some so-called "how-to" or "silver bullet" books instruct readers to manipulate holes in the Google algorithm, which can quickly become out of date, or suggest strategies no longer endorsed or permitted by advertisers.

Outsourced Program Management companies typically combine formal and informal training, providing much of their training through group collaboration and brainstorming. Such companies also try to send each marketing employee to the industry conference of their choice. Other training resources used include online forums, weblogs, podcasts, video seminars, and specialty websites. Affiliate Summit is the largest conference in the industry, and many other affiliate networks host their own annual events.

Code of Conduct

A code of conduct was released by affiliate networks Commission Junction/before and Performance in December 2002 to guide practices and adherence to ethical standards for online advertising.

Threat to Traditional Affiliate Networks

Cost per action networks can be viewed as a threat to "classic" affiliate marketing networks. Traditional affiliate marketing is resource-intensive and requires continual maintenance. Most of the maintenance includes managing, monitoring, and supporting affiliates. The goal of affiliate marketing is directed toward long-term and mutual beneficial partnerships between advertisers and affiliates. Cost per action networks, however, eliminate the need for the advertiser to build and maintain relationships to affiliates, as that task is performed for the advertiser by the cost per action network.

The advertiser makes an offer, almost always CPA-based, and the cost per action networks handle the remainder of the process by mobilizing their affiliates to promote that offer. Cost per sale and revenue sharing are the primary compensation models for classic affiliate marketing, and are rarely found in cost per action networks.

Affiliate marketers typically avoid the topic of cost per action networks; however, if it is being discussed, the debates can become heated and explosive.

Marketing Term

Members of the marketing industry are recommending that "affiliate marketing" be substituted with an alternative name. Affiliate marketing is often confused with either network marketing or multi-level marketing. *Performance marketing* is a common alternative, but other recommendations have been made as well.

Sales Tax Vulnerability

In April 2008 the State of New York inserted an item in the state budget asserting sales tax jurisdiction over Amazon.com sales to residents of New York, based on the existence of affiliate links from New York–based websites to Amazon.

The state asserts that even one such affiliate constitutes Amazon having a business presence in the state, and is sufficient to allow New York to tax all Amazon sales to state residents. Amazon challenged the amendment and lost at the trial level in January, 2009.

The case is currently making its way through the New York appeals courts.

Cookie Stuffing

Cookie stuffing involves placing an affiliate tracking cookie on a website visitor's computer without their knowledge, which will then generate revenue for the person doing the cookie stuffing. This not only generates fraudulent affiliate sales, but also has the potential to overwrite other affiliates' cookies, essentially stealing their legitimately earned commissions.

Click to Reveal

Many voucher code web sites use a click to reveal format, which required the web site user to click to reveal the voucher code. The action of clicking places the cookie on the website visitor's computer. The IAB have stated that "Affiliates must not use a mechanism whereby users are encouraged to click to interact with content where it is unclear or confusing what the outcome will be."

Affiliate Services

- Affiliate programs directories
- Affiliate networks
- Affiliate manager and Outsourced Program Management (OPM or APM) (manages affiliates)
- Category: Internet marketing trade shows.

Cost Per Action

Cost Per Action or CPA (sometimes known as Pay Per Action or PPA) is an online advertising pricing model, where the advertiser pays for each specified action (a purchase, a form submission, and so on) linked to the advertisement.

Direct response advertisers consider *CPA* the optimal way to buy online advertising, as an advertiser only pays for the ad when the desired action has occurred. An *action* can be a product being purchased, a form being filled, etc. The desired *action* to be performed is determined by the advertiser. The *CPA* can be determined by different factors, depending where the online advertising inventory is being purchased.

CPA as "Cost Per Acquisition"

CPA is sometimes referred to as "Cost Per Acquisition", which has to do with the fact that most CPA offers by advertisers are about acquiring something (typically new customers by making sales).

Using the term "Cost Per Acquisition" instead of "Cost Per Action" is not incorrect, it is actually more specific. "Cost Per Acquisition" is included in "Cost Per Action", but not all "Cost Per Action" offers can be referred to as "Cost Per Acquisition".

The Difference between CPA and CPL Advertising

In CPL campaigns, advertisers pay for an interested lead (hence, Cost Per Lead) — i.e. the contact information of a person interested in the advertiser's product or service.

CPL campaigns are suitable for brand marketers and direct response marketers looking to engage consumers at multiple touchpoints— by building a newsletter list, community site, reward program or member acquisition program. In CPA campaigns, the advertiser typically pays for a completed sale involving a credit card transaction.

There are other important differentiators:

1. CPL campaigns are advertiser-centric. The advertiser remains in control of their brand, selecting trusted and contextually relevant publishers to run their offers. On the other hand, CPA and affiliate marketing campaigns are publisher-centric. Advertisers cede control over where their brand will appear, as publishers browse offers and pick which to run on their websites. Advertisers generally do not know where their offer is running.
2. CPL campaigns are usually high volume and light-weight. In CPL campaigns, consumers submit only basic contact information. The transaction can be as simple as an email address. On the other hand, CPA campaigns are usually low volume and complex. Typically, consumer has to submit credit card and other detailed information.

Effective Cost Per Action

A related term, eCPA or Effective Cost Per Action, is used to measure the effectiveness of advertising inventory purchased (by the advertiser) via a CPC, CPI, or CPM basis. In other words, the eCPA tells the advertiser what they would have paid if they had purchased the advertising inventory on a Cost Per Action basis (instead of a Cost Per Click, Cost Per Impression, or Cost Per Mille/Thousand basis).

Companies

- Dozens of smaller companies have addressed the majority of the cost-per-action advertising network market, including companies like Commission Junction, Performance, and others including new entrants such as W4, Advertise.com and Perfect Storm Media.
- Google started testing CPA on 2006. On June 2007 Google expanded its beta trial, opening it to users of AdWords As of October, 2008, Google has discontinued their pay-per-action beta in favour of an offering by Google owned Double Click.
- eBay has moved into CPA advertising with its AdContext system on 2006.
- Snap.com, CPA pioneer and later merged with other to form NBC Internet (NBCi), has long touted the advantages of the CPA model, such as the elimination of click fraud.
- Jellyfish.com was the Internet's first comparison shopping search engine to operate exclusively on a Cost Per Action (CPA) ad model, has a patent pending on an improvement over CPA where part of the ad revenue goes to the customer, and has been bought by Microsoft for integration into Live Search.

Contextual Advertising

Contextual advertising is a form of targeted advertising for advertisements appearing on websites or other media, such as content displayed in mobile browsers. The advertisements themselves are selected and served by automated systems based on the content displayed to the user.

How Contextual Advertising Works

A contextual advertising system scans the text of a website for keywords and returns advertisements to the webpage based on what the user is viewing. The advertisements may be displayed on the webpage or as pop-up ads. For example, if the user is viewing a website pertaining to sports and that website uses contextual advertising, the user may see advertisements for sports-related companies, such as memorabilia dealers or ticket sellers. Contextual advertising is also used by search engines to display advertisements on their search results pages based on the keywords in the user's query.

Service Providers

Google AdSense was the first major contextual advertising program. It works by providing webmasters with JavaScript code that, when inserted into webpages, displays relevant advertisements from the Google inventory of advertisers. The relevance is calculated by a separate Google bot, Mediabot, that indexes the content of a webpage. Recent technology/service providers have emerged with more sophisticated systems that use language-independent proximity pattern matching algorithm to increase matching accuracy. Since the advent of AdSense, Yahoo! Publisher Network, Microsoft adCenter, AOL Sponsored Listings and others have been gearing up to make similar offerings.

Impact

Contextual advertising has made a major impact on earnings of many websites. Because the advertisements are more targeted, they are more likely to be clicked, thus generating revenue for the owner of the website (and the server of the advertisement). A large part of Google's earnings is from its share of the contextual advertisements served on the millions of webpages running the AdSense program. Contextual advertising has attracted some controversy through the use of techniques such as third-party hyperlinking, where a third-party installs software onto a user's computer that interacts with the Web browser. Keywords on a webpage are displayed as hyperlinks that lead to advertisers.

Agency Roles

There are several advertising agencies that help brands understand how contextual advertising options affect their advertising plans. There are three main components to online advertising:

1. creation — what the advertisement looks like
2. media planning — where the advertisements are to be run
3. media buying — how the advertisements are paid for.

Contextual advertising replaces the media planning component. Instead of humans choosing placement options, that function is replaced with computers facilitating the placement across thousands of websites.

Chapter 5

Online Shopping

The use of the Internet as a shopping medium has empowered shoppers with advantages over traditional store front shopping. This paper identifies and discusses these advantages in terms of: 1) convenience and time-saving, 2) powerful research instrument, 3) lower search costs and better product selection, and 4) better price information and lower prices.

Convenience and Time-saving

Shopping on the Internet offers convenience and time-saving benefits to shoppers, as compared to shopping in traditional brick-and-mortar stores. Changing consumer lifestyles and lack of time may make it more difficult for consumers to shop at physical locations such as stores and shopping malls. Shopping on the Internet addresses this problem as shoppers can shop in the comfort and convenience of home. Results of the Master Card Survey 'Internet Shopping' (1996) revealed that consumers viewed the Internet as an "Instrument of Convenience".

The Internet operates 24 hours a week, seven days a week, and can be accessed anywhere in the connected world; shoppers can expect to browse and purchase goods on the Internet anytime, unlike traditional storefronts that have fixed opening hours. Shoppers can also purchase goods that are unavailable at their location, and are able to bypass restrictive import policies, as the Internet allows shoppers to make purchases from vendors in other locations around the world. Ernst and Young's reports 'Internet Shopping' and 'Global Online Retailing' (1998, 2000) noted that in comparison to brick-and-mortar stores, when shopping on the Internet, there were no store lines, surly clerks, pickpockets or panhandlers to contend with, no bad weather to travel under, nor any transportation cost involved; the Internet allows shoppers to develop their own timetables for research and purchasing.

The 'Australian Online Shopping and Future Expenditure Report' (2001) reported that Australian shoppers cited convenience as the leading reason to purchase online, followed by price and product selection. A survey carried out by the Danish E-commerce Association stated similar results, with convenience cited as the most important reason for Danish shoppers to shop online, followed by price and product selection, which were tied in importance (Nielsen 1999). GartnerG2 research director David Schehr mentioned that all of their research shows that consumers are most interested in convenience, not price. According to him, shoppers do still expect bargains online, but fast delivery and a wide selection are more important factors; price comes into the picture along with convenience, but it's no longer the main reason people shop online (Regan 2002).

Powerful Research Instrument

Shoppers are able to use the Internet as a powerful research instrument in the purchasing process. For certain products such as books and Videos/CDs/DVDs, reviews and recommendations are important factors in influencing purchase decision. With such products, shoppers are not only able to browse through a larger selection on the Web in sites such as Amazon.com, but are also able to conveniently obtain reviews and recommendations that are usually unavailable in offline stores.

Shoppers who shop online do not necessarily make the purchase online, but 'offline' from a brick-and-mortar store front, and vice versa. 46 percent of online buyers research online to purchase offline, while 27 percent research offline to purchase online and 17 percent research in both ways, according to Forrester Research (Vigoroso 2001). Ernst and Young's report ('Internet Shopping' 1998) found that more than half of the customers with Internet access gathered information and researched products online and later bought them through traditional channels; 46 percent of consumers with Internet access researched online and them bought products by fax or telephone while 64 percent researched products online and then bought them through traditional stores; these purchases were double of those of consumers (32 percent) who researched online and them bought on the Web. Similar results were found in the 1997 American Internet User Survey conducted by Cyber Dialogue; this research noted that 75 percent of Web consumers sought online product information with 36 percent of those searchers purchasing in traditional stores. The above information gives evidence that the Internet can also be viewed as a supplement to traditional store front purchasing, rather than as a competitor. Ernst and Young's report ('Internet Shopping' 1998) concluded that this ability to shop, research, and view potential purchases on the Internet empowered customers and accelerated their purchase decisions.

Lower Search Costs and Better Product Selection

Shopping using the Internet overcomes the time and pecuniary costs of traditional shopping; shoppers can shop from the comfort and convenience of home, and need not travel to physical storefronts. Shoppers are able to locate many vendors online using search engines and websites designed to navigate shoppers, view detailed product information from a variety of vendors' websites, compare price and quality among different vendors, and make purchases online.

With online shopping, shoppers no longer have to suffer the costs and incomplete information of traditional hierarchical search, making product searches easier and more effective. For example, a shopper is able to search over 3 million titles in Amazon.com from the computer screen at home, as compared to going physically to the bookstore, which carries an average of 80,000 titles

The Internet offers a greater selection for shoppers as compared to physical retail storefronts. According to Sharma and Krishnan (2002), the Internet store can provide a larger inventory of products and sizes, and can virtually guarantee the availability of any type and size of merchandise. According to Ernst and Young's 'Global Online Retailing' survey (2000), 56 percent of consumers surveyed cited the Internet's good selection of items, 14 percent of which were not available in stores, and 40 percent cited its competitive prices as helping to simplify their shopping experiences. Grewal et. al. (2002) state that in the past, retail salespeople had a captive audience; for many merchandise categories, few viable alternatives were available to going to a store; today, the Internet provides an extremely viable alternative shopping mode.

Better Price Information and Lower Prices

The Internet makes it easier for shoppers to compare prices between vendors. Online vendors offer the prices of their goods in their websites. Simply by viewing different vendor websites, shoppers are able to obtain and compare prices easily, as compared to visiting different physical storefronts, which is costly and time consuming. Shoppers are able to find lower prices using the Internet due to the wider reach of information, and navigator websites such as www.autobytel.com that offers prices of competing vendors. With price information on the Internet, shoppers are less vulnerable to overpaying when buying from physical storefronts that may manipulate prices to shopper's disadvantages.

Shoppers are able to obtain lower prices when buying online. According to the Ernst and Young Survey ('Internet Shopping' 1998), prospective shoppers viewed price savings and selection as more important benefits than convenience, which was ranked third. Edgecliffe-Johnson et. al. (2002) reported that online shoppers are more concerned about price than about new features or convenience-the advantage which e-tailers once thought would allow them to charge more than offline stores. Moynagh and Worsley (2002) state that online shopping could transform consumer behaviour, driven by cost saving and convenience and spurred on by competition. Shoppers are able to buy direct from a manufacturer's or wholesaler's website using the Internet. As more manufacturers and wholesalers cut off retail intermediaries to sell direct to consumers via the Internet, costs are lowered and hence they are able to offer lower prices. Examples of such companies are Dell Computer and Amazon.com, which are able to offer its products at lower prices as compared to most physical retail storefronts.

Online stores are not burdened by the costs of running a physical store, such as the rent of the physical premises and operating costs such as the wages of sales staff. The cost savings by online stores lead to lower pricing on the Internet, passing on cost savings to shoppers. The Internet encourages online vendors to compete amongst one another by lowering prices. Sharma and Krishnan (2002) state that in the last three years, the threat of the Internet has increased the competitive pressure that retailers face. According to Evans and Wurster (2000), online vendors are aware that due to the wider informational reach of consumers on the Internet, which leads to low levels of pricing secrecy, they have to focus on low prices to gain the competitive advantage.

Role of E-Commerce in 21st Century

In the past few years, enterprises across the globe have experienced significant changes in their business information system. Huge investments were made in enterprise resource planning system implementations but still they struggle to get timely information that is needed to make effective business decision and to ensure continuous growth of enterprises. Placing "e" in front of any process or function seemed to be the magic prescription for never ending story of success and rapid returns for enterprises. E-business, e-procurement, e-sales, e-payment, e-banking, e-CRM, e-CAD, e-delivery are just a few. Internet, for example is becoming one of the most popular medium in transmitting various data. Users can find any kind of information within a shorter time compared with conventional method that consumes more time.

The emergence of the Internet through out the world has been contributing such a variety medium in doing business as well as people lifestyle. In fact, Internet is the essential prerequisite for the existence of E-commerce. Electronic commerce or e-commerce has been defined as the ability to perform transactions involving the exchange of goods or services between two or more parties using electronic tools and techniques (Yonah, 1997). The explosion of E-commerce has created new phenomena in our lifestyle especially in shopping activities. Consumers can easily buy products or services like magazines and airlines tickets via Internet.

Definition of Electronic Commerce

Besides the earlier definition by Yonah (1997) in the paper, National Office for the Information Economy defines e-commerce as type of business transaction or interaction in which the participants prepare or conduct business electronically. This covers a wide range of activities, ranging from use of electronic mail (e-mail), through to Internet based sales and transactions and web based marketing. Dr. Roger Clarke, Principal Xamas Consultancy Pt Ltd., Canberra said that electronic business (e-business) is defined as the conduct of business with the assistance of electronic devices and telecommunications tools, whereas electronic commerce (e-commerce) is defined as the conduct of commerce in goods and services via electronic devices and telecommunications tools. Different people use different terminology such as 'electronic trading' 'electronic procurement' 'electronic purchasing' or 'electronic marketing'.

From the above definition, we can conclude that electronic commerce is often used in a much broader sense, to mean essentially the same as 'electronic business'. In other words e-commerce includes purchases of goods, services and other financial transactions in which the interactive process is mediated by information or digital technology at both locationally separate, ends of the interchange. Here 'transactions' include both specification of goods and service required and commitment to buy. E-commerce transaction model can be in terms of business to business (B2B), business to customer (B2C) or customer to customer (C2C).

Objective of the Study

The main obstacle now faced by the policy makers and others is lack of comprehensive indicators about the electronic commerce and clear guidelines and consensus on the definition of e-commerce. Thus, several considerable efforts at the international level like Asia-Pacific Economic Cooperation (APEC) and European Union (EU) members to work towards globally accepted guidelines and methodologies for measuring the electronic commerce. They have realized the potential social and economic benefits that could derive from e-commerce as well as the importance of having readily available data, which would highlight the role of e-commerce in their economies.

With the preceding arguments, the paper conceptualizes the role of e-commerce and it sub activities in creating business success. The paper highlights e-commerce milestones in selected countries. The paper further highlights some suggestions and future strategies of e-commerce in specialized industries in years to come. As an explanatory, conceptual, theoretical and descriptive analysis, the paper is expected to benefit large group of users and instigate further study in the area of electronic commerce.

An Overview of E-commerce

E-commerce is the most important application of the new communication technology. Manufacturers, traders and consumers can now reach the market more quickly and get more information than they could ever before. The electronic commerce has penetrated the businesses in many ways. E-commerce has tremendously reduced the transaction costs allied with purchase, sales, operating, holding inventory and financial cost. The application of e-commerce through development of web site enhances the potential global market and sales revenue, product, potential new customers, services and geographical areas. In term of non-financial benefits, e-commerce has significantly helped improving human resources and timeliness, quality of services, customers' satisfaction and some other indirect effects.

The imperative of electronic commerce depends on the evaluation and assessment. To evaluate related data on e-commerce is necessary, since it is not readily available. The available data are collected by different agencies using numerous definitions and methodologies used by the collecting group. In the absence of reliable data, policy makers, governing bodies and business communities are unable to take decisions that reflect the changes brought about by the e-commerce. By employing relevant and accurate data on e-commerce, the policy makers and researchers would be able critically analyse the impact of e-commerce on labor market, market structures and functioning, changes in distribution of goods and services, customers preferences changes in global competition. It permits them to take well-framed decisions about the policies and investments in e-commerce related sector.

Research forecasts that e-commerce will account for 86% of worldwide sales of goods and services by the year 2004. The potential for e-commerce is bright, specifically in those markets where buyers and sellers are motivated to reduce costs, increase efficiency and cut delivery time. By 2003, estimated revenues from e-commerce across the globe will be approximately 1.5 trillion dollars. The rate of growth varies due to the development of infrastructure especially in developing countries. Projected Internet users by the end of 2000 are approximately 48% (North America), 22% (Western Europe), 17% (Asia Pacific) and 7% (Middle East/Africa), which of course stimulate further growth of e-commerce (Sussan and Kassira, 2003).

E-commerce Across the Globe

In Malaysia, the rate of development of e-commerce is quite low compared with other developed countries like Australia, United Kingdom and United States. Table 1 shows the value of e-commerce transactions for Malaysia, Australia and United States.As given in Table 1, value of e-commerce transaction across the globe especially in these three countries increase significantly in 1998 to 2000. It reflected the enhancement of awareness towards the importance of e-commerce in today's business. However the value of e-commerce transaction differs in comparison between the countries.

Table: *Value of E-Commerce Transactions (USD)*

Countries	*1998*	*1999*	*2000*
Malaysia	18.01m	58.89m	164.15m
Australia	123.2m	180.6m	1.2b
United States	25b	75b	250b

Sources:

1. International Data Corporation, 1999
2. Australia Bureau of Statistics, Household Use of Information Technology Report, 1998
3. Forrester Research Report.

While, developed countries like United States and Australia enjoy greater income from doing business electronically, developing countries such Malaysia is gearing up to close the income gap. E-commerce success requires high level of education and technological skills.

The transportation, energy and telecommunication infrastructure also plays important role in ensuring e-commerce success. Without them, e-commerce impact cannot reach wider customers. In addition, the supporting services are also needed in achieving success of e-commerce. These services include banks, hardware manufacturers, programmers, access providers, information providers, web designer, market research organization and also higher learning institution.

In the case of Malaysia, several measures have been taken for past several years to support the progress of e-commerce like Multimedia Super Corridor (MSC) projects, establishing Multimedia University and encouraging banking institutions to venture electronic banking transactions.

Due to those necessary actions undertaken, it is projected that e-commerce will continue to prosper in Malaysian market. The following Table 2 describes and predicts e-commerce earnings in Malaysia for the year 1997-2004.

Table 2:E-commerce Revenues Projection In Malaysia (1997-2004)

Year	*Revenue (USD million)*
1997	6.31
1998	18.01
1999	58.89
2000*	164.15
2001*	426.72
2002*	993.68
2003*	2,066.40
2004*	3,469.85

* Projections

Source: Malaysian Business, April 2000

Meanwhile, developed countries such United States continues to enjoy the success of electronic commerce. It seems that e-commerce development in United States does not been affected by a number of crisis beginning September 11, 2001, downturn of economics and Iraq War.

According to the most recent studies carried out by Forrester Research and Institute for Supply Management (ISM) indicated significant growing of purchasing activities by enterprises using Internet. For instance, average amount of indirect goods and services purchasing via Internet has progressed from 8.3% (Quarter 1, 2002) to 10.5% at then of the year. This momentum resumes till second quarter of 2003. The similar pattern was also found for purchasing of direct goods and services for the same time period. The following Table 3 summarized the indication.

Table: *Average Amount of Purchasing Done Via The Internet (as a % of total company purchasing)*

Period	*Indirect Goods/Services*	*Direct Goods/Services*
Quarter 1, 2002	8.3%	5.7%
Quarter 2, 2002	8.7%	6.6%
Quarter 3, 2002	9.0%	6.5%
Quarter 4, 2002	10.5%	9.4%
Quarter 1, 2003	11.0%	10.0%
Quarter 2, 2003	11.0%	11.7%

Source: Forrester Research, Institute of Supply Management (ISM), January and July, 2003

A report by the Department of Commerce, USA acknowledged the increased use of Internet for commercial activity. In September 2001, 21% of the USA population was using the Internet to make purchase and 8% was using it for online banking as against 135 of both activities in 2000. The Department of Commerce found that 36% of the population used the Internet to search for product or service information in September 2001, an increase of 10% compared to the preceding year.

In addition, United States government has introduced friendly policy and cost guidelines that promotes e-commerce growth. For instance, The USA Department of Trade in 1998 announced the standard transaction costs for some selected e-commerce activities. From the exhibit, it is clearly crystal that US government help to boost e-commerce by charging higher cost for transaction done via conventional and traditional method like booking flight tickets through travel agent. This additional cost is expected to change consumer behaviour and choice of means for doing business from the common ways to the latest and more attractive style, that is by electronic devices.

E-procurement

E-procurement or e-purchasing is a user-friendly, Internet-based purchasing system that offers electronic buying order processing and enhanced administrative functions to buyers that results in operational efficiencies and potential cost savings. Business enterprise can place orders with suppliers on the website. E-marketplace is an online exchange where multiple vendors and buyers meet at one site for dealing in goods, materials and services. A number of websites have been set up in various industries, but they are going under a process of selection with some business withdrawing from e-marketplace operation or merging with other businesses. E-procurement performs all procurement activities such as requisitioning, purchase order transmission, notification of electronic query, request, response to pre-bidding and receipt of goods and processing thereon. Virtually, all types of products, including books, music CDs, toys, household appliances, clothing, foods and other groceries, jewelries are available for sale on the Internet. The founder and Chief Executive Officers (CEO) of amazon.com estimated that the books sold on the Internet accounted for around 15% of the total books market.

Many people believe that e-purchase benefits only certain quarters like large enterprises and multinational companies with very huge investments can afford to meet such expenses. That assumption is untrue. It can be applied to any enterprises of varied size. Quoting from the technology research firm, AMR Research, among businesses with more than 10,000 employees, 40% participate is some form of public B2B exchange while among companies with 1,000 to 2,500 employees more than 80% are expected to be doing so within a year or more.

E-purchase benefits enterprises by cutting a labor costs and improves efficiency by reducing human errors. To reduce errors further, enterprises must not allow purchasing by a single person every time. The benefits obtained by the e-procurement system should not be lost due to maverick purchasing. Since in e-purchase, the transactions conducted are more transparent both within the enterprise and with the suppliers. However, some of the suppliers are not very well equipped with it. E-procurement involves displaying the catalog and other information such as inventory and supplier mark up, are shared with others, which few suppliers are reluctant to do so.

The benefits should not only be to the buyers. It should be balanced with the buyer and the supplier. The purchasing should not be shifted from old to new suppliers. Reliability and the level of service must be enhanced. The relationship and trust that has been developed over a period of time cannot be ignored. The Canadian National Railway Company once had more than 75 000 items in its online catalogs that saved it $10 million in procurement costs. For smaller purchases, the staff used to search paper catalog which did not have the required information and moreover other processes were done through phone, fax and mail services before. The initial teething problems such as issuing multiple requisition orders were resolved and soon the system went live for all suppliers. E-procurement helped in getting better prices from suppliers.

After a trial of six months, the railroad company was able to reduce the cost of processing from an average $50 per order to $4 electronically. The company got larger discounts for bulk-buying and other purchases. The usage of online catalog can help the employees to check the items, which are purchased often. E-procurement focuses on the increasing integration of suppliers' procurement network. It supports all business partners in shortening process chains, speeding up the flow of information and exploiting potential for innovation. Procurement markets are already networked worldwide. A successful procurement system will depend on how well the network functions across the boundaries.

E-sales

One of the ways to measure the companies' performance is by comparing the total revenue with that of previous period, with same industry, with competitors and with other economic resources, which produces the cash flows. A sale is important component of any trading. Performance is always measured with what you put in and what you get back. According to survey of executives, conducted in USA, 46% of retailers cite sales as the primary metric the use to measure a web sites performance and about one in four said they focus on profits.

To e-business, the enterprise should always monitor the customer demand and changes in the market and global developments. Internet is as an avenue for tracking customer demand and customers inventories as well as for sourcing materials, knowing the customers demand for inventory on a real time basis is very difficult. Integrating online and offline systems will become increasingly important for retailers who are focused on driving consumers into their stores with purchase intent. The above survey revealed that while only 31% of retailers already provide visibility of store inventory on their web sites, another 23% expect to offer this capability within the next two years.

A well-developed and integrated web sites connected to their back offices is a requirement to improve the revenue. As the web site has not been properly linked, an order placed by customer could not be attended to and after a considerable delay sold out information was passed on to the customer. Certainly this affects the customer relations. But this system involves some cost, but the benefit is more than the cost spent. An order management and fulfillment software suited for business to business as well as business to customer transactions. The software can do allocation of inventory as an order is being taken online, or inform a customer about an item much be back-ordered and give the customer an estimated shipping date for the back-order. It also confirms the order placed and shipping details to the customer.

The web customers are increasing year after year in spite of uncertainties in global economy. Recent reports say that Internet sales were up is USA by 18% for the quarter ending in July. Some stores improved its Internet sales but stores sales however down by 14%. Even 1-800 flowers.com reported an increase of 33% in revenues compared to the immediate previous period. The results say even though there is an increase in Internet business, it is certainly to some extent at the cost of orders place through other sources such as telephone, stores and by e-mail.

Critical Issues in E-commerce

The two critical issues hampering e-commerce growth are securities and tax environment. As we discussed above, there are two kinds of goods delivery methods after customers put an order via electronic commerce transaction. One through mail or courier and another one is through online itself. The main concern to tax authority is through online. For instance, Mr. X resides in Mumbai bought a Zorro X Play station Software version 5.0 from United States by downloading online from the particular software company. All payments and delivery made through online. In this case, there is no intermediary such as courier officers or customs department at the point of entry (etc. airport, port).

On the other hand, Miss Y also resides in Mumbai purchased the same software, but she wishes to get the software in compact disc (CD) form through courier. If this situation occurs, the Indian tax authority will go for Miss Y but not Mr. X. It means that if someone buys a digital product from other countries and full settlement done through Internet inclusive the payment and delivery, he or she will not be taxed. Traditional tax principle in most of the countries were developed when a transactions involves an identifiable party established in a physical location which delivers goods or services to an identifiable customers. The concept of 'permanent establishment (PE) is used in many tax regulations will typically determine whether or not the transactions or operation constitute a taxable presence in the country concerned.

In the era of e-commerce, there are often no face-to-face customer contacts; there may be no employees or human intervention and no identifiable physical location for either the seller or the customer. Thus, in e-commerce transaction, the analysis of PE becomes less clear. Other examples of e-commerce which could possible erode the tax base are computer software which can be purchased and transferred electronically to the user's personal computer, magazines and postcards which can be transferred digitally and securities trading, which is currently offered by some stocks brokerage firms through the web sites that permit customers to trade share.

The study by Grayson (1998) indicated that if there were no tax in e-commerce, the higher income group of customers who always transact via e-commerce would enjoy high tax saving in long run. As a result, fairness and equity will not be achieved. In addition, a statistic published by Wall Street Journal in 1998 evidenced that in United States of America, 80% of households which annual income exceed USD 100,000 posses personal computer, whereas only 25% of households with annual income less than USD 30,000 posses personal computer. Web Week Magazine (1998) revealed that the most popular group transact through Internet come from at least USD 60,000 annual income earners. These two publications in other way support the findings from Grayson (1998).

The second critical aspect of e-commerce is security. Lack of security is the leading barrier to widespread commerce on the Internet due to the inherent openness of the web (Wen, 2001). The lack of security is experienced in several ways such as unauthorized use of corporate network, packet sniffing, data modification, unregistered transactions, eavesdropping, repudiation and spoofing. The threats and attacks to Internet based enterprises have included such Yahoo, E-trade and Amazon.com. These threats and attacks deteriorated the three main aspects of security that are confidentiality, integrity and availability of data. The absence of these three elements causes lack of confidence for wider customers doing business electronically.

However, some necessary actions have been taken to cushion the lack of security in e-commerce like the introduction of new protocol version 6 (Ipv6), a $100 million initiative by USA government. The new protocol will address the areas of confidentiality, data integrity, non-repudiation and selective application of services. A number of multinational companies like NTT (Japan), Sun, Nortel, 3Com have already got the new version of Ipv6, where as Cisco and Microsoft have it in prototype. The limitations of the new protocol vary from the need of higher bandwidth and some current wireless providers do not support Ipv6. In addition, the new protocol is too costly and the return is expected to yield after three to five years (Wen, 2001).

Suggestions for Improvement

The know how of logistic e-commerce enterprises provide new competencies from which to develop future sustainable competitive disadvantage. The greatest drivers for the future will be duration of relationships, type of contracts conducted and the geographic distribution of customers and vendors (Delfman, 2002). To achieve more efficient e-logistics and e-fulfillment, it is desirable to have a trading environment in which there is perfect information about goods and services as regards their description, origins and destinations, and cost for different origins and destinations. Sellers and buyers should be able to monitor and track goods at every point along the way from the supplier to the consumer. All stakeholders should be able to check on the Internet the availability and status or orders. All this can be achieved if trade information is simplified, automated and fully harmonized in all countries and all restrictive government export/ import regulations and practices are eliminated. It is also requires sophisticated supply chain management systems for compelling and enabling global end to end monitoring of trade information. To achieve these abroad objectives and also to take into account the special problems of developing countries, it is recommended that governments, the international community and the private sector corporate promote the following specific measures:

[a] Taking advantage of the great potential provided by Internet technology in order to capture, transfer and monitor trade information over network of supply chains in an open fashion.

[b] Automating customs declaration systems in order to develop customs to customs information exchange and thereby provide a basis for elimination on unnecessary export/import requirements, which can instead be replaced by fully integrated international transactions.

[c] Harmonizing and improving the classification of commodity tariffs, and facilitating the identification of individual consignment.

[d] Providing investment resources especially for customers' administrations in order to upgrade their efficiency.

[e] Harmonizing and simplifying trade facilitation regulations and procedures, and in particular encouraging greater harmonization of customs procedures through the wide adoption and implementation of the revised Kyoto Convention on the Simplification and Harmonization of Customs Procedures.

[f] Promoting cooperation between authorities of exporting and importing countries in order to provide verification and compatibility in trade information. In this context, the International Trade Prototype (ITP) project develop by the United Kingdom and the United States customs administrations could provide a model to be developed at the international level.

The international community should give support to further development of the project.

[g] Encouraging greater transparency in trade processing activities and taking measures to reduce corruption and other forms of malpractice in customs administration.

[h] Promoting partnership between developing country logistics service providers and developed country logistics services providers that are applying e-logistics systems.

[i] Providing technical cooperation program to developing countries that support e-logistics, for example in customs, transportation services, cargo terminals and related services.

In pursuing greater height of e-procurement, Kevin Williams, purchasing specialist for a major cable network in Bristol, Connecticut, identifies nine steps for developing an e-procurement strategy. It is advisable enterprise adopting e-commerce to follow the recommended approach of implementing e-procurement, which as below:-

[a] Identify the supply change management needs of the organization.

[b] Determine the scope of work.

[c] Perform the Request For Proposal (RFP), Request For Information (RFI), and/or Request for Quotation (RFQ) process.

[d] Identify the major suppliers of e-procurement systems.

[e] Narrow the list of suppliers to a possible few, based on their ability to meet the organization's needs.

[f] Select a supplier who best meets the needs of the organization as well as the choice that the supply manager feels most comfortable with.

[g] Discuss with the supplier the objectives of e-procurement system and the necessary features to achieve those goals.

[h] Commit to working with suppliers based on their ability to meet the needs of the organization's business and e-procurement strategy.

[i] Move forward with the project by preparing the organization's employees and suppliers for the new purchasing process.

Security of the network is an area wherein much emphasis has to be given for e-procurement success. It can be done by creating security at the interfaces of network such as standardized code for identification of materials and services. The responsibilities include initiating and executing cross enterprise optimization programs in purchasing and logistics, developing uniform conventions within the company, controlling cross enterprise purchasing activities and providing key figures and ensuring compliance with legal and internal requirements.

The websites of the enterprise must have in addition to other access options, such as register suppliers to participate in the marketplace of the company, which may further have different options such as free registration and non-free registration of suppliers. This free registration process meets the basic requirements that are prerequisites for all business relationships. Once the registration is made, the suppliers become the registered suppliers of the enterprise and they can be allowed for further communication. The registration provides the suppliers to access information about the structure of purchasing, supplier profiles, and IT tools, download documents and responding queries. The registration also allows them to obtain the market share or purchase volume in the material fields relevant to suppliers and the supplier grading evaluation compared with competitors, worldwide communication, availability of information of past and future e-bidding and e-auctions.

E-business models can benefit from inline communities that are sustaining significant collaborative relationships despite geographical diversity of membership. Meanwhile, e-commerce focuses primarily on enterprise's customers, e-business enlarges the connectivity of the enterprises to include their suppliers, employees and potential investors or partners. The expanded connectivity makes e-business solutions much more prominent compared to e-commerce. As e-business and e-commerce continue to progress, legal issues, security weaknesses and taxation environment remain problematic for future prosperity. While, security aspect is expected to improve such as introduction of new protocol like Ipv6 and it is within enterprise control, tax and legal aspect beyond enterprise's discretion as it involves government intervention and global commitments for more standardize definition and regimes.

While e-business is still in its early development stage in many countries, the experience to date has been positive. In many countries, the collected indicators have highlighter a number of barriers to a wide implementation of e-business, providing government with keys to future policy development. They have also pointed to the areas of commerce, the need for training and security, a key aspect when related to the actual conduct of commercial transactions, especially for small and medium enterprises and individuals.

The rapid growth in e-business around the world has prompted many to look for better ways of measuring the phenomenon. As more and more countries and international agencies become involved, it is important to develop plans to ensure that there is no unnecessary duplication of efforts and that users have the data necessary for informed decision-making at the earliest possible opportunity. Sellers and buyers should be able to monitor and track goods at every point along the way from the suppliers to the consumers. All stakeholders should be able to check on the Internet the availability and status of orders. All this can be achieved if trade information is simplified, automated and fully harmonized in all countries and all restrictive government trading regulations and practices are eliminated.

Economic Implications of E-commerce

The information revolution aided by the revolution in the telecommunications and institutional innovations had initially promised to change the nature of the market altogether. The market's primary role as merely a place where buyers and sellers meet (it had seemed) now has been revolutionized by the impact of the information revolution on its subsidiary role, i.e., as a transmission belt of information. Today market is a place where there is no intermediaries between a seller of a good and its final buyer to the mutual benefit of both parties (Sengupta, 2004). The Internet and its enabled technologies (especially electronic commerce) have caused the costs of many kinds of market mterachon to plummet (Saloner, 2001). Not only cost reduction, e-commerce has the potential to stimulate growth and employment in industrialized as well as developing countries. Further, e-commerce allows economics agents (both buyers and sellers) to interact more effectively by creating new market opportunities (Mukhopadhyay, 2002). Thus, e-commerce has strong economic implications at both micro and macro level.

E-commerce and Economic Growth

While e-commerce clearly has a positive impact on the business sector, doubts have been raised about its impact on the macroeconomic growth, and productive growth (2) in particular. Various studies show that e-commerce had an impressive performance particular in terms of productivity growth. The US, which leads the world in IT and e-commerce, has had a notable economic performance, particularly in terms of productive growth, since 1995. But, the same was not happened with the developing countries as they failed to catch up technologically with the industrialized world. To assess the broader economic impact of e-commerce and the ramifications of developing countries' catching up or not, UNCTAD has conducted a quantitative analysis based on two scenario: one in which the developing countries fall behind technologically and one in which they catch up with the developed countries. The analysis is centred on cost saving and assume that e-commerce can reduce costs of services, particularly in retail and wholesale trade, transport and financial and business services. Cost savings in services are stimulated through a productive growth scenario, which allow for the analysis of such macro-economic variables as GDP, welfare, wages and terms of trade. The analysis is a unique application of a computable general equilibrium model to e-commerce at the global level.

According to the report, under the first scenario developed countries would have welfare gains of $117 billion, while the developing world (excluding Asia) would lose welfare of $ 726 million. The Asian region, on the other hand, would gain $ 802 million, largely attributable to the transport services sector. Besides welfare and GDP losses, developing countries would also experience a reduction in wages and deteriorating terms of trade.

E-Commerce could therefore end up actually widening, and not narrowing, the gap between the developed and developing countries.

Under the second scenario, however, if developing countries were to catch up with developed countries in productivity, they would increase output, wages and welfare.

A 1% productive growth m the service sector in Asia for example, would result in welfare gains of $12 billion, GDP growth of 0.4% and a 2 to 3% growth in the service exports. By reducing costs, increasing efficiency, reducing time and distance, e-commerce could thus become an important tool for development.

Impact of E-commerce on Economy

Business and the economy are inextricably linked with the development and implementation of new technology (Tassabehji, 2003). Growth and development of any modern economy has been recognized by many economic theorists, such as Kondratieff, Schumpeter, Mensch and Porter, to be based on innovation of new technology. In the early twentieth century, the economist Kondratieff introduced his 'Long Wave Theory (3)' of economic growth. He detailed the numbers of years that the economy expanded and contracted during each part of the half-century long cycle, which industries suffer the most during the 'downwave' and how technology plays a role in leading the way out of the contraction into the next 'upwave'. Building on this theory the economist Schumpeter (1961) assigned technological innovation an almost exclusive role, as engine of economic development: the fundamental impulse that sets and keeps the capitalist engine in motion comes from the new consumers' goods, the new methods of production or transportation, the new market, the new forces of industrial organization that capitalist enterprise creates. Mensch (1979) updates the Schumpeter theory, giving it an empirical base in history, where clusters of innovation take place and generate completely new sectors. He stressed that only technological innovations can overcome depression and that government must implement an aggressive innovation policy to stimulate the search for new and basic innovation. Further, Porter (1990), emphasizes that the prosperity and competitive advantage of a nation is no longer as a result of a nation's natural resources and its labour force, but rather the ability of its industry to innovate and upgrade.

This can be seen as a disruptive technology on a macro environmental level. And today, whether economic community subscribes to these economic theories or not, the impact of new technology on the economy of a nation is indisputable. Continuous growth of e-commerce is expected to have deep impact on structure and functioning of economies at various levels and overall impact on macro-economy. Some key areas are discussed below:

Impact on Intermediation

Traditional production, transportation and distribution process is characterized by the liner-point-to-point path (4). In this process intermediaries play an important role. In physical world, because of large distance between production units and consumer units, it is not possible for consumers to approach producers directly and vice versa. The existence of intermediaries namely, distributors, wholesalers and retailers, this increase the transaction costs for both the producers and consumers.

But in the emerging economic scenario, liner-point-to-point information and knowledge flow no longer represent the reality. In the process of e-commerce transactions, it is possible for the consumer to conduct and place an order with the manufacturer instantly and directly (Singla, 2000). And same is possible within the various agents of this process (i.e., between producer and Retailers, Retailers and Distributors, Distributors and Retailers etc.). E-Commerce technology brings about the benefits of more accurate and timely information flow, administrative saving, lowering total distribution cost, closer trading relationship, improved cash flows, and moving closer to the end consumers.

No doubt that online ordering and delivery of product is reducing the role of intermediaries. Therefore, it is also feared that intermediaries would be completely eliminated in the e-commerce economy. However, this fear may be unfounded. In 'e-commerce economy, though it is possible to deliver a number of goods and services online, it may not be possible to eliminate the physical delivery of many goods because of their vary nature. Goods such vegetables and grocery, garments and shoes, toys etc. cannot be delivered online (they have physical existence). Though intermediaries like wholesalers and retailers can be eliminated in such transactions, it may not be possible to eliminate distributors and transporters. The demand for distributors and transporters is in fact expected to increase tremendously (Westland and Clark). Even with the advent of e-commerce technology, the functions of intermediaries will not change, because collecting information is a labour and time intensive task. However, this group can exploit new opportunities and challenges.

Impact on Agriculture

The open access architecture of the Internet, declining information technology costs, and high volume have resulted in progressive steps forward for the entire marketing system. Parallel changes in the structure of agriculture have also contributed to the popularity of the current generation of information technology. Chief among the changes is in the need for closer coordination of the supply chain-both upstream and downstream from the producer-and stretching' from seed, fertilizers, and machinery suppliers, to the food processors and retailers. Thus, technologies like electronic commerce have forced new relationships between and among the buyers of agribusiness to form a complex web interaction (Ehmake et al., 2001)

Various studies show that there is much about the potential success of e-commerce's in agriculture. Common agribusiness business-to-business transactions such as buying, selling, trading, delivering and contracting seem to be natural targets for conversion to e-commerce.

Many theoretical benefits of e-commerce in agriculture have been identified such as: (1) promotion of information flow, market transparency and price discovery (Poole, 2001); (2) facilitation of industry coordination (Nicolaisen, 2001); and reduction or elimination of transaction costs (Porter, 2001; Thompson, 1996). Internet based e-commerce also offer tremendous opportunities to create collaborative marketplaces in low-cost and effective way (Nicolaisen, 2001). E-commerce in agriculture could also potentially tighten the supply chain and cut marketing margins and transactions costs in way that benefit smaller, local producers as well as local agribusinesses. It also enables a vast array of products to be transacted, usually at a price that is competitive with local retailers. E-commerce can also change the situation of hard bargain caused by scattered farmers and lack of information. At the same time, the fast and convenient electronic bargain manner can accelerate the circulation of commodities, and lessen the risk, and increase the competitions of agricultural products in the international market (Cao and Chen, 2001). These theoretical benefits appear to be undisputed. However, these have yet to materialize into profitability. Study of Golman Sachs (2000) discussed the general barriers citied by business to Internet based e-commerce adoption and explained that these barriers also apply to agribusiness as well. These barriers include: (1) unclear return on investment (2) lack of budget (3) lack of stakeholders support and (4) complicated technology. Added to these, there may be some other factors (10) slowing down e-commerce adoption in agriculture. In fact, many of the issues faced by e-agribusinesses are the same as those faced by the firms in other sectors similar to changes brought by other new agricultural technologies (Hooker et al., 2001). However, characteristics of the agricultural sector and its participants present some inherent impediments to the implementation of e-commerce practices. Nonetheless, despite these challenges, there is room for creative solutions potentially leading to successful adoption. Those potential strategies touch on: structure of industry; market and product expertise; and organizational development. At this point of time it is not very clear-the impact of e-commerce on farms, agribusiness firms, markets, and rural communities. Are there only winners or are losers too? If so, who are they? What will government to do, with or against e-commerce in agriculture? Since e-commerce is still evolving, it is too early to definitive answer (Mueller, 2000). An inspection of current practices; however, suggest that success of e-commerce in agribusiness is undeniable. Factors specific to agriculture will create additional challenges, which must be overcome before success may be attained. The ability of each player to work though these challenges will determine the speed of implication of e-commerce in agriculture.

Impact on Labour Market

E-Commerce, consisting of marketing and other business processes conducted over the computer-mediated networks is changing the way organizations in many industries operate. It leads to the automation of some job functions and replaces others with self service operations, raising output per worker and dampening employment requirements in some occupations, as well as in the industries in which these occupations are concerned (Hecker, 2001). The introduction and implementation of new technologies has posed important challenges for the commercial workers and their trade unions worldwide. Among the issues that unions have to deal with are, both B2B and B2C, self-scanning, logistics system, multimedia and other in store sales support applications. In many ways, they are already deeply affecting labour market (Gottardi et al., 2004). In contrast, e-commerce has spurred employment in industries producing software, and systems used by e-commerce and other occupations associated with websites and networks.

Various studies showed that e-commerce has a positive impact on the labour productivity. At the theoretical level, since e-commerce reduces coordination costs between different work processes, they facilitate firms to fragment tasks to enable them to improve the labour productivity. At the same time when the routine tasks can be automated, e-commerce reduces unskilled work. In a recent study, Atrostic and Nguyen (2004) considered the impact of computer networks on the labour productivity in the US manufacturing sector, using micro data predominantly for 1999. They found a positive and significant impact of computer networks on plant level labour productivity, suggested that networks increase labour productivity by around 7.5 per cent. Motohashi (2001) provides evidence for the positive impact of different information networks on labour productivity in Japan. In the UK a recent study by Criscuolo and Waldron (2003), based on Annual Business Inquiry, shows that buying online positively affects the labour and total factors of productivity, while selling online has a negative impact on productivity. But, perhaps the larger impact of e-commerce on labour market can be seen in the form of online job search. However, very little is known about the importance of online job applications or direct employer initiated contracts with potential candidates. Even then, online job posting has grown spectacularly (Autor, 2001). Estimates place the number of online job boards at over 3000, the number of active resumes online at over 7 million, and the number of job posting at 29 million. Kuhn and Skuterud (2000) reported that 7 per cent of employed workers regularly use the web to search for a new job in 1998. The leading job board, Monster.Com, offered 3.9 million resumes and 4, 30,000 jobs in August 2000. Further, the Internet is likely to change how some workers deliver labour services. For example, falling telecommunications traffic regardless of where it originates. Improvements in communication and control technology likely mean that people who monitor equipment or other workers can perform their task at the greater physical remove. Remote access to e-mail and company documents will enable many workers to perform some or all of their work from home to elsewhere.

On the flip side, it has also been feared that the reduction in number of intermediaries and sales persons due to reduction in number of supermarkets and showroom would reduce employment world over. The worst affected are expected to be the unskilled manpower. It is true that unskilled labour is getting displaced in a big way in the e-commerce economy. Internet and e-commerce by facilitating firms to employ home-workers on a contractual basis are seen to promote insecure employment opportunities. In India, as well as in the other low-income economies, the potential of e-commerce is seen to employment from the formal sector to small firms in the unorganized sector where employment is not protected by any legislation. Further, if this feature of e-commerce encourages the formation of small firms that are narrowly specialized, it also implies that there is less room for employee mobility within the firms, transforming the careers paths of employees (Francis, 1986). Added to this, as with other tools, the internet is not without its limitations as a means of attracting qualified candidates. For example, companies listing opportunities on major job boards may receive applications from a much wider geographic region-and sometimes less qualified applicants-requiring additional sorting and review. Firms are also noting that some candidates who post their resumes online may be more passive job seekers; they want to "test the waters" and wait the results, versus proactively applying for open position.

Impact on Transportation

In a very short time span common sense has emerged within the world of transport, about the assumed huge impact of e-commerce and especially the Internet on relationships between companies (and consumers). Dholakia et al, (2000) concluded that in those regions of the world where there is old, established and often congested road infrastructure, any e-commerce-based methods that could lead to trip reduction and/or trip rationalization can contribute to an improvement in the quality of life. At least from a theoretical point of view, it seems quite clear that the online shopping could lead to reduction of transport demand. In some cases, online shopping eliminates any kind of physical transport (when goods can be dematerialized as software, books, music etc.). In other cases, a goods transport is still necessary, but the journeys to shops are eliminated or reduced. Even if the purchase is finally made at the shop, the consumer can have used the Internet, looking for information, instead of visiting different shops. Thus, electronic commerce transactions have strong implications on transportation. In this context, numbers of studies have been conducted to measure the impact of e-commerce on the number of trips. Browne (2001) first quoted the study made by Farahmand and Young (1998). It modelled the effects of the number of trips by switch to home shopping of 10 per cent of the customers of a grocery store and a DIY store (of a typical size) in the UK. They assumed that delivery vans would carry the loads of nine customers on each round trip. In both the cases, the reduction in total trips is around 9 per cent. The vehicle kilometer made by the delivery vans for the 10 per cent of home shoppers suppose a reduction of 87 per cent in comparison with the vehicle kilometers previously made by car. Further, the study (Coirm, 1999) also modelled a case of grocery home delivery in UK and their result shows that if 10-20 per cent of shoppers use home shopping, the reduction in the trips could arrive to 7-16 per cent. For the purchase made from home, the reduction in vehicle kilometers is 70-80 per cent even if each van only carries eight loads. Against this, study of Colin (2001) revealed that commerce has not had as great an impact on transport lows as some had expected, at least in terms of the volumes carried. However, some substitution effects are to be expected.

Not only on the retail transportation, e-commerce does have impact on the companies where heavy transportation is needed. E-transportation tool can enable seamless connectivity, provide dock-to-dock visibility of the supply chain, and deliver real time information that leads to better and faster decisions. E-transportation also enables shippers a choice of carriers to be used for shipments of merchandise varying in weights and service, and identifies all shipping packing, marking, labelling and communications requirements as well. (Vevaldi and Prasad, 2002). But many shippers still are not quite ready to put their faith in this relatively new e-commerce tool. Indeed, as with the introduction of new technology, e-commerce as it relates to the transportation industry, is going to take time to catch on.

For transportation companies it is expected that, with e-commerce, a whole new market will open up for transportation and logistics companies, or whatever they may be called in the future. At present e-commerce is pursued to a fairly high degree between companies, but is still not very developed between companies and private persons. The business-to-consumer (B2C) relation is expected to grow rapidly though, and when this happens it will result in several changes for actors in the logistics area. When delivering to private persons instead of companies, the demand for fast and accurate deliveries will increase.

This is because one or more of the physical nodes will disappear when the goods can be transported directly from the producing company to the end customer. Direct home deliveries will request shorter lead times, and more complex distribution systems will be necessary to make this possible. Expected trends in traffic and distribution from a widely spread use of e-commerce are fewer passenger cars, an increased number of pickup trucks, and smaller consignments, especially on international transports. Further the study of Hultkrantz and Lumsden (2000) concluded that the logistics industry has to face the challenges and opportunities created by e-commerce, both from within the industry and from external players. The industry has always been pressed to cut costs and squeeze margins, and the future will be even more formidable as competition forces most companies to continue the streamlining of their business.

Impact on Taxation

When new technologies evolve, can taxation issues be far behind? If e-commerce is being billed as one of the greatest economic developments of the 21st century the taxation issues arising there from poses the single biggest challenge of the century to both-the businesses and the taxman's. (Girish, 20001) This is particularly true in the context of digitized products because transactions of such products are not backed up by any physical of goods. As e-commerce transcends the barriers of geographical boundaries the concept like the place of transactions and place of consumption become immaterial. Therefore, it is often difficult to determine national jurisdiction and revenue rights

International tax issues in the area of e-commerce are manifold and include nexus 0fthe vendor and tax enforcement agencies. Taxing authorities may have great difficulty collecting revenue form vendors conducting commerce through foreign Internet addresses. The foremost problem associated with Internet based commerce is fixing the place of transaction.

The place where a web-server is located, the place where the user initializes the transaction and the server where payment is collected may be different. Electronic transfer of funds heightens the risk of money being sent to tax havens. Further, many jurisdictions rely on the taxpayer to voluntarily identify himself, herself or itself as falling within its tax system. Tax authorities may not be able to effectively enforce their rights to collect tax in such an environment, especially if a business does not consider itself to be within a tax jurisdiction and simply choose not to disclose its activities to the relevant authority. It is trite, but true, that taxation of e-commerce is a major concern for the international agencies and the tax authorities worldwide.

In Europe, North America, and Australia and in many Asian Countries (particularly India and Singapore) substantial research have been conducted on the impact of the e-commerce on taxation. Among the plethora of books, reports, articles and papers produced on this topic however, the work of Organization for the Economic Co-Operation and Development (OECD) stands out as the most significant, given its commitment to consulting broadly with the governments worldwide as well as with the business community to develop an integrated and comprehensive approach to the taxation of e-commerce.

The identification and analysis of the inter jurisdictional measures imposed by e-commerce is one thing. The formulation of domestic and treaty policies for dealing with e-commerce is another, even more controversial challenge. Perhaps, the most fundamental threat to the international tax system is the erosion of the worldwide tax base.

It is increasingly possible for a company to try to divert income to a tax haven by locating its server there. This raises issues of allocation of business profits between the residence and source countries and leakage to tax haven (Cidambi, 2000).

The debate over how international tax principles ought to be revealed and may be reformed is still in its formulative stage. It would be necessary to equip the tax administration after reviewing the entire procedure in the light of the advent of e-commerce. First, the procedures have to be simplified. Second, it would be necessary top create an environment within the tax department to ensure that the tax laws are implemented appropriately, and that integrity of the tax base is maintained. (Mantravadi and Chowdary, 2002).

For India, it is high time to learn from the experience of the work of OECD, Japan and the US to suggest a strategy to encourage e-commerce and integrate the tax system in such a way that it takes care of the twin problems of determining the sites of sales and also identifies the jurisdiction with regard to its authority to tax transactions. In doing so, we have to keep in mind the associated risk for the tax compliance.

Impact on Cost, Price and Competition

Logically, e-commerce reduces search and transaction cost (Mukhopadhya, 2002). Reducation in transaction costs are motivating businesses to incorporate e-commerce into their business strategy (Garcia, 1995 and Kambil, 1995) The net impact of e-commerce on UK Economy has been estimated to be between 2% to 3% of GDP. It has also been estimated that improved demand forecasting and stock management as a result of e-commerce will enable reduction in overall inventories by as much as 25% in the US. At the micro level, there is evidence that this will provides an one-off sustainable improvement in the profitability by an average of 5% or more for the enterprises currently working with low margin (Goldman Sachs, 1999). The e-commerce lowers costs because, the Internet lowers selling search costs as well as, by allowing seller to communicate product information cost effectively to potential buyers, and by offering sellers new ways to reach buyers through the targeted advertisement and one-on-one advertising. Thus it is helpful in reducing the search costs on both the sides. By reducing search costs on both sides of the market, it appears likely that buyers will be able to consider more product offering and will identify and purchase products that better match their needs, with a resulting increase in economic efficiency. But the reduction in the cost combined with new capabilities of technology can set off more complex market dynamics (Bakos, 2001).

The lower search and information cost should push markets towards a greater degree of price and competition, and this outcome is certainly possible, especially for the homogeneous goods. On the other hand the use of Internet technology to provide differentiate and customized products, and thus avoid competition purely on the price.

Lower search costs in the digitized markets will make it easier for the buyers to find low cost sellers and thus will promote price competition among the sellers. Thus e-commerce economy comes quite close to the features of the prefect competition, as larger numbers of buyers and sellers can instantly interact with each other. Many characteristics of e-commerce should increase competition because buyers will have access to a global marketplace and the ability to easily compare price and product features (Fletcher et al., 2000). E-Commerce technologies have the potential to significantly increase competition by increasing consumers' choice of products and traders (ACCC, 2001). However, some of the distinguishing characteristics of the e-commerce set up also have the potential for creating the monopoly power in the certain lines of products. The e-commerce set up has negligible distribution cost for the intangibles and therefore marginal cost of the production and distribution is almost nil for these goods. Sales of these goods to a particular customer does not reduce its availability to the other potential customers. Economies of scale arising out of negligible marginal cost, along with network externalities and consumer preference for the already acquired skills, provide natural monopoly power to some of the products in the e-commerce set up. Early birds are thus expected to reap the benefits in these lines of production.

Therefore, in the e-commerce environment, monopoly is expected to exist along with the prefect competition. Competition would be especially seen in those areas where goods and services cannot be digitized and economies of scale are not very prominent. Breaking the monopoly power to remain in the competition would require high speed of innovation and making the product visible all the time, whether there is a demand for the products or not. Competition would be basically in the forms of converting ideas, knowledge and brain power into innovation.

Impact on Money

With the new economic landscape now outline, let us return to the money. Not surprisingly, in the intangible (e-commerce based economy) economy, money is also becoming increasingly intangible. The relative weight on non-cash monetary transactions now exceeds the value of cash money by the factor often (Goldfinger, 2002). Money and payments are delivered via electronic networks as data bits and database entries. At the wholesale level, money representation and manipulation are fully automated. Beyond the alteration of the appearance and mechanics of money, there are deeper structural changes. The triumph of markets means that money is increasingly used to settle multilateral transactions rather that the bilateral commercial transactions. The functional evolution in turn leads to profound modification in the design of the clearing system and networks, which need to handle large volume, work in real time, and offer more open access. Growth of e-commerce and development of various payment alternative channels (i.e.. Debit and Credit Cards, E-Cheque, Digital Purse, E-Cash etc.) assist payment channels. The delivery channels greatly impacted the retail banking and the wholesale markets of banks. And today, these new technologies have transformed the banking business almost beyond the belief in the last decade and the half. Most of all the customers have benefited, as have the bank themselves. Added to this, digital currencies have many other advantages; some of the important are: cheaper, faster, safer, global, and more private than traditional credit cards and bank wires. In other words, digital currencies will prove to be as world-changing as the invention of the printing press and gunpowder. Digital currencies link together financial institutions and markets across the globe in a way that allows instantaneous value transfers with a mere fraction of the cost associated with traditional bank wires and credit cards. But, this new forms of money has also posed certain challenges before the banking sector, most of them are related to IT plans (Kamesan, 2003). Many schemes have been piloted or rolled out but the use of e-money is still tiny. This raises the question why e-money has not been more successful. One explanation may be that there is not sufficient demand. Another explanation is that we are merely observing the slow start that is typical for many inventions. Once critical mass has been reached, e-money will take off. Finally, the problems of e-money may stem from regulation.

No doubt, these changes make money more visible and pervasive but also less stable, more volatile in its value and more elusive. Therefore, in the new economy, monetary policy become more important as a lever of economic management at the same time that the classical monetary aggregates—lose their reliability as signals of the future economic growth and inflation' (Goodhar, 1984). Nevertheless, one thing appears certain, electronic money will continue to emerge, rendering the overall money landscape more intricate and multifarious. To facilitate the emergence of electronic money, it is important to be open minded, to accept innovate vision of money and money transaction. At the same time it is also essential to recognize that many of these visions will either never be implemented or fail the critical test of customer acceptance.

Concluding Remarks

The emergence and rapid growth of Internet and E-Commerce has strong implications on economic and social actitivities. It is quite possible that these new technologies might transform the future of economic and societal landscape. At the economic front, there is a clear evidence that E-Commerce and Internet techonolgy have positive impact (UNDP, (2003), Pohjola (2000), Dewan and Kramer (2000), Kraemer and Dedrick (2000)}. To study the economic implications of e-commerce, few areas of economy (transportation, Intermediation, Agriculture, Labour Market, Taxation, Cost, Price and Competition, and money) has been selected.

On the basis of various studies it is revealed that e-commerce technology have strong economic implications. At the general level, there are two types of potential economic gains from the use of E-commerce and IT enabled technologies. First, are the gains in efficiency, both in static and dynamic.

Static gains are one-time, and come from more efficeint use of scarce resources, allowing higher consumption in the present. Dynamics gains come from higher growth, potentially raising the entire future stream of consumption and population. Efficiency gains of e-commerce also come about through the enabling of new digitized goods and services. The second type of potential benefits comes from cost reduction. Studies indicates that e-commerce is helpful in reduction of search cost, administration cost, distribution cost and even the labour costs. However, all these opportuities are yet to materlize in to profitability i.e. in agricultural sector, benefits of e-commerce exists, but, only theortically; not practically, as the implemetnation of e-commerce technolgy in agricultural sector has certin challenges. Addes to this, e-commerce based economic models has also posed number of challenges before the concerned people and community. The area of e-taxation is one of the best example and most controversial issue all over the world. As e-commerce transaccends the barriers of geographical boundaries, the concept like the place of transactions and place of consumption become immaterial. With the emergence and growth of digital money in the economy, the chances of frauds have also incresased. Another most difficult issue is the planning regarding the adoption and implemetation of e-commerce technology in the various economic activities. In nutshall, with the e-commerce based economic models, there is little to lose and more to gain.

What are the Steps in Creating an Online Business

Thinking of starting your online business? Well the Internet has opened up a wide range of business opportunities for one and all. Perhaps this is the reason why almost all the businesses have their own websites. Well if you are still in the planning stages about your online business, then here are some guidelines for you. Most of the people don't know where to start from, for all such people here are some suggestions and tips which will be definitely helpful.

Steps in Creating an Online Business

Step One: The first and most important step in creating an online business would be to get a personal computer and a secure Internet connection. Having a PC and a twenty-four hour uninterrupted Internet service is a prerequisite. An Internet business calls for highermost security since an online business implies online money transfers as well as security of important passwords.

Step Two: The second step is a crucial one. This is the time to establish your identity on the Internet-yes this is the time for domain name registration. You will have to register for a domain name, which will be thereafter your identity on the World Wide Web. You need to think of an appropriate URL which is relevant, catchy and popular in terms of search engine optimization as well.

Step Three: Well, now that you have these things in place, you need to clearly define the goods and services that you plan to offer on the Internet. Create a soft copy of all the things, which you would like to tell your customers.

Step Four: It is now time to design your website. Always remember that the website is often considered as a reflection of the businessman and hence it needs to be clear, precise attractive and convenient to use. You don't need to be an expert in web designing and content writing, all you need to do is hire the right kind of people to do that job for you. Read more about web designing services and web design and development software.

Step Five: Since a large number of online customers will be using their credit cards to pay for your goods and services you need to establish a way to accept credit cards online. Creating a merchant account with a bank or using a third party merchant account can help you accept credit cards from online customers.

Step Six: Try and place your advertisements on closely-related websites. You can also make use of blog advertising by creating a blog to supplement your website. Think of all possible methods of Internet marketing. Make use of online marketing and advertising tools like Google Adsense or Google Adwords.

Step Seven: Well, now that you are all set for a launch, you need to create hype about your website. This is the time to use all the types of advertising to promote your website! Newspaper ads, radio jingles, television advertising, email advertising or even mobile phone advertising-use all the types that suit your needs as well as fit your budget. And launch your website with a big bang!

Step Eight: The final step in making your business a huge success is to focus on improving your customer service and consider customer feedback for further changes and improvements. Maintaining a customer base is as important as expanding the existing customer base.

Internet Business Scams

Get Paid Programs: First and foremost, let me make it clear. There is some good news for all you get paid program enthusiasts. Not all get paid programs are fake.

(You heaved a huge sigh of relief, didn't you?) Now here's the bad news. 99 percent of them ARE fake (sorry!). Consequently, zeroing in on the remaining one percent of legitimate get paid programs is tougher than finding a needle in a haystack.

99 percent of these programs demand a subscription fee or a membership fee upfront in lieu of their subsequent services. Sadly, these 'subsequent services' do not exist.

Work From Home Scams: Once again, a majority of these programs are downright fake. Most of them promise home based business opportunities and jobs involving typing, data entry, etc. However, all of them vanish from existence once they've managed to lay their hands on the 'small' subscription fee that you pay them.

Nigerian Email Scams: I have mentioned about this right at the beginning of this article.

These fraud emails first surfaced a few years ago and are still in circulation. Each and every one of them are fake. People who have fallen prey to these email scams have lost a whole lot of hard earned money to these fraudsters. Some unfortunate ones have also had to pay with their lives. So, the moment you come across any such mail, all you should do is DELETE it.

Bank Scams: It's not what it sounds like. The banks haven't started getting into Internet crime (and thank God for that!). It's just that some cunning fraudsters create duplicate (read FAKE) websites which are complete with the bank's logo, hyperlink, etc. Then they send fake emails on behalf of the 'bank', asking you to visit the bank website (obviously the fake one) and enter your account details as well as other sensitive information.

What subsequently happens is that all this information actually gets sent to the fraudsters who then hack into your account and wipes it clean. This type of scam is popularly known as phishing. There are also cases of identity theft due to this menace of phishing. This is a relatively new Internet scam and one that is potentially very dangerous (since it is so well thought of and executed).

Email Processing: This is another type of scam which involves pure spamming. The user gets tempted by an offer of getting paid a handsome amount for doing a simple job of forwarding emails. A long list of email addresses is also provided to make the offer seem authentic. Little does the user realize that he is being duped.

The whole process involves nothing but spamming and there is absolutely nothing to gain from it, least of all, money.

Chain Emails: This is an online version of the legendary 'envelope stuffing' scam. As a user, you are told to perform a series of nonsensical tasks (which you do, because monetary greed and logic are always inversely proportional to each other).

By the time you realize that you've been conned, the fraudsters are busy laughing all the way to the bank. The Internet has certainly made life very easy and comfortable indeed.

However, one gets to witness the dark side of the Internet through some of these Internet business scams and Internet hoaxes. They are a genuine threat to Internet safety.

My advice to all you Internet users is to be wary of any suspicious emails or links that you may receive.

Do not fall prey to any 'make millions in a minute' sort of offer. It is just not possible. Oh, and those of you thinking of marrying Paris Hilton for a similar reason, you better think twice too!

The Impact on Wholesale Storage by E–commerce

Under the traditional distribution, the merchandise passes through the wholesale and retail channel from producer to consumer.

Serving as superior agency for producer and producer or producer and retailer in merchandise circulation progress, the wholesale trade takes on some functions as conquering conflicts between producing and consuming in time, space, collection, disperse, ownership, information, and effectively transferring wares from producing area to consuming area.

The wholesale trade' independence lies on the theory that it can greatly reduce the bargaining cost in society. The theory reveals that the wholesale reduces the exchanging times and ware storage cost in society.

Radically, the cause that the wholesale' existing can bring whole affiances lies in depression of distribution cost and improvement of distribution efficiency. But the key to the cause is the time and correction in information transferring. The exchanging time has no longer been the deciding factor for exchanging cost.

By the means of E-commerce, the producer could easily obtain operating information through the Internet. Meanwhile, an extra distribution tache of wholesaler shall make the circulation cost increase and circulation efficiency depress.

On the other hand, the tailer marketing' development and further zero storage could be realized through affiliation of the networks information communication' mutuality and the flexible making system.

The wholesaler' concentrated storage function has no more existing meaning than before.

Thereby, with the E-commerce' development the straight combination of producing and consuming has an increasingly challenge to the wholesale trade. This kind of challenge consists of two sectors: one is the producer' self-building commodity marketing system that dominate the products from producing to retail; the other is the large retailer' linkage and stocking system of directly purchase to break away from the jobbers.

For these challenges, the wholesale trade is going to be weakened totally. But the other way round, the possibility depends on the commodities' property. Less taches, storage time, transportation leading to lower circulation cost fits on the fresh, easy-rotten or bulk, low-value per unit, and higher-damage merchandises.

In this case, the wholesale trade is not suitable to intervene even if with perfect efficiency; in other cases that the merchandises have complex ethnology.

It' much better for manufactures to own strong service support and distribute directly lacking specialties as technique, personality, serving means.

The wholesaler should rashly intervene whereas the wholesalers can interpose into the circulation to accelerate with longevity, high-value per unit, fine performance, and simpleness. As an important tache in merchandise circulation, the main functions of storage lie in modulating the production and consumption on quantity, time, space etc. and facilitating the communication between producer and consumer.

The traditional commerce theory supposed that in any society with commodity circulation, commodity storage is a necessity to the circulation, and develop with the social producing and consuming expanding.

Moreover, the basis of traditional storage theory is going to solve the space-time confliction of merchandise' producing and consuming, and also resolve the structure contradiction by producing and consuming demands.

Along with the information economy' coming, the E-commerce and the main business activity clear the condition of storage away. On the one hand, the enterprises must provide product and service in time as to meet the consumer' need in networks era.

The time interval of merchandise' producing and consuming i much shorter.

On the other hand, the Internet provides an entirely new channel for the enterprise to investigate the market. By means of network, realizing the global consumer' demands at any moment, the enterprise can grasp this demand accordingly and settle down the unsuitable producing and consuming structure. The traditional storage industry has been facing the challenge.

The Impact on Retail Trade by E-commerce

The retail trade lies in the eventual phase and serves the intimate consumers directly, the concatenation linking producing and consuming is implemented in retail trade, and then the commodities are flowed from the circulating area into the consuming area.

Because of the appearance of invisible market, the information communication mode from point to point turned into the reality, so the producers and the ultimate consumers are combined, and the stock function by consumers, vending function by producer and wholesaler, the distribution function burned with the traditional retail trade have been replaced by the Internet.

The role of traditional retail has changed from the past substance distributor to the collector, disposer, interpreter and broadcaster, thus the traditional retail has been challenged by the E-commerce. The contradictions between supply and demand in time, space, amount, price, property and variety and the completion of commodity exchanging must be realized through the functions as follows.

(1) The agential function of consumer' stock. Serving as the consumers' stock agent, the retail traders purchase classification, assembling and stocking a great deal of merchandise, in order to conveniently choose and buy to contemporarily fulfill multiple consumption demands.

(2) The agential function of vendition. Using self-characteristic, the retail traders harmonize the relations among producers, wholesalers and consumer s. As a result, the wares of producer and wholesaler can be put into consuming area conveniently.

(3) Distribution function. The essential storage and keeping of commodities can resolve the confliction between consuming demands and producing supply. This function realizes the transfer of merchandises from the producing area to the consuming area.

The exchange in networks promotes the development of invisible market, and the main kind of exchange mode is gradually changing.

Without tangible markets such as emporium, supermarket, etc. the consumer can not accomplish the whole purchasing course of information collection, analysis and comparison, purchasing decision. As the invisible market function that the Internet takes on would partly substitute the tangible market function of retail trade, and then there is infirmness occurred in retail trade.

Firstly, avoiding the medial attaches such as wholesale and retail, the Internet channel depresses the circulation and dealing cost as well as quickening information flowing by means of contacting producer with consumer. The producer can accomplish the commodity circulation process without the retail trade, so the producer and wholesaler' distributional agent of retail trade is weakening.

Secondly, along with the rapid development of modern society and gradual improvement of consumer' living standard, there have been the trends of consumer' individuation and retailer' marketing. Under the environment of invisible market, the cost reduction and retailer marketing will be developed with the one to one information communication and the improvement of the flexible making system. At the same time, the retail trade in Internet has entirely the superiority of space and time.

It has an extended space by the net works' no geographical obstacle, and has extended time decided by the consumers in networks. Therefore, the consumers' demands of the Internet could be satisfied to greater degree and extent. These two situations mentioned above would weaken the stock agent function in retail trade. Thirdly, the condition that there is more osculation between producing and consuming makes the producing relate to the selling simpler. Through t e networks, the enterprises can show the quality, capacity, price and payment term; the clients can send out their order forms based on self-demands; the producers regulate producing and stock layout according to the order information to realize zero storage. Those all can weaken the distribution function of retail trade; the emergence and development of E-commerce have a certain impact on retail trade.

The Challenge on Scale Expanding Mode by E-commerce Along with the differing objects and capital expanding forming system, the modern business enterprises are on the scale extending way in the historic evolvement.

There exist two assumptions in scale extending as the fall of management cost and economy of scale. When the invisible market substitutes the tangible market and the information environments are much improved, the two assumptions occurred to be changed and the scale of modern business enterprise will take on a new trend. The precondition of enterprise' expanding is reducing management cost with greater ratio than market exchanging. This precondition is also changed when the market changes, information transfers quickly and cost decreases greatly.

The Internet is a web utensil promoting the dealing such as network purchase, network trade and so on. Having lower cost and time effectiveness, the invisible market agencies take competition superiorities on ascertaining exchanging object, contract negotiating and executing in helping dealing sides. Sequentially, the bargain cost is lower and much more depressed than the management cost. The enterprise would discover that it' much efficient to replace part management mechanism with market mechanism. In such case, the enterprise with portrait expands and the project will dwindle in scale.

Along with the progress of modern enterprises, because of dimension-economy caused by specialization and cosmically yield, the modern enterprise continuously expand in landscape orientation to enhance circulating effectiveness and lower cost.

However, due to the consumption individuation in modern society, in many industries the production trends to be non-standardization, small-batch and variety. This wobbles the base of specialization and cosmically circulation. Contemporarily in the network era, the networks clients contacted by the business enterprises have qualitative varieties with traditional consumers. With consuming demands of brand diversification and product individuation, the main approach lies not in simply enlarging business area to widen marketing scale. Therefore, the scale-economy effect caused by the traditional landscape orientation is becoming weakened under invisible market environment.

Furthermore, the application of E-commerce provides a lot of developing opportunities for small enterprises and the technique becomes the most important factor for obtaining competition advantage as the substitution of scale. Through the Internet, the small companies can enter international market and do international marketing despite the bulwark built with minute advertising charge. Whereas large enterprises encounter many new problems, such as organization structures' adjustment, supervision mode' change, etc. there have been obstacles in the way of the large enterprises' development. So, under the condition of E-commerce, the two preconditions of business enterprise' expanding are challenged and the modern business enterprises must reconsider its problem of management scale.

Chapter 6

Electronic Payment Systems

Electronic Payment is a financial exchange that takes place online between buyers and sellers. The content of this exchange is usually some fom of digital financial instrument (such as encrypted credit card numbers, electronic cheques or digital cash) that is backed by a bank or an intermediary, or by a legal tender.

The various factors that have lead the financial institutions to make use of electronic payments are:

1. *Decreasing technology cost:* The technology used in the networks is decreasing day by day, which is evident from the fact that computers are now dirt-cheap and Internet is becoming free almost everywhere in the world.
2. *Reduced operational and processing cost:* Due to reduced technology cost the processing cost of various commerce activities becomes very less. A very simple reason to prove this is the fact that in electronic transactions we save both paper and time.
3. *Increasing online commerce:* The above two factors have lead many institutions to go online and many others are following them.

We began E-Commerce with EDI, this was primarily for large business houses not for the common man. Many new technologies, innovations have lead to use of E-Commerce for the common man also. We will now briefly enumerate these innovations based on whom they affected:

1. *Affecting the consumers:* Credit cards, Debit Cards, ATMs (Automated Teller Machines), Stored value cards, E-Banking.

2. *Enabling online commerce:* Digital Cash, E-Cash, Smart cards (or Electronic Purse) and encrypted Credit cards.
3. *Affecting Companies:* The payment mechanisms that a bank provides to a company have changed drastically. The Company can now directly deposit money into its employee's bank account. These transfers are done through Automated Transfer Houses.

There are also many problems with the traditional payment systems that are leading to its fade out. Some of them are enumerated below:

1. *Lack of Convenience:* Traditional payment systems require the consumer to either send paper cheques by snail-mail or require him/her to physically come over and sign papers before performing a transaction. This may lead to annoying circumstances sometimes.
2. *Lack of Security:* This is because the consumer has to send all confidential data on a paper, which is not encrypted, that too by post where it may be read by anyone.
3. *Lack of Coverage:* When we talk in terms of current businesses, they span many countries or states. These business houses need faster transactions everywhere. This is not possible without the bank having branch near all of the companies offices. This statement is self-explanatory.
4. *Lack of Eligibility:* Not all potential buyers may have a bank account.
5. *Lack of support for micro-transactions:* Many transactions done on the Internet are of very low cost though they involve data flow between two entities in two countries. The same if done on paper may not be feasible at all.

We will now focus attention on the various ways available to pay online these methods of payment are still new even when seen as a technology. Each has its own benefits and shortcomings:

1. *Electronic Tokens:* An electronic token is a digital analog of various forms of payment backed by a bank or financial institution. There are two types of tokens:
   i. Real Time: (or Pre-paid tokens)-These are exchanged between buyer and seller, their users pre-pay for tokens that serve as currency. Transactions are settled with the exchange of these tokens. Examples of these are DigiCash, Debit Cards, Electronic purse etc.

   ii. Post Paid Tokens – are used with fund transfer instructions between the buyer and seller. Examples– Electronic cheques, Credit card data etc.

2. *Electronic or Digital Cash:* This combines computerized convenience with security and privacy that improve upon paper cash. Cash is still the dominant form of payment as: The consumer still mistrusts the banks. The non-cash transactions are inefficiently cleared. In addition, due to negative real interests rates on bank deposits. Now we will enumerate some qualities of cash:
   a. Cash is a legal tender i.e. payee is obligatory to take it.
   b. It is negotiable i.e. can be given or traded to someone else.
   c. It is a bearer instrument i.e. possession is proof of ownership.
   d. It can be held & used by anyone, even those without a bank certificate.
   e. It places no risk on part of acceptor.

The following are the limitations of Debit and Credit Cards:

i. They are identification cards owned by the issuer & restricted to one user i.e. cannot be given away.

ii. They are not legal tender

iii. Their usage requires an account relationship and authorization system.

Properties of Digital Cash

- *Must have a monetary value:* It must be backed by cash (currency), bank authorized credit or a bank certified cashier's check.
- Must be interoperable or exchangeable as payment for other digital cash, paper cash, goods or services, lines of credit, bank notes or obligations, electronic benefit transfers and the like.
- *Must be storable and retrievable:* Cash could be stored on a remote computer's memory, in smart cards, or on other easily transported standard or special purpose devices. Remote storage or retrieval would allow users to exchange digital cash from home or office or while travelling.
- Should not be easy to copy or tamper with while it is being exchanged. This is achieved by using the following technologies, these are nothing but new and very efficient versions of the old art of cryptography.

- Digital cash is based on cryptographic systems called "Digital Signatures" similar to the signatures used by banks on paper cheques to authenticate a customer.
- Purchase of digital cash from an online currency server (or bank) involves 2 steps:
- Establishment of an account in this step we are given a unique digital number which also becomes our digital signature. As it is a number known only to the customer and the bank, forgery, which may be done in paper cheques becomes very difficult.
- Maintenance of sufficient money in the account is required to back any purchase.

Electronic Cheques

The electronic cheques are modeled on paper checks, except that they are initiated electronically. They use digital signatures for signing and endorsing and require the use of digital certificates to authenticate the payer, the payer's bank and bank account. They are delivered either by direct transmission using telephone lines or by public networks such as the Internet.

Benefits of electronic Cheques:

- o Well suited for clearing micro payments. Conventional cryptography of e-cheques makes them easier to process than systems based on public key cryptography (like digital cash).
- o They can serve corporate markets. Firms can use them in more cost-effective manner.
- o They create float and the availability of float is an important requirement of Commerce.

E-Banking

Banking as a business can be divided into five broad types:

1. Retail
2. Domestic wholesale
3. International Wholesale
4. Investment
5. Trust.

Of all these types, retail and investment banking are most affected by online technological innovations and are the ones that stand to profit most from e-commerce.

Role of e-commerce in banking is multifaceted – impacted by:

1. Changes in technology.
2. Rapid deregularization of many parts of finance.
3. Emergence of new banking institutions.
4. Basic economic restructuring.

E-Banking offers an inexpensive alternative to branching to expand a bank's customer base, and many banks are using e-banking to increase services to their customers. Many banks have started websites on the Internet and many plan to offer banking services over the Internet.

Smart Cards and other forms of electronic cash could be the key to consumer acceptance of home banking, eventually allowing banks to reduce the number of their physical branches.

Four major categories of home banking are:

1. *Proprietary bank dial-up services:* A home banking service in combination with a Computer and Modem lets the bank become and electronic gateway to consumer's accounts, enabling them to transfer funds or pay bills directly to creditor's accounts.
2. *Off-the-shelf home finance Software:* This category is a key player in making relationships between current customers and helping banks gain new customers. Example: Microsoft's Money and Bank of America's MECA Software.
3. *Online Service Based Banking:* This category allows banks to setup retail branches or subscriber based online services such as Prodigy, Compu Serve and America Online.
4. *WWW Based Banking;* This allows banks to bypass subscriber based online services and reach the customer's browser directly through worldwide web. Advantage of this model is its flexibility to adapt to new online transaction processing models facilitated by e-commerce and elimination of the constricting intermediary.

E-Commerce and Retailing

Retailing is expected to change with the rapid development of new online sales and distribution channels that literally can be used from anywhere, anytime – from work, school, a hotel, car or airplane. As an example of the Electronic retailing we can see Amazon which sells books online and Dell computers who sell computers online. These retailers started as small players in a market, which did not trust them. However, they have become major players after taking over some small retailers.

Almost every retailer is now re-evaluating every aspect of its operation from customer service to advertising, merchandising to store design and logistics to order fulfillment and further more reacting to the pressure of retailers, suppliers are assessing technology based solutions to drive down costs and become more efficient producers of goods.

Online channels are impacting traditional retail business models with online retailing constraints of time and space disappear.

Electronic Retailing

Today electronic retailing is still far from being a competitive threat to more traditional store retailing but it is becoming increasingly attractive as technology and application improve and retailers gain experience.

Some traditional retail outlets:

1. Shopping malls and departmental stores.
2. Super Centres
3. Factory outlets
4. Warehouses
5. Mail order and catalogue shopping.

Television Retailing

The T.V. retail marketing and programming are divided into segments that are televised live, with a show host who presents the merchandise and conveys information relating to the product including price, quality, features and benefits.

Success of T.V. shopping is the result of effective utilization of electronic media for capturing the power and influence of celebrity and the magic of showmanship and bringing them to bear on a sale.

CD-ROM Based Shopping has the following advantages:

- o A CD-ROM catalogue has multimedia capability and can enable a merchant to add sound, photographs an a full motion video to a product presentation.
- o It can be interactive enabling the customer to select which category to view.
- o Relatively inexpensive to produce and distribute.

It has the following disadvantages:

- o Not all possible customers may have a CD-ROM drive or software to see it.

- o It is a static device to catalogue a company's products, but the list or style of the products a company makes may vary from time to time.

Electronic Publishing

Publishing is another area where the Internet has impacted. With all web sites having web pages that show some content or other visitors, get hordes of web page based information on almost any topic. In fact, the web has become a very big virtual information library. Taking advantage of this are some web sites like the www.rocketlibrary.com. These web sites encourage people to write for them free and encourage members to get e-books free. E-Books are nothing but electronic forms of paper books, these books are a part of a wave of innovation, these include Palmtop computers, E-Book readers etc. These readers and Palmtops can store thousands of books in a very small size as compared to paper books.

The big publishing houses are taking hue and are now offering some chapters or complete books online. This has also lead to a new trend in which authors are now offering their books online without actually going to publishing houses, eg. Stephen King is offering one chapter of his new book The Plant at a dollar.

All this has become due to the fact that Internet can handle micro-payments. Like retailing it may appear that books may vanish one day due to these online publishers but it is not so as books are still a favourite pastime of many, but e-books will become a supplement to the paper books this is for sure.

Online publishing can be viewed in two ways:-

- o Activity of disseminating information.
- o Activity of publishing for sale. In order to realize revenue from their information, publishers package their product as a bundled commodity rather than disjointed information.

There is a fundamental difference between information and commodity. A commodity such as digital book needs to be sold in volume in order to generate revenue, so publishers must keep their material from spreading freely all over the planet. On the other hand, value of information is not lost when it is sold because the contents are not limited by their medium of expression.

Technical Issues:

1. How to improve and enforce copyright protection.
2. How to create compelling content using the available technology.

3. How to conduct financial transactions for individual articles (Micropayments).
4. Publishers have to constantly innovate and challenge present concepts if this form of commerce is to become widely accepted and popular.

The following factors are to be considered for a successful online publishing business:

1. Content
2. Incentive
3. Services
4. Quality
5. Price
6. Speed of delivery
7. Bundling of products
8. Diversity of choice.

The following approaches are to be followed for online publishing:

1. *Online Archive Approach:* (Includes bibliography databases and full text searches). This is new to the web and appeals to corporate publishers and to some extent, commercial publishers (such as academic or journal publishers) who have an existing digital archive that they want to deliver over the web, as well as on paper, CD-ROM or other media.
2. *The new medium approach:* (Including real-time news delivery, personalized news delivery and entertainment). It aims to create new material for the web; to treat the web, as its own medium. This will appeal mostly to commercial publishers, such as magazines, that view web as an alternative, not a replacement for print publication. This approach is more controversial and more difficult to implement, but also more exciting.
3. *The Publishing Intermediation Approach:* This approach (including online directories) exploits new service opportunities for intermediaries. The future is bright for the publishing intermediaries who offer case of operation speed & details information because there will always be a need for a good directory to help people locate goods, service & products.
4. *The dynamics & Just-in-Time Publishing Approach:* In the approach, content is assembled is real-time and transmitted in the format best suited to the user's faster and perfection. It is

just in time publishing i.e. the stories, applets and content flow into the computer just as consumer need and then self-destruct after usage.

Digital Copyrights

A key issue in online publishing relates to digital copyrights. Effective technological protection mechanisms are vital to ensuring the availability of quality of quality content online. Protecting intellectual property rights (copyrights, trademarks and licenses) and collecting dues from online users is proving to be quite challenging. The Internet makes it extremely easy to copy, retransmit and alter works without the permission of the copyright holder. Moreover, the digital world has no international boundaries, and policing is impossible since the levels of protection and sanctions against infringement vary widely in countries across the globe, which makes the risk even greater. Without effective protection, publishers are not willing to risk their investment and hard work.

The following two methods are used to copyright online data:

1. Restricting access to the source of the work:
   a. Controlling web server access.
   b. Controlling individual document access.
2. Restricting manipulation of the electronic file containing the work.

Advertising & Online Publishing

Magazines & Newspapers have also set up sites on the Web with the interaction of attracting advertising dollars. Many online periodicals include traditional advertisements as well as icons, which display an advertiser's logo & when clicked with mouse, send a user across the web to the advertiser's website.

Advertising spending is expected to increase for 5 reasons.

1. *Shorter Access Times:* The bandwidth available is constantly increasing so that the user now has to wait less to access a web site. This means that the user can spend more time on the web site. This in turn means that he will be seeing more ads.
2. *Reduced Access Fees:* We are all seeing that Internet usage has now almost become free, companies like CalTiger are offering it in India. This reduction in prices has lead to tremendous growth in the number of users.
3. *Increasing convenience to access information:* The web has now become sort of the worlds biggest encyclopedia, it is the largest

source of all information. We all refer to the web for information. We know how easy it is search the web.

4. *Increasingly valuable information:* With so much information available the competition among the publishers increases, this leads to better content and service.

Now that we have discussed E-Commerce we will try to see how does a site actually implement it, what tools are necessary to implement an online store.

E-Commerce Phases

Let us now look at each of these phases closely:

- *Marketing:* Marketing is not a new term, to sell anything companies have to market it. But to use the Internet, as a medium of marketing is new as the bandwidth is still limited so no commercials can be shown as on T.V. Internet marketing has a different approach. We market things on the net by showing small banner ads that everyone who surfs the net is familiar. Also web sites like Amazon pay other web sites if someone from their web site comes to Amazon's web site by clicking on a banner ad or a link. The whole business on the web is *sticky* the term refers to the fact that the customer has to be sold a product and also the web site should be so attractive that the customer keeps coming back to it for further buying. This is done by sending attractive offer mails and referrals.
- *Customer/Visitor:* Here we have to make distinction between the type of commerce web site. There actually exist three broad types of commerce web sites:
  - B2C – These web sites provide business to consumer. These are micro-payment based web sites. They have to attractive and should be able to show the products properly. As an example, you may visit www.fabmart.com and www.firstandsecond.com to see the feel of a B2C site.
  - B2B – These are web sites that provide business to the business, that is their function is similar to the stock exchanges, i.e. they are meeting points for a buyer and a seller. These do not focus on content but rather on service. Functions of such web sites are online order processing, tender filling, tracking of orders etc.
  - Auction Sites – These are sites that let you auction or sell something online it may be an old motorcycle or bed or books.

- Web Site Visit: Once a user visits a web site the site begins tracking him/her, by presenting him/her with products based on his/her preference. Some means of doing this are cookies, registration forms, surveys etc.

o *Product Browsing:* A user will typically browse through departments and then various products; he/she may be attracted by sowing blinking new offers and other discounts.

o *Shopping Basket:* Shopping basket is a term taken straight from regular shopping, as in a store the user adds the items of need to a basket the online store also implement a shopping basket, in which we can keep on adding items o our need.

o *Checkout:* Once we have added all items we need to the basket the web site lists all the items that we intend to purchase, we also have to fill in all the billing related information here. We enter the credit card numbers here. Other things such as gift-wrapping etc. are also specified here.

o *Tax & Shipping:* Once it has been decided where the product has to go and who is going to pay for it, we now decide on various taxex and shipping routes the product may take. These become very challenging especially in international orderings as countries have different taxes and shipping rates.

o *Payment:* This is the most important part of the purchasing online. The user is presented with a list of all the items purchased, and a total of the payments he has to make then he has to decide on the mode of payment whether by credit card or cash on delivery etc.

o *Receipt:* Once an order has been placed and confirmed, we may want to place a copy of the order with the user. This may be done either by snail mail or e-mail.

o *Process Order:* At this stage the consumer leaves the picture, we now begin to check the credit card number and other data. This may be done online or offline, then the product is made and prepared for shipping to the customer.

o *Fulfill Order:* Once the order has been processed it has to be fulfilled duly. Even though 90% of the transactions are online but the product has to reach the consumer physically and in well shape.

o *Ship Order:* Once we have processed the order fully it is ready to be sent to the consumer it is then shipped to the consumer.

The tools that go into the making of a web site depend on the platform or OS being used to develop the store:

1. Windows NT platform:
    a. Database support – A must, either in form of Access or SQL Server.
    b. ASP support – this is the technology from Microsoft that will enable dynamic content on the web site.
    c. MTS support – Every transaction should pass the ACID test (i.e. it should be Atomic Consistent Isolated and Durable) MTS has built in transaction objects that can be used.
    d. Site Server – has a rich set of tools to build a site, these help to engage a customer.
    e. Commerce Server – This has a rich set of tools that can help in commerce transactions.
2. Unix/Linux platforms:
    a. MySQL support – this is the database supported by sites on this platform.
    b. Perl – is the scripting language that enables dynamic content on these web sites.
3. JAVA:
    a. Java is a platform independent package, so JAVA has Java Server Pages for scripting and can interact with most of the databases with the use of some third party addons etc.

Case Studies

E-Banking Case Study

Intuit: Intuit is a leading provider of financial software it pioneered the concept of e-banking by making a personal finance software called Quicken in 1984. It launched online bill payment services in the year 1990, IntelliCharge credit card service in 1993 and Quicken Quotes a portfolio price update service in 1994.

At the forefront was the company's software Quicken; it allows users to organize, understand and manage their personal finance. Quicken looks and works like a cheque-book, it allows users to enter their financial transactions and then generate meaningful reports and graphs. It allows users to reconcile their bank accounts and also track their credit card purchases. It also enables users to print cheques from the computer and allows them to make online payments.

The company also offers to its customers online banking, bill payment and credit management.

How it Works

Customers will have to sign up with a local bank and then use Quicken software to get the desired information. Quicken users then dial a local number and all transactions between Quicken and the banks are done through an Intuit subsidiary National Payment Clearing House, which changed its name to Intuit Service Corporation. ISC is basically an intermediary between the Quicken software and the banks. ISC's network design is based on "burst and disconnect" i.e. the user connects to ISC gets his desired information and disconnects. This strategy allows full utilization of the network and allows maximum number of users. The network applies the RSA security method. Intuit's banking partners download all bank related information like bank balances and statements into ISC's servers. So that all information is available to the user from his computer and modem. In case of credit card payments the request is passed to the credit card company which feeds the details about the latest transactions to ISC which then gets back to the user. In case of Bill Payment the user just logs into the ISC server and feeds the details of the bills he has to pay. ISC then sees the most appropriate method of payment of the bill. There may be many possible ways, like some companies may have tied up with ISC itself, some may have tied up with other networks etc. If the bill cannot be paid over the network then Intuit prints a physical cheque and sends it to the party.

The figure on the following page shows graphically with the help of block diagrams how Intuit's services work.

Intuit is one of the oldest and leading players in this market the other leading service providers are:

- Citibank and Prodigy: This is a tie up between a major bank and an Internet service provider to benefit the user.
- Intuit and America Online: Similar to one above.
- Security First Network Bank: (SFNB) this is different from the rest as the complete bank is online and you do not have to purchase any proprietary software, the browser is the only software needed. This service also clearly distinguishes between Internet Banking and Online Banking.
    - Internet banking: is banking with the use of just a browser and nothing else. You can download statements and other information and print them as you like it. This type of

banking allows banks to break free of software developers, as no proprietary software is needed.

- Online Banking as we saw relies on proprietary software. This software is responsible for all transactions that take place on with the bank.

SFNB is one such Internet based bank. After registering at the banks secure servers the user gets an account and can operate this account just like the normal account.

A Case Study on Online Retailing

The intricacies of online retailing can be explain through following case study of *Peapod CUC International,* based in Evanston, Illinois which is using the online medium for food retailing services. Founded in 1989 by two brothers, Peapod is a member of online grocery/drug store shopping and delivery service that already has thousands of customers in the Chicago, San Francisco, and Boston Area.

Peapod is performing as a middleman supply chain management, which was founded on the idea that people do not want to go to the grocery store and without leaving the room they can avail the facility of the modern Internet communication. Peapod has an online database over 25,000 grocery and drugstore items, and allows comparison-shopping based on price, nutritional content, fat or Calories. Other feature includes electronic coupons retailer preferred customer discounts, and other benefit like recipes, tips, and home delivery service. Peapod has a staff of professional shoppers; produce specialists, and delivery people who fulfill the order

In the online retailing we will discuss the following in view of Peapod's online retailing management through the supermarket:

1) The Mechanism behind online retailing.
2) The Business Model.

The Mechanism Behind Online Retailing

Peapod initially had a DOS – Based system with little Graphics. Later in 1995, they introduced a new version of the software – based on the windows platform, in which product pictures were available.

Peapod's back office is linked with the mainframe databases of the supermarkets at which it ships for its customers, allowing it to provide the supermarkets' storekeeping units and shelf tag prices electronically to its customers where they need to buy a software application that enables them to access peapod database through an online computer service. By executing the Peapod software and entering the user ID & password. On verification, user gets access whole grocery store and drugstore items the supermarket online. Then Peapod provides customers with home shopping services.

After accessing, the customers can virtually visit to the grocery store and according to provide information as well as delivery services then can find the item by brand name or product type or can be sorted out item by various categories. Within categories, they can choose to have the item arranged alphabetically by brand stored by lowest per ounce, package size, unit price, or nutritional value. Customer can make selection for goods to be purchase and can subtotal the amount.

Peapod customers create their own grocery aisles in their own virtual store. Customers can a make request for list of item by category (cereals), by item (Frosted Flakes), by brand (Kellogg's), or even by what is on sale in the store on a given day. And even there last history to goods purchase.

After having finished shopping, user can choose a Pinpoint delivery time period with featuring 60 minutes or 90 minutes time slots. Now clicking on *done* button the order is electronically routed to Peapod. Where all order are taken centrally, and then lined to the respective store. The store gets a printout with the order including delivery address and payment instruction mode.

At the customer services availability, customer can avail the facility from Membership Service Cell, where their representative will try to resolve the matter. For example, service representative found that customer receiving five bags of apples instead of five apples. In response, Peapod began asking to its virtual customer to confirm order in which order-entry error may occur.

The Business Model

The formula for Peapod's success is the busy American lifestyle. So on the basis of good demographics, which can do better things among the American to, delivers the goods across the homes. The behind-the-scenes logistics are central to what Peapod is all about; that means make sure the orders get to the stores correctly and that they are shopped correctly. With the overcome of traditional retailer Peapod need to crate the supply chain after identifying a specific demand from a target customer for a particular item, and then it feeds off the existing infrastructure to do it. But, Peapod has to option to switch over the food supply management then need to re-plan all the way of their online retailing with compare to food retailer who have the shopper's resistance to switching food stores because of familiarity with the shelf location of the products purchased. Apart from this scene on-line customer feel inconvenience to relearn dozen of product location at a new store. Online environment must offer significant advantage to overcome shopper enteria and induce trial.

As some new retail format emerge in the market, and once Peapod gain enough customers, Peapod need to create extra warehouse to avoid the extra overhead because costing does a matter to go to the store and pick the product off the shelf. At the end of each shopping interaction Peapod's customer feedback can give a boost to institute a variety of changes and option.

Clearly, Peapod stands as testament to the power of new ideas in retailing. The service, which has about 15000 customers has customer-retention rate of more than 80 per cent. However with competition heating up from their entrants Peapod has to find new way to be efficient in order to make money in low-margin business.

Some Online Marketing Company

Amazon.com

Amazon.com, Inc. (NASDAQ: AMZN) is an American-based multinational electronic commerce company. Headquartered in Seattle, Washington, it is America's largest online retailer, with nearly three times the Internet sales revenue of the runner up, Staples, Inc., as of January 2010.

Jeff Bezos founded Amazon.com, Inc. in 1994 and launched it online in 1995. It started as an online bookstore, but soon diversified to product lines of VHS, DVD, music CDs and MP3s, computer software, video games, electronics, apparel, furniture, food, toys, and so on. Amazon has established separate websites in Canada, the United Kingdom, Germany, France, Japan, and China. It also provides international shipping to certain countries for some of its products.

On January 15, 2009, a survey published by Verdict Research found that Amazon was the UK's favourite music and video retailer, and came third in overall retail rankings.

History

Amazon was founded in 1994, spurred by what Bezos called "regret minimization framework," his effort to fend off regret for not staking a claim in the Internet gold rush. While company lore says Bezos wrote the business plan while he and his wife drove from New York to Seattle, that account appears to be apocryphal. The company began as an online bookstore; while the largest brick-and-mortar bookstores and mail-order catalogs for books might offer 200,000 titles, an online bookstore could offer more. Bezos named the company "Amazon" after the world's largest river. Since 2000, Amazon's logotype is an arrow leading from A to Z, representing customer satisfaction (as it forms a smile); the goal was to have every product in the alphabet.

In 1994, the company incorporated in the state of Washington, beginning service in July 1995, and was reincorporated in 1996 in Delaware. The first book Amazon.com sold was Douglas Hofstadter's *Fluid Concepts and Creative Analogies: Computer Models of the Fundamental Mechanisms of Thought*. Amazon.com issued its initial public offering of stock on May 15, 1997, trading under the NASDAQ stock exchange symbol AMZN, at an IPO price of US$18.00 per share ($1.50 after three stock splits in the late 1990s).

Amazon's initial business plan was unusual: the company did not expect a profit for four to five years; the strategy was effective. Amazon grew steadily in the late 1990s while other Internet companies grew blindingly fast. Amazon's "slow" growth provoked stockholder complaints: that the company was not reaching profitability fast enough. When the dot-com bubble burst, and many e-companies went out of business, Amazon persevered, and finally turned its first profit in the fourth quarter of 2001: $5 million, just 1¢ per share, on revenues of more than $1 billion, but the profit was symbolically important.

In 1999, *Time* magazine named Bezos Person of the Year, recognizing the company's success in popularizing online shopping.

Merchant Partnerships

The Web site CDNOW is powered and hosted by Amazon. Until June 30, 2006, typing ToysRUs.com into a browser would similarly bring up Amazon.com's Toys & Games tab; however, this relationship was terminated as the result of a lawsuit. Amazon also used to host and run the website for Borders bookstores, but this ceased in 2008.

Amazon.com powers and operates retail web sites for Target, Sears Canada, Benefit Cosmetics, bebe Stores, Timex Corporation, Marks & Spencer, Mothercare, and Lacoste. For a growing number of enterprise clients, currently including the UK merchants Marks & Spencer, Benefit Cosmetics' UK entity, and Mothercare, Amazon provides a unified multichannel platform where a customer can seamlessly interact with the retail website, standalone in-store terminals, or phone-based customer service agents. Amazon Web Services also powers AOL's Shop@AOL.

Business Results

The company remains profitable: net income was $35.3 million in 2003, $588.50 million in 2004, $359 million in 2005, and $190 million in 2006 (including a $662 million charge for R&D in 2006). The firm's retained earnings were negative $1.8 billion in 2006, negative $1.4 billion in 2007, negative $730 million in 2008, and $172 million in 2009. Revenues increased thanks to product diversification and an international presence: $3.9 billion in 2002, $5.3 billion in 2003, $6.9 billion in 2004, $8.5 billion in 2005, and $10.7 billion in 2006.

On November 21, 2005, Amazon entered the S&P 500 index, replacing AT&T after it merged with SBC Communications. On December 31, 2008, Amazon entered the S&P 100 index, replacing Merrill Lynch after it was taken over by Bank of America. As of March 26,2010, Amazon has a higher market cap than that of Target, Home Depot, Costco, Barnes and Noble, and Best Buy, only lagging that of Walmart among American brick and mortar retailers.

Locations

Amazon.com has offices, fulfillment centres, customer service centres and software development centres across North America, Latin America, Europe and Asia.

Headquarters

The company's global headquarters are located on Seattle's Beacon Hill. It has offices throughout other parts of greater Seattle, including Union Station and The Columbia Centre.

Amazon has announced plans to move its headquarters to the South Lake Union neighborhood of Seattle beginning in mid-2010, with full occupancy by 2011. This move will consolidate all Seattle employees onto the new 11-building campus.

Software Development Centres

The company employs software developers in medium-to large-sized centres across the globe. While much of Amazon's software development is in Seattle, other locations include:

- Slough (United Kingdom)
- Edinburgh (United Kingdom)
- Dublin (Ireland)
- Bangalore, Chennai, and Hyderabad (India)
- Cape Town (South Africa)

- Shibuya, Tokyo (Japan)
- Beijing (China)
- Tempe, Arizona (United States).

Fulfillment and Warehousing

Fulfillment centres are located in the following cities, often near airports. Amazon offers warehousing and order-fulfillment for third-party sellers including large companies such as Target Corporation:

- North America:
- Arizona, USA: Phoenix, Goodyear
- Delaware, USA: New Castle
- Indiana, USA: Whitestown and Plainfield
- Kansas, USA: Coffeyville
- Kentucky, USA: Campbellsville, Hebron (near CVG), Lexington, and Louisville
- Nevada, USA: Fernley and North Las Vegas
- New Hampshire, USA: Nashua
- Pennsylvania, USA: Carlisle, Chambersburg, Hazleton, Allentown, and Lewisberry
- Texas, USA: Dallas/Fort Worth
- Virginia, USA: Sterling
- Ontario, Canada: Mississauga (a Canada Post facility).

In March 2009, Amazon announced plans to close three U.S. distribution centres: Red Rock, Nevada; Chambersburg, Pennsylvania; and Munster, Indiana.

Europe

- Bedfordshire, England: Marston Gate, near Brogborough
- Inverclyde, Scotland: Gourock
- Fife, Scotland: Glenrothes
- Swansea, Wales: Crymlyn Burrows near Jersey Marine
- Loiret, France: Orleans-Boigny (2000)
- Loiret, France: Orleans-Saran (2007)
- Hessen, Germany: Bad Hersfeld
- Saxony, Germany: Leipzig.

Asia

- Ichikawa, Chiba, Japan
- Yachiyo, Chiba, Japan

- Sakai, Osaka, Japan
- Guangzhou, China
- Suzhou, China
- Beijing, China.

Product Lines

Amazon has steadily branched into retail sales of music CDs, videotapes and DVDs, software, consumer electronics, kitchen items, tools, lawn and garden items, toys & games, baby products, apparel, sporting goods, gourmet food, jewelry, watches, health and personal-care items, beauty products, musical instruments, clothing, industrial & scientific supplies, groceries, and more.

The company launched Amazon.com Auctions, its own Web auctions service, in March 1999. However, it failed to chip away at industry pioneer eBay's juggernaut growth. Amazon.com Auctions was followed by the launch of a fixed-price marketplace business called zShops in September 1999, and a failed Sotheby's/Amazon partnership called *sothebys.amazon.com* in November.

Amazon no longer mentions either Auctions or zShops on its main pages and the help page for sellers now only mentions the Marketplace. Old links to zShops now simply redirect to the Amazon home page, while old links to Auctions take users to a transactions history page. New product listings are no longer possible for either service.

Although zShops failed to live up to its expectations, it laid the groundwork for the hugely successful Amazon Marketplace service launched in 2001 that let customers sell used books, CDs, DVDs, and other products alongside new items. Today, Amazon Marketplace's main rival is eBay's Half.com service.

Beginning August 2005, Amazon began selling products under its own private label, "Pinzon"; the initial trademark applications suggested the company intended to focus on textiles, kitchen utensils, and other household goods. In March 2007, the company applied to expand the trademark to cover a larger and more diverse list of goods, and to register a new design consisting of the "word PINZON in stylized letters with a notched letter O whose space appears at the "one o'clock" position.". The list of products registered for coverage by the trademark grew to include items such as paints, carpets, wallpaper, hair accessories, clothing, footwear, headgear, cleaning products, and jewelry. On September 2008], Amazon filed to have the name registered. While the USPTO has finished its review of the application, Amazon has yet to receive an official registration for the name.

On May 16, 2007 Amazon announced its intention to launch Amazon MP3, its own online music store. The store launched in the US in public beta September 25, 2007, selling downloads exclusively in MP3 format without digital rights management. This is especially notable as it was the first online offering of DRM-free music from all four major record companies.

In August 2007, Amazon announced Amazon Fresh, a grocery service offering perishable and nonperishable foods. Customers can have orders delivered to their homes at dawn or during a specified daytime window. Delivery was initially restricted to residents of Mercer Island, Washington, and was later expanded to several ZIP codes in Seattle proper. Amazon Fresh also operated pick-up locations in the suburbs of Bellevue and Kirkland from summer 2007 through early 2008.

In 2008 Amazon expanded into film production and is currently funding the film *The Stolen Child* with 20th Century Fox.

Website

The domain *amazon.com* attracted at least 615 million visitors annually by 2008 according to a Compete.com survey. This was twice the numbers of *walmart.com*. According to the Internet audience measurement website Compete.com, Amazon attracts approximately 50 million U.S. consumers to its website on a monthly basis.

Reviews

Amazon allows users to submit reviews to the web page of each product. As part of their review, users must rate the product on a rating scale from one to five stars. In 2004 a software error accidentally showed the names behind reviews that were submitted anonymously, and some authors were shown to have written glowing reviews of their own books. Amazon created a feature in recent years that allowed users to comment on reviews. Amazon provides an optional badging option for reviewers which indicate the real name of the reviewer (based on confirmation of a credit card account) or which indicate that the reviewer is one of the top reviewers by popularity. The U.S. site generally has the most reviews. A review posted on one site is not necessarily visible on another site.

Amazon.com's customer reviews are monitored for all negative or indecent comments that are directed at anything, or anyone, but the product itself. In regards to the reviews lacking relative restrictions, Robert Spector, who is the author of the book *Amazon.com*, describes how "when publishers and authors asked Bezos why Amazon.com would publish negative reviews, he defended the practice by claiming that Amazon.com was 'taking a different approach...we want to make every book available – the good, the bad, and the ugly...to let truth loose'" (Spector 132). Reviews for different media of the same product are grouped together (for example, the review page for a particular film, whether on VHS, Blu-Ray, or DVD, will feature reviews from all three media formats). Currently, there is no way to look at reviews only for one version of a product.

Content Search

"Search Inside the Book" is a feature which allows customers to search for keywords in the full text of many books in the catalog. The feature started with 120,000 titles (or 33 million pages of text) on October 23, 2003. There are currently about 250,000 books in the program. Amazon has cooperated with around 130 publishers to allow users to perform these searches.

To avoid copyright violations, Amazon.com does not return the computer-readable text of the book. Instead, it returns a picture of the matching page, disables printing, and puts limits on the number of pages in a book a single user can access. One author observed that his entire book could be read online by searching a few words. Additionally, customers can purchase online access to the some books via the "Amazon Upgrade" program, although the selection is currently quite limited.

Third-party Sellers

According to information in Amazon.com discussion forums, Amazon derives about 40 percent of its sales from affiliates whom they call Associates and third-party sellers who list and sell products on the Amazon websites. Associates receive a commission for referring customers to Amazon by placing links on their websites to the Amazon homepage or to specific products. If a referral results in a sale, the Associate receives a commission from Amazon. Worldwide, Amazon has "over 900,000 members" in its affiliate programs. Associates can access the Amazon catalog directly on their websites by using the Amazon Web Services (AWS) XML service. A new affiliate product, aStore, allows Associates to embed a subset of Amazon products within, or linked to from, another website.

Amazon reported over 1.3 million sellers sold products through Amazon's World Wide Web sites in 2007. Selling on Amazon has become more popular as Amazon expanded into a variety of categories beyond media and built a variety of features to support volume selling. Unlike eBay, Amazon sellers do not have to maintain separate payment accounts; all payments and payment security are handled by Amazon itself.

Acquisitions and Spinoffs

- In April 1998, Amazon bought the Internet Movie Database (IMDb).
- In August 1998, Amazon bought Cambridge, Massachusetts-based Planet All for 800,000 shares of Amazon stock. Planet All operated a web-based address book, calendar, and reminder service. In the same deal, Amazon acquired Sunnyvale-based Junglee.com, an XML-based data mining startup for 1.6 million shares of Amazon stock. The two deals together were valued at about $280 million at the time.
- In June 1999, Amazon bought Alexa Internet, Accept.com, and Exchange.com in a set of stock deals worth approximately $645 million.
- In 2003, Amazon purchased the rival online music retailer CD Now.
- In 2004, Amazon purchased Joyo.com, a Chinese e-commerce website. It also debuted A9.com, a company focused on researching and building innovative technology.
- In March 2005, Amazon acquired BookSurge, a print on demand company, and Mobipocket.com, an eBook software company.
- On July 30, 2007, the National Archives announced that it would make thousands of historic films available for purchase through Create Space.
- In February 2006, Amazon acquired Shopbop, a Madison, Wisconsin-based retailer of designer clothing and accessories for women.
- In May 2007, Amazon acquired dpreview.com, a London-based digital photography review website created by Phil Askey as his personal hobby website and Brilliance Audio, the largest independent publisher of audiobooks in the United States.
- In January 2007 created Endless.com, a separate e-commerce brand focusing on shoes.
- In January 2008, Amazon announced that it would acquire audiobook provider Audible.com for $300 million in cash.
- In June 2008, Amazon announced that it had acquired Fabric.com, an online fabric store.
- In July 2008, Amazon's IMDb subsidiary purchased Box Office Mojo, a site that tracks movie sales in theatres.

- In August 2008, Amazon announced it had an agreement to purchase Victoria, B.C. based Abe Books, seller of new, used, out-of-print and rare books. Later that month Amazon announced that it would acquire Seattle-based Shelfari, a book-based social network site, for an undisclosed sum. As part of its acquisition of Abe Books Amazon also got an additional stake in Shelfari's competitor Library Thing, which Abe Books had previously purchased a 40 percent stake in, and whole ownership of Bookfinder.com, Gojaba.com, and listing-management service FillZ, all owned by Abe Books at the time of acquisition.
- In October 2008 acquired Reflexive Entertainment, a casual video game development company.
- In July 2009 Amazon agreed to acquire Zappos, an online shoe and apparel retailer. The deal is expected to close in fall 2009.
- In January 2010 is said to buy Touchco·

Products and Services

Amazon.com has incorporated a number of products and services into its shopping model, either through development or acquisition. The Honor System was originally launched in 2001 to allow customers to make donations or buy digital content, with Amazon collecting 2.9 percent of the payment plus a flat fee of 30¢. The service was discontinued on December 11, 2008. It has been superseded by Amazon Payments. Amazon launched Amazon Web Services (AWS) in 2002. The service provides programmatic access to many features leveraged behind the scenes on its website. Amazon also created "channels" to benefit certain causes.

In 2004, Amazon's "Presidential Candidates" allowed customers to donate $5–200 to the campaigns of 2004 U.S. presidential hopefuls. Amazon has periodically reactivated a Red Cross donation channel after such tragedies as 9/11 and Hurricane Katrina. After the 2004 earthquake and tsunami in the Indian Ocean, Amazon set up an online donation channel to the American Red Cross, waiving its processing fee. By January 2005, nearly 200,000 individuals had donated over $15.7 million in the US alone.

Amazon Prime offers customers unlimited expedited shipping with no minimum purchase amount for a flat annual fee. The service also offers discounted priority shipping rates. Amazon launched the program in the continental United States in 2005, in Japan in June 2007, in the United Kingdom and Germany in November 2007, and in France (as

"Amazon Premium") in October 2008. Launched in 2005, Amazon Shorts offers exclusive short form content, including short stories and nonfiction pieces from best-selling authors, all available for immediate download at 49¢. As of June 2007, the program has over 1,700 pieces and is adding about 50 new pieces per week. In November 2005, Amazon.com began testing Amazon Mechanical Turk, an application programming interface (API) allowing programs to dispatch tasks to human processors. In March 2006, Amazon launched an online storage service called Amazon Simple Storage Service (Amazon S3). An unlimited number of data objects, from 1 byte to 5 gigabytes in size, can be stored in S3 and distributed via HTTP or BitTorrent. The service charges monthly fees for data stored and for data transferred. In April 2006, Amazon introduced Amazon Simple Queue Service (Amazon SQS), a distributed queue messaging service. In August 2006, Amazon launched product wikis (later folded into Amapedia) and discussion forums for certain products using guidelines that follow standard message board conventions. In August 2006, Amazon introduced Amazon Elastic Compute Cloud (Amazon EC2), a virtual site farm, allowing users to use the Amazon infrastructure with its high reliability to run diverse applications ranging from running simulations to web hosting. In 2008, Amazon improved the service adding Elastic Block Store (EBS), offering persistent storage for Amazon EC2 instances and Elastic IP addresses, static IP addresses designed for dynamic cloud computing.

In January 2007 Amazon launched Amapedia, a collaborative wiki for user-generated content to replace ProductWiki. In March 2007, Amazon launched an online video on demand service, Amazon Unbox. In September 2007, Amazon launched a new music store (currently in beta) called Amazon MP3, which sells downloadable tracks, all in the MP3 format and most recorded at 256 kilobits per second variable bitrate (VBR). Amazon's terms of use agreements legally restrict use of the music, but Amazon does not use DRM to enforce those terms: Amazon MP3 sells music from the Big 4 record labels: EMI, Universal, Warner Bros. Records, and Sony BMG, as well as many independents. Previous to the launch of this service, Amazon made an investment in Amie Street, a similar music store with a variable pricing model based on demand. In August 2007 Amazon launched Amazon Vine, which allows top product reviewers free access to pre-release products from vendors participating in the program. Reviewers may either return the used product to Amazon, or post a review and keep the product, within a few months of receipt. In August 2007 Amazon launched a payment service specifically targeted at developers called Flexible

Payment Service FPS. Amazon FPS has facilities for developing many different charging models including micro-payments. The service also gives developers easy access to Amazon customers.

In November 2007, Amazon launched Amazon Kindle, an e-book reader which downloads content over "Whispernet", a free EV-DO wireless service on the Sprint Nextel network. The screen uses E Ink technology to reduce battery consumption. In 2008 Amazon claimed its library had grown to 200,000 titles. In December 2007, Amazon introduced SimpleDB, a database system, allowing users of its other infrastructure to utilize a high reliability high performance database system. In August 2007, Amazon launched an invitation-only beta-test for online grocery delivery. It has since rolled out in several Seattle, Washington suburbs.

In January 2008 Amazon announced they would be rolling out their MP3 service to their subsidiary websites worldwide throughout the year. On December 1, 2008, Amazon MP3 was made available in the UK. At the beginning of September, IMDB and Amazon.com launched a Music metadata browsing site with wiki-like user contribution. In November, Amazon partnered with manufacturers including Fisher-Price, Mattel, Microsoft and electronics manufacturer Transcend to offer products in minimal packaging. This reduces environmental impact of the packaging and frustration with opening "clamshell" type security packaging. Amazon Web Services launched a public beta of Amazon Elastic Compute Cloud running Microsoft Windows Server and Microsoft SQL Server. Amazon Connect enables authors to post remarks on their book pages to customers who have bought their books. WebStore by Amazon allows businesses to create e-commerce websites using Amazon technology. Merchants can customize their sites using their own photos and branding. Sellers pay a commission of 7 percent, which includes credit-card processing fees and fraud protection, and a subscription fee of $59.95/month for an unlimited number of webstores and listings.

Controversies

Competition

The company has been controversial for its alleged use of patents as a competitive hindrance. The "1-click patent" is perhaps the best-known example of this. Amazon's use of the one-click patent against competitor Barnes and Noble's website led the Free Software Foundation to announce a boycott of Amazon in December 1999. The boycott was discontinued in September 2002. On February 22, 2000, the company was granted a patent covering an Internet-based customer referral system, or what is commonly called an "affiliate program". Reaction was swift and negative. Industry leaders Tim O'Reilly and Charlie Jackson spoke out against the patent, and O'Reilly published an open letter to Bezos protesting the 1-click patent and the affiliate program patent, and petitioning him to "avoid any attempts to limit the further development of Internet commerce". O'Reilly collected 10,000 signatures with this petition. Bezos responded with his own open letter. The protest ended with O'Reilly and Bezos visiting Washington, D.C. to lobby for patent reform. On February 25, 2003, the company was granted a patent titled "Method and system for conducting a discussion relating to an item on Internet discussion boards". On May 12, 2006, the USPTO ordered a re-examination of the "One-Click" patent, based on a request filed by Peter Calveley, who cited as prior art an earlier e-commerce patent and the Digicash electronic cash system.

Amazon has a Canadian site in both English and French, but is prevented from operating any headquarters, servers, fulfillment centres or call centres in Canada by that country's legal restrictions on foreign-owned booksellers. Instead, Amazon's Canadian site originates in the United States, and Amazon has an agreement with Canada Post to handle distribution within Canada and for the use of the Crown corporation's Mississauga, Ontario shipping facility. The launch of Amazon.ca generated controversy in Canada. In 2002, the Canadian Booksellers Association and Indigo Books and Music sought a court ruling that Amazon's partnership with Canada Post represented an attempt to circumvent Canadian law, but the litigation was dropped in 2004.

In March 2008, sales representatives of Amazon's Book Surge division started contacting publishers of print on demand titles to inform them that for Amazon to continue selling their POD-produced books, they were required to sign agreements with Amazon's own BookSurge POD company. Publishers were told that eventually, the only POD titles that Amazon would be selling would be those printed by their own company, BookSurge. Some publishers felt that this ultimatum amounted to monopoly abuse, and questioned the ethics of the move and its legality under anti-trust law.

In 2008, Amazon UK came under criticism for attempting to prevent publishers from direct selling at discount from their own websites. Amazon's argument was that they should be able to pay the publishers based on the lower prices offered on their websites, rather than on the full RRP.

In June 2008 Amazon UK drew criticism in the British publishing community following their withdrawal from sale of key titles published by Hachette Livre UK. The withdrawal is apparently intended to put pressure on the publisher to provide levels of discount described by the trade as unreasonable. Curtis Brown's managing director Jonathan Lloyd was quoted in *The Bookseller* magazine as saying: "I think the entire industry of publishers, authors and agents are 100% behind [Hachette]. Someone has to draw a line in the sand. Publishers have given 1% a year away to retailers, so where does it stop? Using authors as a financial football is disgraceful."

Kindle Content Removal

In July 2009, *The New York Times* reported that Amazon.com deleted all customer copies of certain books published by Mobile Reference, including the books *1984* and *Animal Farm* from users' Kindles. This action was taken with neither prior notification nor specific permission of individual users. Customers did receive a refund of the purchase price and, later, an offer of an Amazon gift certificate or a cheque for $30.

Products Sold and not Sold

Amazon at one time carried two cockfighting magazines and two dog fighting videos although the Humane Society of the United States (HSUS) contends that the sale of these materials is a violation of U.S. Federal law. The Humane Society of the United States has filed a lawsuit against Amazon. A campaign to boycott Amazon purchases gained momentum in August 2007 after the much publicized dog fighting case involving NFL quarterback Michael Vick. On May 21, 2008, Marburger Publishing agreed to settle with the Humane Society by requesting that Amazon stop offering their magazine *The Game Cock* for subscription. The second magazine named in the Humane Society lawsuit, *The Feathered Warrior*, remains available. On April 12, 2009, it was revealed that some erotic, lesbian, gay, bisexual, transgender, feminist and politically liberal books were being excluded from Amazon's sales rankings. Various books and media were flagged as "Adult content" (including children's books, self-help books, non-fiction, and non-explicit fiction), with the result that works by established authors like E. M. Forster, Gore Vidal, Jeanette Winterson and D. H. Lawrence were now unranked. The change first received publicity on the blog of author Mark R. Probst, who reproduced an e-mail from Amazon customer service describing a policy of de-ranking "adult" material. However, Amazon later said that there was no policy of de-ranking LGBT material and blamed the change first on a "glitch" and then on "an embarrassing and ham-fisted cataloging error" that had affected 57,310 books.

In September 2009 it emerged that Amazon was selling defamatory MP3 music downloads falsely suggesting a well-known Premier League football manager was a child sex offender. Despite a campaign urging the retailer to withdraw the item, they refused to do so citing freedom of speech. The company was finally forced to withdraw the item when legal action was threatened. However, they continued to sell the item on their American, German and French websites.

Collection of Sales Tax

Amazon has been criticized for its refusal to collect sales taxes from consumers in states in which it does not have a physical presence, thus giving it an unfair advantage over brick-and-mortar retailers. In theory, such consumers should pay the equivalent amount in use tax directly to their state, however in reality few consumers do so. In 2008 New York passed a law that would force online retailers to collect sales taxes on shipments to New York State residents. Shortly after the law was signed, Amazon.com filed a complaint in the New York Supreme Court objecting to the law. The complaint wasn't based on whether instate customers should pay tax, but upon the long-standing practice of it being the responsibility of the customer to report the sales tax (known as use tax in this case) and not that of the out-of-state businesses. The lawsuit was tossed out of court in January, 2009, when New York State Supreme Court Justice Eileen Bransten stated "there is no basis upon which Amazon can prevail." Amazon has created wholly owned subsidiaries for parts of the company that are treated separately for tax matters, a legal technique called "entity isolation". For example, the subsidiary that developed the Kindle is in California, but because it doesn't sell the Kindle directly to consumers, Amazon's legal position is that it isn't required to collect sales taxes in California. In the company's financial report for the quarter ending September 30, 2009, the company told investors in its discussion of risk factors that the imposition of sales-tax collection by more states or Congress could "decrease our future sales."

Other

In 1999, the Amazon Bookstore Cooperative of Minneapolis, Minnesota sued Amazon.com for trademark infringement. The cooperative had been using the name "Amazon" since 1970, but reached an out-of-court agreement to share the name with the on-line retailer.

A 2004 glitch in Amazon.ca's review system temporarily revealed that many well-established authors were anonymously giving themselves glowing reviews, with some revealed to be anonymously giving "rival" authors terrible reviews. According to Amazon, those reviews have since been removed or made non-anonymous. In April 2009, *Business Week* magazine reported that Amazon.com was one of 25 US companies that paid the least US taxes. Amazon.com paid a 4.1 percent annual tax rate, far less than the standard 35 percent corporate rate, based on an analysis of the company's financial figures for 2005-2008. According to SEC filings, this rate was caused in part by lower tax rates for Amazon.com's international subsidiaries.

Amazon has opposed efforts by trade unions to organize in both the United States and the United Kingdom. In 2001, 850 employees in Seattle were laid off by Amazon.com after a unionization drive. The Washington Alliance of Technological Workers (Wash Tech) accused the company of violating union laws, and claimed Amazon managers subjected them to intimidation and heavy propaganda. Amazon denies any link between the unionization effort and the layoffs. Also in 2001, Amazon.co.uk hired a US management consultancy organization, The Burke Group, to assist in defeating a campaign by the Graphical, Paper and Media Union (GPMU, now part of Amicus) to achieve recognition in the Milton Keynes distribution depot. It was alleged that the company victimized or sacked four union members during the 2001 recognition drive and held a series of captive meetings with employees.

Following the announcement of the Apple iPad on January 27, 2010, Macmillan Publishers entered into a pricing dispute with Amazon.com regarding electronic publications. Macmillan asked Amazon to accept a new pricing scheme it had worked out with Apple, raising the price of e-books from $9.99 to $15. Amazon responded by pulling all Macmillan books, both electronic and physical, from their website (although affiliates selling the books were still listed). On January 31, 2010, Amazon "capitulated" to Macmillan's pricing request.

Entrepreneurship by Former Employees

A number of companies have been started and founded by former Amazon.com employees. This is despite a non-compete agreement Amazon employees must sign that prohibits starting a company with another Amazon employee.

- BankBazaar.com was founded by Arjun Shetty, a former Senior product manager at Amazon.com
- Evri was led by Neil Roseman, a former VP at Amazon.com.
- Foodista was founded by Barnaby Dorfman
- Hulu is led by Jason Kilar, a former SVP at Amazon.com.

- Jambool/Social Gold was co-founded by former Amazon engineers Vikas Gupta and Reza Hussein.
- Mind Bloom was founded by Brent Poole
- Quora was co-founded by ex-Amazon (and Facebook) engineer Charlie Cheever
- Teach Street was founded by Dave Schappell, an early Amazon.com product manager.
- Track Simple was founded by Jon Ingalls and Ajit Banerjee.
- Trusera was founded by Keith Schorsch, an early Amazonian.
- Twilio was founded by Jeff Lawson, an Amazon Technical Product Manager.
- Vittana was co-founded by Kushal Chakrabarti and Brett Witt.
- Pelago was co-founded by Jeff Holden, a former SVP at Amazon.com.
- Wikinvest was founded by Michael Sha.

eBay

eBay Inc. is an American Internet company that manages eBay.com, an online auction and shopping website in which people and businesses buy and sell a broad variety of goods and services worldwide.

The majority of the sales take place through a set-time auction format, but subsequent methods include a substantial segment of listings in the "Buy It Now" category.

In addition to its original U.S. website, eBay has established localized websites in thirty other countries. eBay Inc. also owns PayPal, StubHub, Kijiji, and other businesses.

Origins and History About Ebay/Ebay Motors

The online auction website was founded as Auction Web in San Jose, California, on September 3, 1995, by French-born Iranian computer programmer Pierre Omidyar as part of a larger personal site that included, among other things, Omidyar's own tongue-in-cheek tribute to the Ebola virus. The very first item sold on eBay was a broken laser pointer for $14.83. Astonished, Omidyar contacted the winning bidder to ask if he understood that the laser pointer was broken. In his responding email, the buyer explained: "I'm a collector of broken laser pointers." The frequently repeated story that eBay was founded to help Omidyar's fiancee trade Pez candy dispensers was fabricated by a public relations manager in 1997 to interest the media. This was revealed in Adam Cohen's 2002 book, *The Perfect Store*, and confirmed by eBay.

Chris Agarpao was hired as eBay's first employee and Jeffrey Skoll was hired as the first president of the company in early 1996. In November 1996, eBay entered into its first third-party licensing deal, with a company called Electronic Travel Auction to use Smart Market Technology to sell plane tickets and other travel products. Growth was phenomenal; in January 1997 the site hosted 2,000,000 auctions, compared with 250,000 during the whole of 1996. The company officially changed the name of its service from Auction Web to eBay in September 1997.

Originally, the site belonged to Echo Bay Technology Group, Omidyar's consulting firm. Omidyar had tried to register the domain name echobay.com, but found it already taken by the Echo Bay Mines, a gold mining company, so he shortened it to his second choice, *eBay.com*. (Echobay.com is now owned by Echobay Partners, Ltd., a private equity firm based in Nevis.)

In 1997, the company received approximately $5 million in funding from the venture capital firm Benchmark Capital.

Meg Whitman was hired as eBay President and CEO in March 1998. At the time, the company had 30 employees half a million users and revenues of $4.7 million in the United States. eBay went public on September 21, 1998, and both Omidyar and Skoll became instant billionaires. eBay's target share price of $18 was all but ignored as the price went to $53.50 on the first day of trading.

As the company expanded product categories beyond collectibles into almost any saleable item, business grew quickly. In February 2002, the company purchased IBazar, a similar European auction web site founded in 1995 and then bought PayPal on October 14, 2002.

In early 2008, the company had expanded worldwide, counted hundreds of millions of registered users, 15,000+ employees and revenues of almost $7.7 billion. After nearly ten years at eBay, Whitman made the decision to enter politics. On January 23, 2008 the company announced that Whitman would step down on March 31, 2008 and John Donahoe was selected to become President and CEO. Whitman remained on the Board of Directors and continued to advise Donahoe through 2008. In late 2009, eBay completed the sale of Skype for $2.75 Billion, but will still own 30% equity in the company.

Items

Millions of collectibles, decor, appliances, computers, furnishings, equipment, vehicles, and other miscellaneous items are listed, bought, or sold daily. In 2005, eBay launched its Business & Industrial category, breaking into the industrial surplus business. Some items are rare and valuable, while many others are dusty gizmos that would have been discarded if not for the thousands of eager bidders worldwide. Anything may be offered for sale as long as it is not illegal and does not violate the eBay Prohibited and Restricted Items policy. Services and intangibles can be sold, too. Large international companies, such as IBM, sell their newest products and offer services on eBay using competitive auctions and fixed-priced storefronts. Separate eBay sites such as eBay US and eBay UK allow the users to trade using the local currency. Software developers can create applications that integrate with eBay through the eBay API by joining the eBay Developers Program. In June 2005, there were more than 15,000 members in the eBay Developers Program, comprising a broad range of companies creating software applications to support eBay buyers and sellers as well as eBay Affiliates.

Controversy has arisen over certain items put up for bid. For instance, in late 1999, a man offered one of his kidneys for auction on eBay, attempting to profit from the potentially lucrative (and, in the United States, illegal) market for transplantable human organs. On other occasions, people and even entire towns have been listed, often as a joke or to garner free publicity. In general, the company removes auctions that violate its terms of service agreement.

PayPal-only Categories

Beginning in August 2007, eBay required listings in "Video Games" and "Health & Beauty" to accept its payment system PayPal and sellers could only accept PayPal for payments in the category "Video Games: Consoles". Starting January 10, 2008, eBay said sellers can only accept PayPal as payment for the categories "Computing > Software", "Consumer Electronics > MP3 Players", "Wholesale & Job Lots > Mobile & Home Phones", and "Business, Office & Industrial > Industrial Supply/MRO". eBay announced that starting in March 2008, eBay had added to this requirement that all sellers with fewer than 100 feedbacks must offer PayPal and no merchant account may be used as an alternative. This is in addition to the requirement that all sellers from the United Kingdom have to offer PayPal.

Further, and as noted below, it is a requirement to offer Paypal on all listings in Australia and the UK.

eBay Express

In April 2006, eBay opened its new eBay Express site, which is designed to work like a standard Internet shopping site for consumers with United States addresses. It closed in 2008. Selected eBay items were mirrored on eBay Express, where buyers shop using a shopping cart to purchase from multiple sellers. The UK version was launched to eBay members in mid-October 2006 but on January 29, 2008 eBay announced its intention to close the site. The German version, eBay Express Germany, was also opened in 2006 and closed in 2008.

Selling Manager Applications

At the 2008 eBay Developer's Conference, eBay announced the Selling Manager Applications program (SM Apps). The program allows approved developers to integrate their applications directly into the eBay.com interface. The applications created by developers are available for subscription by eBay members who also subscribe to Selling Manager.

eBay Specialty Sites

eBay maintains a number of specialty sites. eBay Pulse, for example, provides information about popular search terms, trends, and most-watched items. Other ebay Community Content includes the Discussion Boards, Groups, Answer Centre, Chat Rooms, and Reviews & Guides. eBay has a robust mobile offering, including SMS alerts, a WAP site, J2ME clients, and an Apple iPhone application available in certain markets. Best of eBay is a specialty site for finding the most-unusual items on the eBay site. Users can vote on and nominate listings that they find.

Auction Types

eBay offers several types of auctions.

- Auction-style listings allow the seller to offer one or more items for sale for a specified number of days. The seller can establish a reserve price.
- Fixed price format allows the seller to offer one or more items for sale at a *Buy It Now* price. Buyers who agree to pay that price win the auction immediately without submitting a bid.
- Fixed price format with best offer allows the seller to accept best offers. If a buyer submits a best offer, the seller either rejects or accepts the best offer. If the best offer is not satisfactory, a seller may submit a counter offer to the buyer. Best offer is not available for auction style listings. In addition, best offer is not available in every category. Sellers also meet specific requirements in order to sell with best offer.

Bidding

Auction-style Listings

Bidding on eBay's auction-style listings is called proxy bidding and is essentially equivalent to a Vickrey auction, with the following exceptions.

- The winning bidder pays the second-highest bid plus one bid increment amount (i.e., some small predefined amount relative to the bid size), instead of simply the second-highest bid. However, since the bid increment amounts are relatively insignificant compared to the bid size, they are not considered from a strategic standpoint.
- The current winning bid is not sealed, but instead is always displayed. However, at any given moment, the highest bidder's bid is not necessarily displayed, since this amount may be higher than the amount required to win the auction.

Example of Bidding on an Auction-style Listing

Suppose bidding for an item placed by Anne starts at $1.00 and that the bid increment amount in this price range is $.25. Khalid bids $3.00 for the item, and since no one else has bid yet, eBay displays that the current winner is Khalid, with a bid of $1.00, and that the minimum allowable bid is $1.25, which is equal to one bidding increment above the winning bid. Suppose then that Sanjeev bids $2.00 for the item. Since Khalid has already bid more than Sanjeev, eBay will display that the current winner is Khalid, with a bid of $2.25, which equals the second-highest bid ($2.00) plus the bid increment amount ($.25). Again, eBay will also display that the minimum allowable bid is $2.50, one bid increment above the winning bid. Suppose that Sanjeev bids again, this time at $2.75. Again, since Khalid's bid is higher than Sanjeev's, eBay will display that the current winning bidder is Khalid, with a bid of $3.00, which is equal to the second-highest bid ($2.75) plus the bid increment ($.25). eBay will also display that the minimum allowable bid is $3.25, one bidding increment above the current winning bid. Suppose Sanjeev bids one more time, at $10.00. Since Sanjeev's bid is now higher than Khalid's, eBay will display that the current winning bidder is Sanjeev, with a bid of $3.25, which is equal to the second-highest bid ($3.00) plus the bid increment ($.25). If Sanjeev were to win the auction, he would have to pay the amount equal to the winning bid ($3.25), even though his previous bid was much larger than that.

Seller Ratings

In 2007, eBay began using detailed seller ratings with four different categories. When leaving feedback, buyers are asked to rate the seller in each of these categories with a score of one to five stars, with five being the highest rating and one the lowest. Unlike the overall feedback rating, these ratings are anonymous; neither sellers nor other users learn how individual buyers rated the seller. The listings of sellers with a rating of 4.3 or below in any of the four rating categories appear lower in search results.

Profit and Transactions

eBay generates revenue from a number of fees. The eBay fee system is quite complex; there are fees to list a product (Insertion Fee) and fees when the product sells (Final Value Fee), plus several optional adornment fees, all based on various factors and scales. The U.S.-based eBay.com takes $0.10 to $4 (based on the opening price) for a basic listing without any adornments and 8.75% or less of the final price (as of May 2009). The UK based ebay.co.uk (ebay.co.uk offices) takes from GBP £0.15 to a maximum rate of GBP £3 per £100 for an ordinary listing and from 0.75 percent to 10% (writing as of June 2009) percent of the final price. Reduced FVF's are available to business registered customers. In addition, eBay now owns the PayPal payment system which has fees of its own. Under current U.S. law, a state cannot require sellers located outside the state to collect a sales tax, making deals more attractive to buyers. Although some state laws require purchasers to pay sales tax to their own states on out-of-state purchases, it is not a common practice. However, most sellers that operate as a full time business do follow state tax regulations on their eBay transactions. However for the tax called Value added tax (VAT), eBay requires sellers to include the VAT fees in their listing price and not as an add-on and thus eBay profits by collecting fees based on what governments tax for VAT.

The company's current business strategy includes increasing international trade. eBay has already expanded to over two dozen countries including China and India. The only places where expansion failed were Taiwan and Japan, where Yahoo! had a head start, and New Zealand where TradeMe, owned by the Fairfax media group is the dominant online auction website.

A more recent strategy involves the company increasingly leveraging the relationship between the eBay auction site and PayPal: The impact of driving buyers and sellers to use PayPal means not only does eBay turn buyers into clients (as a pure auction venue its clients used to be predominantly sellers) but for each new PayPal registration it achieves via the eBay auction site it also earns offsite revenue when the resulting PayPal account is used in non-eBay transactions. In its Q1 2008 results, total payment volume via PayPal increased 17 percent, but off the eBay auction site it was up 61 percent. eBay runs an affiliate program under the name eBay Partner Network. eBay affiliate marketers were originally paid a percentage of the eBay seller's transaction fees, with commissions ranging from 50% to 75% of the fees paid for an item purchased. In October 2009, eBay changed to an affiliate payout system that it calls Quality Click Pricing, in which affiliates are paid an amount determined by an undisclosed algorithm. The total earnings amount is then divided by the number of clicks the affiliate sent to eBay and is reported as Earnings Per Click, or EPC.

Acquisitions

Economics

As eBay is a huge, publicly visible market, it has created a great deal of interest from economists, who have used it to analyse many aspects of buying and selling behavior, auction formats, etc., and compare these with previous theoretical and empirical findings.

Controversy and Criticism

eBay has its share of controversy, including cases of fraud, its policy of requiring sellers to use PayPal, and concerns over forgeries and intellectual property violations in auction items.

Prohibited or Restricted Items

In its earliest days, eBay was essentially unregulated. However, as the site grew, it became necessary to restrict or forbid auctions for various items. Note that some of the restrictions relate to eBay.com (the U.S. site), while other restrictions apply to specific European sites (such as Nazi paraphernalia). Regional laws and regulations may apply to the seller or the buyer. Generally, if the sale or ownership of an item is regulated or prohibited by one or more states, eBay will not permit its listing. Among the hundred or so banned or restricted categories:

- Tobacco (tobacco-related items and collectibles are accepted.)
- Alcohol (alcohol-related collectibles, including sealed containers, as well as some wine sales by licensed sellers are allowed)
- Drugs and drug paraphernalia
- Nazi paraphernalia
- Bootleg recordings
- Firearms and ammunition, including any parts that could be used to assemble a firearm as well as (as of July 30, 2007) any firearm part that is required for the firing of a gun, including bullet tips, brass casings and shells, barrels, slides, cylinders, magazines, firing pins, trigger assemblies, etc. Crossbows and various types of knives are also forbidden.

- Police and Emergency Service vehicular warning equipment such as red or blue lights and sirens (antique or collectible items are exempt)
- Used underwear and dirty used clothing
- Forged, Illegal, Stolen, or Confidential Documents which include Passports, Social Security Cards, Drivers Licences, Voter Registration Cards, Birth Certificates, School Documents, Medical Records, Financial Information, Government License Plates, Government Classified Information, or CarFax documents. Any Item which is used to modify documents are restricted as well.
- Human parts and remains (with an exception for skeletons and skulls for scientific study, provided they are not Native American in origin)
- Live animals (with certain exceptions)
- Certain copyrighted works or trademarked items.
- Lock-picking tools, accessories, and practice locks fall into the category of burglar tools.
- Lottery tickets, sweepstakes tickets, or any other gambling items.
- Military hardware such as working weapons or explosives.
- Any items of a sexual nature must be listed in the Adult Only category, which prohibits:
  - Child Pornography
  - Obscene Materials including bestiality, necrophilia, rape, coprophilia, and incest
  - Pre-owned sex toys
  - Services including any sexual activity
  - Links to sites that contain prohibited items
  - Adult products that are delivered digitally
- Virtual items from massively multiplayer online games, restrictions which vary by country
- Non-physical items no longer can be sold through eBay. They can only be advertised through classified ads on eBay and do not get feedback.
- Ivory products.
- Teachers' edition textbooks

- Knives, other than cutlery, are prohibited in the UK following media pressure about the sale of items assessed by police to be 'illegal'
- Many other items are either wholly prohibited or restricted in some manner.

Unusual Sale Items

- In May 2006, the remains of U.S. Fort Montgomery, a stone fortification in upstate New York built in 1844, were put up for auction on eBay. The first auction ended on June 5, 2006, with a winning bid of $5,000,310. However, the sale was not completed, and the fort and lands surrounding it remain for sale and have been relisted on the site several times since.
- In February 2004, a scrapped F/A-18 Hornet fighter jet was listed on eBay by Mike Landa, of Landa and Associates, with a starting bid of $1,000,000. He was the legal owner of the plane after purchasing it from a scrap yard and also offered to have the plane restored for flying condition for a Buy It Now price of $9,000,000. Landa also told potential buyers that maintenance of the plane would cost roughly $40,000 a month for just 2 to 3 hours of flying time. The FBI told Landa that he could only sell the plane to an American citizen residing in the United States, and that the plane must not leave U.S. airspace. The auction ended without a sale.
- In December 2005, a brussels sprout cooked on Christmas Day was listed by "crazypavingpreacher" (Andrew Henderson of Darlington, England). It sold for £99.50 on 4 January 2006. The sprout had been frozen and was sent by first class post in insulated packaging to the buyer, "5077phil". The listing was reported in the Daily Star, making the front page (and was followed by a series of "copycat" listings of various vegetables). The proceeds of the sale were donated to Tearfund, a major Christian relief and development agency working in the third world. This sprout was the first cooked brussels sprout to be sold on eBay.
- In January 2006, a British man named Leigh Knight sold an unwanted brussels sprout left over from his Christmas dinner for £1550 in aid of cancer research.
- In May 2006, a Chinese businessman named Zhang Cheng bought a former Czech Air Force MIG-21 fighter jet from a seller in the United States for $24,730. The seller, "inkgirle", refused to ship it. It is not known whether he was refunded.

- In June 2005, the wife of Tim Shaw, a British radio DJ on Kerrang! 105.2, sold Tim's Lotus Esprit sports car with a Buy It Now price of 50 pence after she heard him flirting with model Jodie Marsh on air. The car was sold within 5 minutes, and it was requested that the buyer pick it up the same day.
- In May 2005, a Volkswagen Golf that had previously been registered to Joseph Ratzinger (then a cardinal, who had since been elected pope and chose the regnal name Benedict XVI on April 19, 2005) was sold on eBay's German site for €188,938.88 ($277,171.12 USD). The winning bid was made by the GoldenPalace.com online casino, known for their outrageous eBay purchases.
- A seaworthy 16,000-ton aircraft carrier, formerly the British HMS *Vengeance*, was listed early in 2004. The auction was removed when eBay determined that the vessel qualified as ordnance, even though all weapons systems had been removed.
- Water that was said to have been left in a cup Elvis Presley once drank from was sold for $455. The few tablespoons came from a plastic cup Presley sipped at a concert in North Carolina in 1977.
- Coventry University student Bill Bennett got £1.20 for a single cornflake.
- A man from Brisbane, Australia, attempted to sell New Zealand at a starting price of $0.01AUD. The price had risen to $3,000 before eBay closed the auction.
- An Australian newspaper reported in December 2004 that a single piece of the Kellogg's breakfast cereal Nutri-Grain sold on eBay for AUD$1,035 because it happened to bear a slight resemblance to the character E.T. from the Steven Spielberg movie. Apparently the seller went on to make even more money in relation to the sale for his appearance on a nationally televised current affairs program.
- One of the tunnel boring machines involved in the construction of the Channel Tunnel was auctioned on eBay in 2004.
- A group of four men from Australia auctioned themselves to spend the weekend with the promise of "beers, snacks, good conversation and a hell of a lot of laughs" for AU$1,300
- Disney sold a retired Monorail Red (Mark IV Monorail) for $20,000

- The German Language Association sold the German language to call attention to the growing influence of English in modern German.
- In late November 2005, the original Hollywood Sign was sold on eBay for $450,400.
- In February 2007, after Britney Spears shaved all of her hair off in a Los Angeles salon, it was listed on eBay for 1 million USD before it was taken down.
- In September 2004, the Indiana Firebirds arena football team was auctioned off, first in a regular auction that failed to reach the reserve price, and again as a "Buy it Now" item for $3.9 million.
- Bridgeville, California was the first town to be sold on eBay in 2002, and has been up for sale 3 times since.
- In April 2005, American entrepreneur Matt Rouse sold the right to choose a new middle name for him. After receiving an $8,000 "Buy It Now" bid, the Utah courts refused to allow the name change. He currently still has his original middle name "Jean".
- In 2004, a partially eaten, 10-year-old grilled cheese sandwich said to bear the image of the Virgin Mary sold on eBay for $28,000.
- In January 2008, four golf balls were auctioned on eBay after being surgically removed from the carpet python which had inadvertently swallowed them whilst raiding eggs in a chicken enclosure. The story attracted considerable international attention and the balls eventually sold for more that AUD$1,400. The python recovered and was released.
- In May 2008, Paul Osborn of the UK listed his wife Sharon for sale on eBay, alleging that she had an affair with a coworker.
- In June 2008, Ian Usher put up his "entire life" on auction. The auction included his house in Perth, belongings, introduction to his friends, and a trial at his job. When bidding closed, his "life" sold for $384,000.
- In August 2008, Dr. Richard Harrington, Vice President of the UK Royal Entomological Society, announced that a fossilized aphid he bought for £20 from a seller in Lithuania, was a previously unknown species. It has been named *Mindarus harringtoni* after Dr. Harrington. He had wanted to name it *Mindarus ebayi*, but this name was disallowed as being too flippant. The 45-million-year-old aphid, preserved in a piece of Baltic amber, is now housed in the Natural History Museum in London.

- In October 2008, amidst the 2008–2009 Icelandic financial crisis one seller had put up Iceland for sale. Auction started with 99 pence but had reached 10 million pounds (US $17.28 million). However, singer Björk was "not included" in the sale. The notice read *Located in the mid-Atlantic ridge in the North Atlantic Ocean, Iceland will provide the winning bidder with — a habitable environment, Icelandic Horses and admittedly a somewhat sketchy financial situation.* Bidders' questions included: "Do you offer volcano/earthquake insurance?"
- In November 2008, a Swedish man put a digitally hand-drawn picture of a 7-legged spider onto eBay. The picture stemmed from an article on the site 27bslash6.com wherein David Thorne claims to have attempted to pay a chiropractor's bill with a picture of a 7-legged spider, which he valued at $233.95. On eBay, the bidding price started at $233.95, with bidding ended at a sale price of US$10,000. Both the e-mail exchange and the picture have become internet hits.
- In July 2009 Dornoch Capital Advisors placed England's Coca Cola League One Side Tranmere Rovers F.C. on eBay without permission for them to do so from owner and chairman Peter Johnson. This led to Johnson issuing a statement on the team's website saying that the team was not for sale and that he had contacted eBay to have the listing removed.
- In August 2009, a mother of six from South Arkansas auctioned off the legal rights to name her unborn child.
- In December 2009, a woman auctioned the copyright for a never before seen four-minute home video of Marilyn Monroe smoking a joint.

Charity Auctions

Using Mission Fish as an arbiter, eBay allows sellers to donate a portion of their auction proceeds to a charity of the seller's choice. The program is called eBay Giving Works in the US, and eBay for Charity in the UK. eBay provides a partial refund of seller fees for items sold through charity auctions. As of March 4, 2010, $154 million has been raised for U.S. nonprofits by the eBay Community since eBay Giving Works began in 2003. Some high-profile charity auctions have been advertised on the eBay home page, and have raised large amounts of money in a short time. For example, a furniture manufacturer raised over $35,000 for Ronald McDonald House by auctioning off beds that had been signed by celebrities.

To date the highest successful bid on a single item for charity was for a letter sent to Mark P. Mays, CEO of Clear Channel (parent company of Premiere Radio Networks the production company that produces The Rush Limbaugh Show and Glenn Beck Program) by United States Senator Harry Reid and forty other Democratic senators, complaining about comments made by conservative talk show host Rush Limbaugh. The winning bid was $2,100,100, with 100 percent of the proceeds going to the Marine Corps-Law Enforcement Foundation, benefiting the education of children of men and women who have died serving in the armed forces. The winning bid was matched by Limbaugh in his largest charity donation to date.

In 2007, eBay Canada partnered with Montreal-based digital branding agency Cloud Raker to develop a campaign to raise money for Quebec's national children's hospital, Sainte-Justine. They aligned themselves with internet phenomenon Tetes a Claques to create an eBay auction based on popular T-A-C character Uncle Tom, an infomercial host who pitches absurd products. eBay and Cloud Raker reproduced Uncle Tom's imaginary products, The Body Toner Fly Swatter, The Willi Waller Potato Peeler, and the LCD Shovel and sold them online. In 6 weeks, they raised $15,000 for Hopital St-Justine with one fly swatter, one potato peeler, and one shovel, a world record. The Body Toner Fly Swatter sold for $8,600, the Willi Waller Potato Peeler sold for $3,550, and the LCD Shovel sold for $2,146.21.

Environmental Record

On May 8, 2008, eBay announced the opening of its newest building on the company's North Campus in San Jose, which is the first structure in the city to be built from the ground up to LEED Gold standards. The building, the first the company has built new in its 13-year existence, uses an array of 3,248 solar panels, spanning 60,000 square feet (5,600 m), and providing 650 kilowatts of power to eBay's campus. All told the array can supply the company with 15-18 percent of its total energy requirements, reducing the amount of greenhouse gases that would be produced to create that energy by other means. Solar City, the company responsible for designing the array, estimates that the solar panels installed on eBay's campus will prevent 37 million pounds of carbon dioxide from being released into the environment as a result of replaced power production over the next three decades. Creating an equivalent impact to remove the same amount of carbon dioxide from the atmosphere would require planting 322 acres (1.30 km^2) of trees. The design of the building also incorporates other elements to reduce its impact on the environment. The building is equipped with a lighting system that detects natural ambient light sources and automatically dims artificial lighting to save 39 percent of the power usually required to light an office building. eBay's newest building also reduces demand on local water supplies by incorporating an eco-friendly irrigation system, low-flow shower heads, and low-flow faucets. Even during construction, more than 75 percent of the waste from construction was recycled. eBay also runs buses between San Francisco and the San Jose campus to reduce the number of commuting employees.

Craigslist

In the summer of 2004, eBay acknowledged that it had acquired 25% of classified listings website, Craigslist. Former Craigslist executive Phillip Knowlton was the seller, and he insisted that his former employer was aware of his plans to divest his holdings. Initially, eBay assured Craigslist that they would not ask the company to change the way it does business. eBay spokesman Hani Durzy stated that the "investment was really for learning purposes; it gives us access to learn how the classified market online works."

The classifieds service Kijiji was launched by eBay in March 2005. In April 2008, eBay sued Craigslist to "safeguard its four-year financial investment", claiming that in January 2008, Craigslist took actions that "unfairly diluted eBay's economic interest by more than 10%." Craigslist countersued in May 2008 "to remedy the substantial and ongoing harm to fair competition" that Craigslist claims is constituted by eBay's actions as a Craigslist shareholder. The case will be tried in Delaware and is scheduled for late June, 2009.

Overstock.com

Overstock.com (NASDAQ: OSTK) is an online retailer headquartered in Cottonwood Heights, Utah, near Salt Lake City. Founded in 1997 by Robert Brazell, under the name D2: Discounts Direct, it pioneered the online sale of surplus merchandise. It now features a combination of surplus, returned, and new items.

After Discounts Direct declared bankruptcy in 1999, the company was purchased and relaunched as Overstock.com by Patrick M. Byrne. Overstock.com then began selling surplus and returned merchandise on an online E-commerce marketplace, buying the surplus inventory of at least 18 failed dot-com companies at below-wholesale prices. In recent years it has expanded to sell new merchandise. Overstock went public in May 2002 at an IPO price of $13. After achieving significant growth and profits in some early quarters, the company's stock traded as high as $77, but following recent losses the company has traded as low as single digits. Its major rivals are thought to be Amazon.com and eBay.

Business Model

Part of Overstock.com's merchandise is purchased by or manufactured specifically for Overstock.com. Among their products are handmade goods produced for Overstock by workers in developing nations. The company also manages the inventory supply for other retailers. In addition to its direct retail sales, Overstock.com has also offered online auctions on its website since September 24, 2004.

After initially relying solely on word-of-mouth marketing from customers, the company turned to distinctive television advertisements starring German actress Sabine Ehrenfeld. Newer advertisements feature Briana Walker.

Since 1999, when Byrne took control and relaunched the company as Overstock the company has never achieved an annual profit, losing $240 million. Byrne projected in May 2008 that Overstock would be profitable in the fourth quarter of 2008, and would achieve a $10 million profit. The company indeed was profitable in Q4/2008, but resumed making losses in Q1 and Q2/2009.

Naked Short Selling Campaign

The company has received attention stemming from CEO Patrick Byrne's battle against alleged naked short selling of his company's shares. Beginning in 2005, Byrne has contended that a number of companies, including Overstock.com, have been the targets of this practice, which involves selling a stock short but without the usual step of initially borrowing or locating the shares. Byrne alleges that the practice circumvents safeguards of conventional shorting, and has been used in large schemes devised to profit from driving down the prices of companies' shares, in many cases leading to these companies' failure. With Overstock, Byrne contends that the company's longstanding appearance on the Regulation SHO Threshold Security list, an SEC-mandated list showing companies with a high number of "fails to deliver," along with high trading volumes that sometimes surpass total quantity of the company's stock, establish that it has been targeted by this practice.

Byrne's campaign has been controversial, including criticism in the financial press that Byrne is seeking to divert attention from Overstock's share price declines and failure to turn a profit. New York Times columnist Joseph Nocera has said in 2006 that, "Except for a few fellow-travelling Web sites, where Mr. Byrne is viewed as a heroic figure, most people who understand the issue or have looked into it think it's pretty bogus." Others have suggested that the problem is real, but that the SEC acts to prevent it and that it does not happen on any scale such as Byrne suggests. SEC Chairman Christopher Cox called abusive naked short selling "a fraud that the commission is bound to prevent and to punish."

Lawsuits

Overstock filed a lawsuit against the hedge fund Rocker Partners in 2005, for libel, unfair business practices and tortious interference, saying it colluded with a research firm, Gradient Analytics, in short-selling the company while paying Gradient Analytics to publish negative reports about Overstock.com and supplying pre-publication copies to Rocker. Naked short-selling was not alleged in that suit. In a conference call with analysts in August 2005, a day after the suit was filed, Byrne said that "there's been a plan since we were in our teens to destroy our stock, drive it down to $6—$10... and even a plan for how the company would then get whacked up." He said that the conspirators were part of a "Miscreants Ball," headed by a "Sith Lord," who he refused to identify but said "he's one of the master criminals from the 1980s." Byrne said the conspiracy included hedge funds, journalists, investigators, trial lawyers, the SEC, and Eliot Spitzer."

Rocker Partners, renamed Copper River Management, filed a counterclaim against Overstock in November 2007, alleging overstatement of profits, false projections, and misrepresentations about the company's ventures. Copper River also alleges that Byrne tried to silence critics by suing them. A portion of this suit was settled out of court on October 13, 2008, when Overstock.com and Gradient dropped the claims against each other after Gradient retracted allegations that Overstock's reporting methods did not comply with rules established by the FASB, stated they believed Overstock.com complied with GAAP standards, and that three directors were independent according to NASD standards, and apologized. Byrne has said the apology and settlement "represents a great step forward in our case", while Copper River's attorney stated that "If somehow this improved Overstock's case, then Gradient would admit to doing something wrong and they haven't.", and that he expected the settlement to help Copper River's case.

On Dec. 8, 2009, it was announced that Copper River had reached an out of court settlement with Overstock. As part of the agreement, Copper River, which closed in December 2008, agreed to pay Overstock $5 million. In a letter to his shareholders, Patrick Byrne said, "The good guys won". Copper River said in a statement that it continued to deny Overstock's allegations. Copper River managing general partner Marc Cohodes said "Although settlement deprives us of the ability to disprove Overstock's case and prosecute our counterclaims, we decided that the litigation costs did not justify passing up a practical way to end four-and-half years of meritless litigation by Overstock."

In February 2007, Overstock.com launched a $3.5 billion lawsuit against Morgan Stanley, Goldman Sachs and other large Wall Street firms, alleging a "massive illegal stock market manipulation scheme" involving naked short selling. Among its allegations, Overstock stated that since at least January 2005, naked short selling has accounted for large portions of Overstock stock, in some cases exceeding the 23.4 million total shares outstanding. The lawsuit alleged that this had created "immense downward pressure" on share prices over time. Kerry Fields, associate professor of law and business ethics at the University of Southern California, said, "Byrne may be able to help set new law if he handles this right." Fields said, Byrne's "best approach now is probably to persuade the SEC, which continues to wander around the issue, or the government to serve subpoenas and let them decide whether or not his company was wronged." However, Joseph Nocera criticized the lawsuit, while John Coffee, director of the Centre on Corporate Governance at Columbia University Law School, described it as overly ambitious and "extremely unpromising." Two members of the Overstock.com board of directors, John Fisher and Ray Groves, resigned in disagreement over the lawsuit.

SEC and Regulatory Action

A Securities and Exchange Commission investigation of Gradient Analytics was initiated but then dropped in February 2007. An SEC investigation of Overstock.com and Byrne, seeking information as to the company's accounting policies, targets, projections, and estimates relating to its financial performance, continued but was dropped in June 2008.

In July 2007, two American Stock Exchange options market makers were fined and suspended for using Regulation SHO exemptions to "impermissibly engage in naked short selling" in trades involving options and stocks for their own account. Overstock shares were believed to be among the stocks traded. The market makers settled without admitting or denying the allegations. None of the defendants sued by Overstock were named in the decision, but the Dow Jones News Service said that the decision was likely to be used by Byrne in pursuing his case.

New SEC Investigation and Auditor Dispute

On September 17, 2009, Reuters News Agency reported Overstock's announcement that the SEC is investigating its "history of financial restatements." The company completed an earlier investigation in 2008 without taking action. The new probe involved the financial restatements in 2006 and 2008 and "other matters".

In November 2009, the company took the unusual step of filing a quarterly financial statement not reviewed by an independent accounting firm, after firing its second auditor in nine months. Byrne defended the decision, and criticized the company's auditor, Grant Thornton, which had just been fired by Overstock prior to filing of the financial statement. The filing did not did not contain the certifications required under the Sarbanes-Oxley Act. The NASDAQ stock market notified Overstock on November 20 that it violated its market listing rule, and gave it until Jan. 18 to submit a plan to gain compliance. Overstock said it would hire an independent auditor to gain compliance. Grant Thornton subsequently became embroiled in a heated dispute with Overstock, with each accusing the other of not being truthful concerning the company's third quarter 2009 restatement.

Board of Directors

Overstock.com's current Board of Directors includes Patrick Byrne, Allison H. Abraham, Clay Corbus and Joseph J. Tabacco, Jr.

In July 2006, John J. Byrne, the father of Overstock's chief executive, resigned from the board of directors, after a public airing of the elder Byrne's unhappiness with his son's crusade against naked short-selling. In August 2008, Jack Byrne said that after "much initial skepticism" he believed his son was "right all along" about the battle and lawsuits with short-sellers and analysts.

In early 2007, John A. Fisher and Ray Groves resigned from the Overstock board of directors over disagreement with the company's prime broker suit.

On January 2, 2008, Overstock announced that cofounder Jason Lindsey had resigned as President, COO, and as a Director of Overstock effective from December 31, 2007. Byrne said Lindsey had "played a decisive role getting [Overstock] back on track" after "I screwed it up a couple years ago".

Overstock stock dropped to a four-year low following the announcement, which an analyst for investment bank Broadpoint Capital described as a "key loss".

Information Security

Information Security Components: or qualities, i.e., Confidentiality, Integrity and Availability (CIA). Information Systems are decomposed in three main portions, hardware, software and communications with the purpose to identify and apply information security industry standards, as mechanisms of protection and prevention, at three levels or layers: Physical, personal and organizational. Essentially, procedures or policies are implemented to tell people (administrators, users and operators)how to use products to ensure information security within the organizations. Information security means protecting information and information systems from unauthorized access, use, disclosure, disruption, modification or destruction.

The terms information security, computer security and information assurance are frequently incorrectly used interchangeably. These fields are interrelated often and share the common goals of protecting the confidentiality, integrity and availability of information; however, there are some subtle differences between them.

These differences lie primarily in the approach to the subject, the methodologies used, and the areas of concentration. Information security is concerned with the confidentiality, integrity and availability of data regardless of the form the data may take: electronic, print, or other forms.

Computer security can focus on ensuring the availability and correct operation of a computer system without concern for the information stored or processed by the computer.

Governments, military, corporations, financial institutions, hospitals, and private businesses amass a great deal of confidential information about their employees, customers, products, research, and financial status. Most of this information is now collected, processed and stored on electronic computers and transmitted across networks to other computers.

Should confidential information about a business' customers or finances or new product line fall into the hands of a competitor, such a breach of security could lead to lost business, law suits or even bankruptcy of the business. Protecting confidential information is a business requirement, and in many cases also an ethical and legal requirement. For the individual, information security has a significant effect on privacy, which is viewed very differently in different cultures.

The field of information security has grown and evolved significantly in recent years. As a career choice there are many ways of gaining entry into the field. It offers many areas for specialization including: securing network(s) and allied infrastructure, securing applications and databases, security testing, information systems auditing, business continuity planning and digital forensics science, to name a few. This article presents a general overview of information security and its core concepts.

History

Since the early days of writing, heads of state and military commanders understood that it was necessary to provide some mechanism to protect the confidentiality of written correspondence and to have some means of detecting tampering.

Julius Caesar is credited with the invention of the Caesar cipher c50 B.C., which was created in order to prevent his secret messages from being read should a message fall into the wrong hands.

World War II brought about many advancements in information security and marked the beginning of the professional field of information security.

The end of the 20th century and early years of the 21st century saw rapid advancements in telecommunications, computing hardware and software, and data encryption. The availability of smaller, more powerful and less expensive computing equipment made electronic data processing within the reach of small business and the home user. These computers quickly became interconnected through a network generically called the Internet or World Wide Web.

The rapid growth and widespread use of electronic data processing and electronic business conducted through the Internet, along with numerous occurrences of international terrorism, fueled the need for better methods of protecting the computers and the information they store, process and transmit. The academic disciplines of computer security, information security and information assurance emerged along with numerous professional organizations-all sharing the common goals of ensuring the security and reliability of information systems.

Basic Principles

Key Concepts

For over twenty years, information security has held confidentiality, integrity and availability (known as the CIA triad) as the core principles of information security. Many information security professionals firmly believe that Accountability should be added as a core principle of information security.

Confidentiality

Confidentiality is the term used to prevent the disclosure of information to unauthorized individuals or systems. For example, a credit card transaction on the Internet requires the credit card number to be transmitted from the buyer to the merchant and from the merchant to a transaction processing network. The system attempts to enforce confidentiality by encrypting the card number during transmission, by limiting the places where it might appear (in databases, log files, backups, printed receipts, and so on), and by restricting access to the places where it is stored. If an unauthorized party obtains the card number in any way, a breach of confidentiality has occurred.

Breaches of confidentiality take many forms. Permitting someone to look over your shoulder at your computer screen while you have confidential data displayed on it could be a breach of confidentiality. If a laptop computer containing sensitive information about a company's employees is stolen or sold, it could result in a breach of confidentiality. Giving out confidential information over the telephone is a breach of confidentiality if the caller is not authorized to have the information. Confidentiality is necessary (but not sufficient) for maintaining the privacy of the people whose personal information a system holds.

Integrity

In information security, integrity means that data cannot be modified without authorization. This is not the same thing as referential integrity in databases. Integrity is violated when an employee accidentally or with malicious intent deletes important data files, when a computer virus infects a computer, when an employee is able to modify his own salary in a payroll database, when an unauthorized user vandalizes a web site, when someone is able to cast a very large number of votes in an online poll, and so on. There are many ways in which integrity could be violated without malicious intent. In the simplest case, a user on a system could mis-type someone's address. On a larger scale, if an automated process is not written and tested correctly, bulk updates to a database could alter data in an incorrect way, leaving the integrity of the data compromised. Information security professionals are tasked with finding ways to implement controls that prevent errors of integrity.

Availability

For any information system to serve its purpose, the information must be available when it is needed. This means that the computing systems used to store and process the information, the security controls used to protect it, and the communication channels used to access it must be functioning correctly. High availability systems aim to remain available at all times, preventing service disruptions due to power outages, hardware failures, and system upgrades. Ensuring availability also involves preventing denial-of-service attacks. In 2002, Donn Parker proposed an alternative model for the classic CIA triad that he called the six atomic elements of information. The elements are confidentiality, possession, integrity, authenticity, availability, and utility. The merits of the Parkerian hexad are a subject of debate amongst security professionals.

Authenticity

In computing, e-Business and information security it is necessary to ensure that the data, transactions, communications or documents (electronic or physical) are genuine. It is also important for authenticity to validate that both parties involved are who they claim they are.

Non-repudiation

In law, non-repudiation implies one's intention to fulfill their obligations to a contract. It also implies that one party of a transaction cannot deny having received a transaction nor can the other party deny having sent a transaction.

Electronic commerce uses technology such as digital signatures and encryption to establish authenticity and non-repudiation.

Risk Management

A comprehensive treatment of the topic of risk management is beyond the scope of this article. However, a useful definition of risk management will be provided as well as some basic terminology and a commonly used process for risk management.

The CISA Review Manual 2006 provides the following definition of risk management: "Risk management is the process of identifying vulnerabilities and threats to the information resources used by an organization in achieving business objectives, and deciding what countermeasures, if any, to take in reducing risk to an acceptable level, based on the value of the information resource to the organization."

There are two things in this definition that may need some clarification. First, the *process* of risk management is an ongoing iterative process. It must be repeated indefinitely. The business environment is constantly changing and new threats and vulnerability emerge every day. Second, the choice of countermeasures (controls) used to manage risks must strike a balance between productivity, cost, effectiveness of the countermeasure, and the value of the informational asset being protected.

Risk is the likelihood that something bad will happen that causes harm to an informational asset (or the loss of the asset). A vulnerability is a weakness that could be used to endanger or cause harm to an informational asset. A threat is anything (man made or act of nature) that has the potential to cause harm.

The likelihood that a threat will use a vulnerability to cause harm creates a risk. When a threat does use a vulnerability to inflict harm, it has an impact. In the context of information security, the impact is a loss of availability, integrity, and confidentiality, and possibly other losses (lost income, loss of life, loss of real property). It should be pointed out that it is not possible to identify all risks, nor is it possible to eliminate all risk. The remaining risk is called *residual risk.*

A risk assessment is carried out by a team of people who have knowledge of specific areas of the business. Membership of the team may vary over time as different parts of the business are assessed. The assessment may use a subjective qualitative analysis based on informed opinion, or where reliable dollar figures and historical information is available, the analysis may use quantitative analysis. The ISO/IEC 27002:2005 Code of practice for information security management recommends the following be examined during a risk assessment:

- security policy,
- organization of information security,
- asset management,
- human resources security,
- physical and environmental security,
- communications and operations management,
- access control,
- information systems acquisition, development and maintenance,
- information security incident management,
- business continuity management, and
- regulatory compliance.

In broad terms the risk management process consists of:

1. Identification of assets and estimating their value. Include: people, buildings, hardware, software, data (electronic, print, other), supplies.

2. Conduct a threat assessment. Include: Acts of nature, acts of war, accidents, malicious acts originating from inside or outside the organization.
3. Conduct a vulnerability assessment, and for each vulnerability, calculate the probability that it will be exploited. Evaluate policies, procedures, standards, training, physical security, quality control, technical security.
4. Calculate the impact that each threat would have on each asset. Use qualitative analysis or quantitative analysis.
5. Identify, select and implement appropriate controls. Provide a proportional response. Consider productivity, cost effectiveness, and value of the asset.
6. Evaluate the effectiveness of the control measures. Ensure the controls provide the required cost effective protection without discernible loss of productivity.

For any given risk, Executive Management can choose to accept the risk based upon the relative low value of the asset, the relative low frequency of occurrence, and the relative low impact on the business. Or, leadership may choose to mitigate the risk by selecting and implementing appropriate control measures to reduce the risk. In some cases, the risk can be transferred to another business by buying insurance or out-sourcing to another business. The reality of some risks may be disputed. In such cases leadership may choose to deny the risk. This is itself a potential risk.

Controls

When Management chooses to mitigate a risk, they will do so by implementing one or more of three different types of controls.

Administrative

Administrative controls (also called procedural controls) consist of approved written policies, procedures, standards and guidelines. Administrative controls form the framework for running the business and managing people.

They inform people on how the business is to be run and how day to day operations are to be conducted. Laws and regulations created by government bodies are also a type of administrative control because they inform the business. Some industry sectors have policies, procedures, standards and guidelines that must be followed-the Payment Card Industry (PCI) Data Security Standard required by Visa and Master Card is such an example.

Other examples of administrative controls include the corporate security policy, password policy, hiring policies, and disciplinary policies. Administrative controls form the basis for the selection and implementation of logical and physical controls. Logical and physical controls are manifestations of administrative controls. Administrative controls are of paramount importance.

Logical

Logical controls (also called technical controls) use software and data to monitor and control access to information and computing systems. For example: passwords, network and host based firewalls, network intrusion detection systems, access control lists, and data encryption are logical controls.

An important logical control that is frequently overlooked is the principle of least privilege. The principle of least privilege requires that an individual, program or system process is not granted any more access privileges than are necessary to perform the task. A blatant example of the failure to adhere to the principle of least privilege is logging into Windows as user Administrator to read Email and surf the Web. Violations of this principle can also occur when an individual collects additional access privileges over time. This happens when employees' job duties change, or they are promoted to a new position, or they transfer to another department. The access privileges required by their new duties are frequently added onto their already existing access privileges which may no longer be necessary or appropriate.

Physical

Physical controls monitor and control the environment of the work place and computing facilities. They also monitor and control access to and from such facilities. For example: doors, locks, heating and air conditioning, smoke and fire alarms, fire suppression systems, cameras, barricades, fencing, security guards, cable locks, etc. Separating the network and work place into functional areas are also physical controls. An important physical control that is frequently overlooked is the separation of duties. Separation of duties ensures that an individual can not complete a critical task by himself. For example: an employee who submits a request for reimbursement should not also be able to authorize payment or print the check. An applications programmer should not also be the server administrator or the database administrator-these roles and responsibilities must be separated from one another.

Security Classification for Information

An important aspect of information security and risk management is recognizing the value of information and defining appropriate procedures and protection requirements for the information. Not all information is equal and so not all information requires the same degree of protection. This requires information to be assigned a security classification.

The first step in information classification is to identify a member of senior management as the owner of the particular information to be classified. Next, develop a classification policy. The policy should describe the different classification labels, define the criteria for information to be assigned a particular label, and list the required security controls for each classification.

Some factors that influence which classification information should be assigned include how much value that information has to the organization, how old the information is and whether or not the information has become obsolete. Laws and other regulatory requirements are also important considerations when classifying information.

The type of information security classification labels selected and used will depend on the nature of the organisation, with examples being:

- In the business sector, labels such as: Public, Sensitive, Private, Confidential.
- In the government sector, labels such as: Unclassified, Sensitive But Unclassified, Restricted, Confidential, Secret, Top Secret and their non-English equivalents.
- In cross-sectoral formations, the Traffic Light Protocol, which consists of: White, Green, Amber and Red.

All employees in the organization, as well as business partners, must be trained on the classification schema and understand the required security controls and handling procedures for each classification. The classification a particular information asset has been assigned should be reviewed periodically to ensure the classification is still appropriate for the information and to ensure the security controls required by the classification are in place.

Access Control

Access to protected information must be restricted to people who are authorized to access the information. The computer programs, and in many cases the computers that process the information, must also be authorized. This requires that mechanisms be in place to control the access to protected information. The sophistication of the access control mechanisms should be in parity with the value of the information being protected-the more sensitive or valuable the information the stronger the control mechanisms need to be. The foundation on which access control mechanisms are built start with identification and authentication.

Identification is an assertion of who someone is or what something is. If a person makes the statement *"Hello, my name is John Doe."* they are making a claim of who they are. However, their claim may or may not be true. Before John Doe can be granted access to protected information it will be necessary to verify that the person claiming to be John Doe really is John Doe.

Authentication is the act of verifying a claim of identity. When John Doe goes into a bank to make a withdrawal, he tells the bank teller he is John Doe (a claim of identity). The bank teller asks to see a photo ID, so he hands the teller his driver's license. The bank teller checks the license to make sure it has John Doe printed on it and compares the photograph on the license against the person claiming to be John Doe. If the photo and name match the person, then the teller has authenticated that John Doe is who he claimed to be.

There are three different types of information that can be used for authentication: something you know, something you have, or something you are. Examples of *something you know* include such things as a PIN, a password, or your mother's maiden name. Examples of *something you have* include a driver's license or a magnetic swipe card. *Something you are* refers to biometrics. Examples of biometrics include palm prints, finger prints, voice prints and retina (eye) scans. Strong authentication requires providing information from two of the three different types of authentication information. For example, something you know plus something you have. This is called two factor authentication.

On computer systems in use today, the Username is the most common form of identification and the Password is the most common form of authentication. Usernames and passwords have served their purpose but in our modern world they are no longer adequate. Usernames and passwords are slowly being replaced with more sophisticated authentication mechanisms.

After a person, program or computer has successfully been identified and authenticated then it must be determined what informational resources they are permitted to access and what actions they will be allowed to perform (run, view, create, delete, or change). This is called authorization.

Authorization to access information and other computing services begins with administrative policies and procedures. The policies prescribe what information and computing services can be accessed, by whom, and under what conditions. The access control mechanisms are then configured to enforce these policies.

Different computing systems are equipped with different kinds of access control mechanisms-some may even offer a choice of different access control mechanisms. The access control mechanism a system offers will be based upon one of three approaches to access control or it may be derived from a combination of the three approaches.

The non-discretionary approach consolidates all access control under a centralized administration. The access to information and other resources is usually based on the individuals function (role) in the organization or the tasks the individual must perform. The discretionary approach gives the creator or owner of the information resource the ability to control access to those resources. In the Mandatory access control approach, access is granted or denied basing upon the security classification assigned to the information resource.

Examples of common access control mechanisms in use today include Role-based access control available in many advanced Database Management Systems, simple file permissions provided in the UNIX and Windows operating systems, Group Policy Objects provided in Windows network systems, Kerberos, RADIUS, TACACS, and the simple access lists used in many firewalls and routers.

To be effective, policies and other security controls must be enforceable and upheld. Effective policies ensure that people are held accountable for their actions. All failed and successful authentication attempts must be logged, and all access to information must leave some type of audit trail.

Cryptography

Information security uses cryptography to transform usable information into a form that renders it unusable by anyone other than an authorized user; this process is called encryption. Information that has been encrypted (rendered unusable) can be transformed back into its original usable form by an authorized user, who possesses the cryptographic key, through the process of decryption. Cryptography is used in information security to protect information from unauthorized or accidental disclosure while the information is in transit (either electronically or physically) and while information is in storage.

Cryptography provides information security with other useful applications as well including improved authentication methods, message digests, digital signatures, non-repudiation, and encrypted network communications. Older less secure application such as telnet and ftp are slowly being replaced with more secure applications such as ssh that use encrypted network communications.

Wireless communications can be encrypted using the WPA or WEP protocols. Wired communications (such as ITU-T G.hn) are secured using AES for encryption and X.1035 for authentication and key exchange. Software applications such as GNUPG or PGP can be used to encrypt data files and Email.

Cryptography can introduce security problems when it is not implemented correctly. Cryptographic solutions need to be implemented using industry accepted solutions that have undergone rigorous peer review by independent experts in cryptography.

The length and strength of the encryption key is also an important consideration. A key that is weak or too short will produce weak encryption. The keys used for encryption and decryption must be protected with the same degree of rigor as any other confidential information. They must be protected from unauthorized disclosure and destruction and they must be available when needed. PKI solutions address many of the problems that surround key management.

Defence in Depth

Information security must protect information throughout the life span of the information, from the initial creation of the information on through to the final disposal of the information. The information must be protected while in motion and while at rest. During its life time, information may pass through many different information processing systems and through many different parts of information processing systems. There are many different ways the information and information systems can be threatened. To fully protect the information during its lifetime, each component of the information processing system must have its own protection mechanisms. The building up, layering on and overlapping of security measures is called defence in depth. The strength of any system is no greater than its weakest link. Using a defence in depth strategy, should one defensive measure fail there are other defensive measures in place that continue to provide protection.

Recall the earlier discussion about administrative controls, logical controls, and physical controls. The three types of controls can be used to form the basis upon which to build a defence-in-depth strategy. With this approach, defence-in-depth can be conceptualized as three distinct layers or planes laid one on top of the other. Additional insight into defence-in-depth can be gained by thinking of it as forming the layers of an onion, with data at the core of the onion, people as the outer layer of the onion, and network security, host-based security and application security forming the inner layers of the onion. Both perspectives are equally valid and each provides valuable insight into the implementation of a good defence-in-depth strategy.

Process

The terms reasonable and prudent person, due care and due diligence have been used in the fields of Finance, Securities, and Law for many years. In recent years these terms have found their way into the fields of computing and information security. U.S.A. Federal Sentencing Guidelines now make it possible to hold corporate officers liable for failing to exercise due care and due diligence in the management of their information systems.

In the business world, stockholders, customers, business partners and governments have the expectation that corporate officers will run the business in accordance with accepted business practices and in compliance with laws and other regulatory requirements. This is often described as the "reasonable and prudent person" rule. A prudent person takes due care to ensure that everything necessary is done to operate the business by sound business principles and in a legal ethical manner. A prudent person is also diligent (mindful, attentive, and ongoing) in their due care of the business.

In the field of Information Security, Harris offers the following definitions of due care and due diligence:

"Due care are steps that are taken to show that a company has taken responsibility for the activities that take place within the corporation and has taken the necessary steps to help protect the company, its resources, and employees." And, [Due diligence are the] "continual activities that make sure the protection mechanisms are continually maintained and operational."

Attention should be made to two important points in these definitions. First, in due care, steps are taken to *show*-this means that the steps can be verified, measured, or even produce tangible artifacts. Second, in due diligence, there are continual activities-this means that people are actually doing things to monitor and maintain the protection mechanisms, and these activities are ongoing.

Security Governance

The Software Engineering Institute at Carnegie Mellon University, in a publication titled "Governing for Enterprise Security (GES)", defines characteristics of effective security governance. These include:

- An enterprise-wide issue
- Leaders are accountable
- Viewed as a business requirement
- Risk-based
- Roles, responsibilities, and segregation of duties defined
- Addressed and enforced in policy
- Adequate resources committed
- Staff aware and trained
- A development life cycle requirement
- Planned, managed, measurable, and measured
- Reviewed and audited.

Incident Response Plans

1 to 3 paragraphs (non technical) that discuss:

- Selecting team members
- Define roles, responsibilities and lines of authority
- Define a security incident
- Define a reportable incident
- Training
- Detection
- Classification
- Escalation
- Containment
- Eradication
- Documentation.

Change Management

Change management is a formal process for directing and controlling alterations to the information processing environment. This includes alterations to desktop computers, the network, servers and software. The objectives of change management are to reduce the risks posed by changes to the information processing environment and improve the stability and reliability of the processing environment as changes are made. It is not the objective of change management to prevent or hinder necessary changes from being implemented.

Any change to the information processing environment introduces an element of risk. Even apparently simple changes can have unexpected effects. One of Managements many responsibilities is the management of risk. Change management is a tool for managing the risks introduced by changes to the information processing environment. Part of the change management process ensures that changes are not implemented at inopportune times when they may disrupt critical business processes or interfere with other changes being implemented. Not every change needs to be managed. Some kinds of changes are a part of the everyday routine of information processing and adhere to a predefined procedure, which reduces the overall level of risk to the processing environment. Creating a new user account or deploying a new desktop computer are examples of changes that do not generally require change management. However, relocating user file shares, or upgrading the Email server pose a much higher level of risk to the processing environment and are not a normal everyday activity. The critical first steps in change management are (a) defining change (and communicating that definition) and (b) defining the scope of the change system.

Change management is usually overseen by a Change Review Board composed of representatives from key business areas, security, networking, systems administrators, Database administration, applications development, desktop support and the help desk. The tasks of the Change Review Board can be facilitated with the use of automated work flow application. The responsibility of the Change Review Board is to ensure the organizations documented change management procedures are followed. The change management process is as follows:

- *Requested:* Anyone can request a change. The person making the change request may or may not be the same person that performs the analysis or implements the change. When a request for change is received, it may undergo a preliminary review to determine if the requested change is compatible with the organizations business model and practices, and to determine the amount of resources needed to implement the change.

- *Approved:* Management runs the business and controls the allocation of resources therefore, Management must approve requests for changes and assign a priority for every change. Management might choose to reject a change request if the change is not compatible with the business model, industry standards or best practices. Management might also choose to reject a change request if the change requires more resources than can be allocated for the change.
- *Planned:* Planning a change involves discovering the scope and impact of the proposed change; analysing the complexity of the change; allocation of resources and, developing, testing and documenting both implementation and backout plans. Need to define the criteria on which a decision to back out will be made.
- *Tested:* Every change must be tested in a safe test environment, which closely reflects the actual production environment, before the change is applied to the production environment. The backout plan must also be tested.
- *Scheduled:* Part of the change review board's responsibility is to assist in the scheduling of changes by reviewing the proposed implementation date for potential conflicts with other scheduled changes or critical business activities.
- *Communicated:* Once a change has been scheduled it must be communicated. The communication is to give others the opportunity to remind the change review board about other changes or critical business activities that might have been overlooked when scheduling the change. The communication also serves to make the Help Desk and users aware that a change is about to occur. Another responsibility of the change review board is to ensure that scheduled changes have been properly communicated to those who will be affected by the change or otherwise have an interest in the change.
- *Implemented:* At the appointed date and time, the changes must be implemented. Part of the planning process was to develop an implementation plan, testing plan and, a back out plan. If the implementation of the change should fail or, the post implementation testing fails or, other "drop dead" criteria have been met, the back out plan should be implemented.
- *Documented:* All changes must be documented. The documentation includes the initial request for change, its approval, the priority assigned to it, the implementation, testing and back out plans, the results of the change review board critique, the date/time

the change was implemented, who implemented it, and whether the change was implemented successfully, failed or postponed.

- *Post change review:* The change review board should hold a post implementation review of changes. It is particularly important to review failed and backed out changes. The review board should try to understand the problems that were encountered, and look for areas for improvement.

Change management procedures that are simple to follow and easy to use can greatly reduce the overall risks created when changes are made to the information processing environment. Good change management procedures improve the over all quality and success of changes as they are implemented. This is accomplished through planning, peer review, documentation and communication.

Business Continuity

Business continuity is the mechanism by which an organization continues to operate its critical business units, during planned or unplanned disruptions that affect normal business operations, by invoking planned and managed procedures.

Unlike what most people think business continuity is not necessarily an IT system or process, simply because it is about the business. Today disasters or disruptions to business are a reality. Whether the disaster is natural or man-made (the TIME magazine has a website on the top 10), it affects normal life and so business. So why is planning so important? Let us face reality that "all businesses recover", whether they planned for recovery or not, simply because business is about earning money for survival.

The planning is merely getting better prepared to face it, knowing fully well that the best plans may fail. Planning helps to reduce cost of recovery, operational overheads and most importantly sail through some smaller ones effortlessly.

For businesses to create effective plans they need to focus upon the following key questions. Most of these are common knowledge, and anyone can do a BCP.

1. Should a disaster strike, what are the first few things that I should do? Should I call people to find if they are OK or call up the bank to figure out my money is safe? This is Emergencey Response. Emergency Response services help take the first hit when the disaster strikes and if the disaster is serious enough the Emergency Response teams need to quickly get a Crisis Management team in place.

2. What parts of my business should I recover first? The one that brings me most money or the one where I spend the most, or the one that will ensure I shall be able to get sustained future growth? The identified sections are the critical business units. There is no magic bullet here, no one answer satisfies all. Businesses need to find answers that meet business requirements.
3. How soon should I target to recover my critical business units? In BCP technical jargon this is called Recovery Time Objective, or RTO. This objective will define what costs the business will need to spend to recover from a disruption. For example, it is cheaper to recover a business in 1 day than in 1 hour.
4. What all do I need to recover the business? IT, machinery, records...food, water, people...So many aspects to dwell upon. The cost factor becomes clearer now...Business leaders need to drive business continuity. Hold on. My IT manager spent $200000 last month and created a DRP (Disaster Recovery Plan), whatever happened to that? a DRP is about continuing an IT system, and is one of the sections of a comprehensive Business Continuity Plan.
5. And where do I recover my business from... Will the business centre give me space to work, or would it be flooded by many people queuing up for the same reasons that I am.
6. But once I do recover from the disaster and work in reduced production capacity, since my main operational sites are unavailable, how long can this go on. How long can I do without my original sites, systems, people? this defines the amount of business resilience a business may have.
7. Now that I know how to recover my business. How do I make sure my plan works? Most BCP pundits would recommend testing the plan at least once a year, reviewing it for adequacy and rewriting or updating the plans either annually or when businesses change.

Disaster Recovery Planning

While a business continuity plan (BCP) takes a broad approach to dealing with organizational-wide effects of a disaster, a disaster recovery plan (DRP), which is a subset of the business continuity plan, is instead focused on taking the necessary steps to resume normal business operations as quickly as possible.

A disaster recovery plan is executed immediately after the disaster occurs and details what steps are to be taken in order to recover critical information technology infrastructure.

Laws and Regulations

Below is a partial listing of European, United Kingdom, Canadian and USA governmental laws and regulations that have, or will have, a significant effect on data processing and information security. Important industry sector regulations have also been included when they have a significant impact on information security.

- UK Data Protection Act 1998 makes new provisions for the regulation of the processing of information relating to individuals, including the obtaining, holding, use or disclosure of such information. The European Union Data Protection Directive (EUDPD) requires that all EU member must adopt national regulations to standardize the protection of data privacy for citizens throughout the EU.
- The Computer Misuse Act 1990 is an Act of the UK Parliament making computer crime (e.g. cracking-sometimes incorrectly referred to as hacking) a criminal offence. The Act has become a model upon which several other countries including Canada and the Republic of Ireland have drawn inspiration when subsequently drafting their own information security laws.
- EU Data Retention laws requires Internet service providers and phone companies to keep data on every electronic message sent and phone call made for between six months and two years.
- The Family Educational Rights and Privacy Act (FERPA) (20 U.S.C. § 1232 g; 34 CFR Part 99) is a USA Federal law that protects the privacy of student education records. The law applies to all schools that receive funds under an applicable program of the U.S. Department of Education. Generally, schools must have written permission from the parent or eligible student in order to release any information from a student's education record.
- Health Insurance Portability and Accountability Act (HIPAA) of 1996 requires the adoption of national standards for electronic health care transactions and national identifiers for providers, health insurance plans, and employers. And, it requires health care providers, insurance providers and employers to safeguard the security and privacy of health data.

- Gramm-Leach-Bliley Act of 1999 (GLBA), also known as the Financial Services Modernization Act of 1999, protects the privacy and security of private financial information that financial institutions collect, hold, and process.
- Sarbanes-Oxley Act of 2002 (SOX). Section 404 of the act requires publicly traded companies to assess the effectiveness of their internal controls for financial reporting in annual reports they submit at the end of each fiscal year. Chief information officers are responsible for the security, accuracy and the reliability of the systems that manage and report the financial data. The act also requires publicly traded companies to engage independent auditors who must attest to, and report on, the validity of their assessments.
- Payment Card Industry Data Security Standard (PCI DSS) establishes comprehensive requirements for enhancing payment account data security. It was developed by the founding payment brands of the PCI Security Standards Council, including American Express, Discover Financial Services, JCB, Master Card Worldwide and Visa International, to help facilitate the broad adoption of consistent data security measures on a global basis. The PCI DSS is a multifaceted security standard that includes requirements for security management, policies, procedures, network architecture, software design and other critical protective measures.
- State Security Breach Notification Laws (California and many others) require businesses, nonprofits, and state institutions to notify consumers when unencrypted "personal information" may have been compromised, lost, or stolen.
- Personal Information Protection and Electronics Document Act (PIPEDA)-An Act to support and promote electronic commerce by protecting personal information that is collected, used or disclosed in certain circumstances, by providing for the use of electronic means to communicate or record information or transactions and by amending the Canada Evidence Act, the Statutory Instruments Act and the Statute Revision ActThant is in fact the case.

Sources of Standards

International Organization for Standardization (ISO) is a consortium of national standards institutes from 157 countries with a

Central Secretariat in Geneva Switzerland that coordinates the system.

The ISO is the world's largest developer of standards. The ISO-15443: "Information technology-Security techniques-A framework for IT security assurance", ISO-17799: "Information technology-Security techniques-Code of practice for information security management", ISO-20000: "Information technology-Service management", and ISO-27001: "Information technology-Security techniques-Information security management systems" are of particular interest to information security professionals.

The USA National Institute of Standards and Technology (NIST) is a non-regulatory federal agency within the U.S.

Department of Commerce. The NIST Computer Security Division develops standards, metrics, tests and validation programs as well as publishes standards and guidelines to increase secure IT planning, implementation, management and operation. NIST is also the custodian of the USA Federal Information Processing Standard publications (FIPS).

The Internet Society is a professional membership society with more than 100 organization and over 20,000 individual members in over 180 countries.

It provides leadership in addressing issues that confront the future of the Internet, and is the organization home for the groups responsible for Internet infrastructure standards, including the Internet Engineering Task Force (IETF) and the Internet Architecture Board (IAB).

The ISOC hosts the Requests for Comments (RFCs) which includes the Official Internet Protocol Standards and the RFC-2196 Site Security Handbook.

The Information Security Forum is a global nonprofit organization of several hundred leading organizations in financial services, manufacturing, telecommunications, consumer goods, government, and other areas.

It provides research into best practice and practice advice summarized in its biannual Standard of Good Practice, incorporating detail specifications across many areas.

The IT Baseline Protection Catalogs, or IT-Grundschutz Catalogs, ("IT Baseline Protection Manual" before 2005) are a collection of documents from the German Federal Office for Security in Information Technology (FSI), useful for detecting and combating security-relevant weak points in the IT environment ("IT cluster"). The collection encompasses over 3000 pages with the introduction and catalogs.

Professionalism

In 1989, Carnegie Mellon University established the Information Networking Institute, the United States' first research and education centre devoted to information networking. The academic disciplines of computer security, information security and information assurance emerged along with numerous professional organizations during the later years of the 20th century and early years of the 21st century.

Entry into the field can be accomplished through self-study, college or university schooling in the field, or through week long focused training camps. Many colleges, universities and training companies offer many of their programs on-line.

The GIAC-GSEC and Security+ certifications are both entry level security certifications. Membership of the Institute of Information Security Professionals (IISP) is gaining traction in the U.K. as the professional standard for Information Security Professionals.

The Certified Information Systems Security Professional (CISSP) is a mid-to senior-level information security certification. The Information Systems Security Architecture Professional (ISSAP), Information Systems Security Engineering Professional (ISSEP), Information Systems Security Management Professional (ISSMP), and Certified Information Security Manager (CISM) certifications are well-respected advanced certifications in information-security architecture, engineering, and management respectively.

Within the UK a recognised senior level information security certification is provided by CESG.

CLAS is the CESG Listed Adviser Scheme-a partnership linking the unique Information Assurance knowledge of CESG with the expertise and resources of the private sector.

CESG recognises that there is an increasing demand for authoritative Information Assurance advice and guidance. This demand has come as a result of an increasing awareness of the threats and vulnerabilities that information systems are likely to face in an ever-changing world.

The Scheme aims to satisfy this demand by creating a pool of high quality consultants approved by CESG to provide Information Assurance advice to government departments and other organisations who provide vital services for the United Kingdom.

CLAS consultants are approved to provide Information Assurance advice on systems processing protectively marked information up to, and including, SECRET.

Potential customers of the CLAS Scheme should also note that if the information is not protectively marked then they do not need to specify membership of CLAS in their invitations to tender, and may be challenged if equally competent non-scheme members are prevented from bidding.

The profession of information security has seen an increased demand for security professionals who are experienced in network security auditing, penetration testing, and digital forensics investigation.

In addition, many smaller companies have cropped up as the result of this increased demand in information security training and consulting.

Bibliography

Aaker, David A. : *Managing Brand Equity*, New York: The Free Press, 1991.

Allen C. Benson: *The Complete Internet Companion for Librarians,* New York: Neal-Schuman, 1995.

Allen, T., and M.S. Morton: *Information Technology and the Corporation of the 1990s*, Oxford University Press, New York, 1994.

Ansoff, H.I.: *The New Corporate Strategy*, John Wiley & Sons, Chichester, 1988.

Bardsley, N., Cubitt: *Assessing Experimental Marketing*, Princeton, Princeton University Press, 2009.

Bazilevskii, Y. Y.: *The Theory of Marketing Management*, Pergamon Press, Macmillan Co., New York, 1963.

Byrne, Deborah J.: *MARC Manual: Understanding and Using MARC Records*, Libraries Unlimited, Englewood, 1998.

Carroll, A. : *Business and Society: Managing Corporate Social Performance*, Boston: Little, Brown & Company, 1981.

Center, Allen & Jackson, Patrick: *Public Relations Practices : Managerial Case Studies and Problems*, Prentice-Hall, UK, 1990.

Cootner, Paul : *The Random Character of Stock Market Prices*, MIT Press, 1964.

Dillon, W. R., Madden, T. S : *Marketing Research in a Marketing Environment,* Irwin, 1994.

Dudeja V.D.: *International Marketing and Trade*, Commonwealth, Delhi, 2001.

Edmund Jeffrey Curry : *A Short Course in International Marketing*, Laxmi Pub., Delhi, 2010.

George J. Kress : *Forecasting and Market Analysis Techniques: A Practical Approach,* Westport, CT: Quorum Books, 1994.

Granger, Clive W. J.: *Empirical Marketing in Economics, Specification and Evaluation,* London, Cambridge University Press, 1999.

Hayek, F. A. *Individualism and Economic Order*, The University of Chicago Press, Chicago, 1948.

Jain J.N. and Singh P.P. : *Modern Retail Management : Principles and Techniques*, Regal Pub, Delhi, 2007.

Jain, Abhinandan K. *: Marketing of Information Products and Services,* Indian Institute of Management, Ahmedabad, 1995.

Kasper, Larry J.: *Business Valuations, Advanced Topics*, Westport, CT, Quorum Books, 1997.

Lindblom, C. E.: *A Strategy of Decision: Policy Evaluation as a Social Process*, New York, The Free Press, 1970.

Manuel, G. Velasquez : *Business Ethics Concepts and Cases,* Delhi, Pearson Education, 2002.

Marris, R. L., and Wood, A.: *The Corporate Marketing Economy*, London: Macmillan, 1971.

Meyer, M. W.: *Theory of Organizational Structure*, Indianapolis, 1977.

Purohit H.C. *: Rural Marketing : Challenges and Opportunities*, Shree Pub, Delhi, 2006.

Rappaport, A.: *Creating Shareholder Value, The New Standard for Business Performance,* New York, Free Press, 1986.

Richard, DeGeorge : *Business Ethics,* New York, MacMillan Publishing, 1990.

Russell Parr, *Valuation of Intellectual Property and Intangible Assets,* New York: Wiley, 1994.

Saee, J. : *Contemporary Corporate Strategy, Global Perspectives,* Routledge Publishing, Francis Taylor Group of Publishing, UK, USA and Canada, 2007.

Salancik, G. R.: *The External Control of Organizations, A Resource Dependence Perspective*, New York, 1978.

Scott, W. R.: *Organizations: Rational, Natural, and Open Systems*, Englewood Cliffs, 1981.

Tinbergen, Jan.: *On the Theory of Economic Policy*; Amsterdam, North-Holland 1952.

Trugman, Gary R., *Guide to Conducting a Valuation of a Closely Held Business*, New York, American Institute of Certified Public Accountants, 1993.

Ullman, D. G.: *Making Robust Decisions,* Trafford, 2006.

Waller, Robert: *Preservation of Collections: Assessment, Evaluation, and Mitigation Strategies,* American Institute for Conservation of Historic and Artistic Works, Washington, D.C., 1996.

Webster, Frank, and Robins, Kevin: *Information Technology—A Luddite Analysis*, Ablex, Norwood, NJ, 1986.

Williamson, Judith : *Decoding Advertisements,* Marion Boyars Publishers Ltd., 1994.

Wooldridge, J.M.: *Econometric Analysis of Cross Section and Panel Data*, Cambridge, MA: MIT Press, 2002.

Index

❑❑❑